The Privacy Advocates

The Privacy Advocates

Resisting the Spread of Surveillance

Colin J. Bennett

The MIT Press
Cambridge, Massachusetts
London, England

For information about special quantity discounts, please email special_sales@mitpress.mit.edu.

This book was set in Times New Roman and Syntax on 3B2 by Asco Typesetters, Hong Kong. Printed and bound in the United States of America.

Library of Congress Cataloging-in-Publication Data

Bennett, Colin J. (Colin John), 1955–
The privacy advocates : resisting the spread of surveillance / Colin J. Bennett
    p.   cm.
Includes bibliographical references and index.
ISBN 978-0-262-02638-3 (hardcover : alk. paper) 1. Privacy, Right of. 2. Human rights advocacy. 3. Human rights movements. 4. Human rights workers. I. Title.
JC596.B46   2008
323.44′82—dc22   2008013819

10 9 8 7 6 5 4 3 2 1

To privacy advocates (anywhere and everywhere)—however they are defined

Contents

Introduction

If one enters the term *privacy advocates* into any major Internet search engine, roughly half a million hits arise. In any one week, numerous media stories quote privacy advocates arguing this or protesting that. Privacy advocates are the people who, at least in journalistic parlance, challenge the development of the increasingly intrusive ways by which personal information is captured and processed: identity cards, video surveillance, biometric identifiers, the retention of communications traffic data, the use of cookies and spyware by Web sites, unsolicited marketing practices, data matching and profiling, the monitoring of employees in the workplace, the use of tracking devices in vehicles, the spread of radio frequency identification devices (RFIDs), and a host of other practices. There are a bewildering variety of ways that personal data can be captured, processed, and disseminated. Some people are deeply concerned about these trends and have been trying to do something about them. They tend to be identified as "privacy advocates."

So who are these "privacy advocates"? Who gets mobilized when new surveillance systems rise to governmental and corporate agendas? How do they organize? What do they do? What do they believe? Privacy advocates operate within a range of institutions. They work within nongovernmental organizations (such as civil liberties groups, human rights organizations, and consumer associations). They can also be employed by government, in the case of staff within the official privacy and data protection authorities. They are also found within the corporate sector, as with the chief privacy officers (CPOs) of major corporations, and within some of the major law firms. And sometimes they work on their own.

This book is not about all the people who self-identify as privacy advocates. It is rather about those individuals and groups that have emerged from civil society, spontaneously and without official sanction, rather than about those within the state or the market. This distinction is imperfect, but it will serve to place some initial delimitation around a huge subject matter. Consequently, and unfortunately, some very important individuals within the privacy movement have to be excluded, or at least marginalized, including those who have current employment within either government or the private sector. The decision to assign these "advocates" to the margins and the footnotes should not be read as signifying that they do not play very important roles in promoting the privacy value within their respective organizations and jurisdictions. Rather, the decision is prompted by practical considerations about the scope of the study.

The focus on the more organized and collective forms of social action should also not obscure the fact that resistance to surveillance practices occurs in many less visible ways by ordinary people who would not necessarily identify as privacy advocates. Gary Marx (2003) has explored the many inventive ways that individuals have found to avoid or thwart surveillance, by obscuring their identities, distorting their data, refusing to comply, and so on. The everyday and ubiquitous realities of contemporary surveillance mean that resistance is demonstrated in many locales by ordinary individuals who might quietly, but insistently, refuse to provide personal information, or subtly try to subvert organizational demands. These patterns of everyday resistance are undeniably important elements of antisurveillance politics. By and large, however, these scattered responses have not translated into collective action. And that is one of the central puzzles of this book.

Based on key informant interviews with over thirty advocates in the United States, Canada, Australia, and Europe, as well as on extensive documentary analysis, this research seeks to fill an important gap in the vast literature on privacy. There exists a long tradition of philosophizing about the privacy value, of debating the various legal, technical, and self-regulatory solutions, of warning about the steady slide toward the "surveillance society" and of dissecting nationally and comparatively what mass publics think about the subject. Nobody, however, has attempted to examine the advocacy groups—the disparate individuals and organizations in civil society who have consciously and purposefully attempted to advance the cause for privacy protection. Nobody has asked the question: when surveillance practices emerge, who mobilizes against them, how, and with what effect? Those are my central questions.

The Justification

Many books have been published on privacy in the last twenty years, most of which have claimed a gradual erosion of personal privacy in the face of some relentless social, political, and technological forces (e.g., Sykes 1999; Whitaker 1999; Garfinkel 2000; Rosen 2000; O'Harrow 2005; Rule 2007). As most of the literature notes, privacy is an elusive and multidimensional concept whose meaning is culturally and historically contingent. Yet, it is still the concept that tends to define the policy issue in advanced industrial societies, and it is still the concept around which challenges to excessive surveillance get framed. At root, it has tended to mean the extent to which individuals have control over the circulation of their personal information. Surveillance, broadly defined, challenges that right or interest. It connotes not only visual observation or monitoring but, according to David Lyon, any "collection or processing of personal data, whether identifiable or not, for the purposes of influencing or managing those whose data have been garnered" (2001, 2). Surveillance is, therefore, a routine condition of modern societies to which we are all subjected when we engage in everyday activities. It is also, therefore, a global condition, because personal information can now flow freely and instantaneously across digital networks.

Privacy protection as a public policy question rose to the agendas of advanced industrial states in the late 1960s and 1970s. In those years, there was an abiding assumption that the enactment of law based on a set of common statutory principles, together with credible oversight and enforcement machinery, was both necessary and sufficient to redress the balance between the vulnerable individual and the power of public and private institutions (Flaherty 1989). In the 1990s, however, those assumptions shifted, and experts began to speak of a more complicated inventory of "policy instruments" in addition to properly enforced domestic data protection or privacy legislation: international agreements for the secure processing or personal data when it crosses national borders; the proper implementation of self-regulatory mechanisms, such as codes of practice, standards, and Internet Web seals; privacy impact assessments; and the application of appropriate privacy-enhancing technologies (Bennett and Grant 1999; Bennett and Raab 2006). All are necessary policy instruments; none is sufficient.

At the same time, others have argued that the progress of privacy protection will depend less on policy mechanisms devised and implemented by elites, and more on the extent to which resistance to surveillance practices can be mobilized through social movements (Lyon 2001, 131–135). Some have even contended that instruments for privacy protection often do little more than legitimate existing surveillance practices, rather than stem the seemingly relentless collection and processing of individually identifiable information (Rule et al. 1980). For some of the more radical

privacy activists, the progress of the issue depends on the building of a
more coherent activist network, which not only uses available means of
redress but continuously exposes overly intrusive practices and "outs"
the organizations that are responsible for them (Davies 1999).

There is some evidence that the concerted efforts of privacy advocates
are producing more frequent and public protests against overly intrusive
methods of personal information collection. In the 1970s and 1980s, there
were some sporadic protests in Western Europe against certain censuses.
And in the late 1980s, the proposed introduction of a national identity
card in Australia provoked a storm of controversy. More recently, however, we have witnessed high-profile campaigns against the capture of
personal information on the Internet. There have been very visible protests and boycotts against some companies for the use of RFIDs in their
products. In Canada, a 1999 controversy over a database managed by
Human Resources and Development Canada provoked front-page head-
lines, a parliamentary uproar, and the near resignation of the responsible
Minister. A proposal in Japan for a centralized national identity system
(Juki Net) was met with street protests and government embarrassment.
In the United Kingdom, the Blair government's proposals for a national
identity card became one of the most controversial and partisan issues of
modern British politics. In Germany, there have been high levels of activism against new laws mandating the retention of communications data by
telecommunications companies and Internet service providers, including
a rally in Berlin in September 2007 in which fifteen thousand people par-
ticipated. There is at least anecdotal evidence that new private-sector and
public-sector schemes for personal information processing can provoke
more intense and widespread protest than has occurred in the past.

Whereas there is a sprawling and multidisciplinary literature on the
appropriate policy responses to this concern, there has been very little
analysis of how demands for privacy protection are articulated and aggre-
gated in different societies and internationally. But who are the privacy
advocates, and can they be distinguished from others in the policy community such as consultants, journalists, lawyers, and organizational privacy officers? What do they believe? How do they organize and obtain
resources? How do they make decisions about strategies and priorities?
Do they direct their appeals to mass publics, or to political and business
elites? This book attempts to gain a better purchase on the organization,
resources, and strategies of these advocacy groups, and thus to determine
whether the conditions are present for a different form of social movement or transnational activist network to develop.

The Organization

Chapter 1 provides a broad historical overview of the nature of the social problem to be confronted. How has the issue been "framed," both by academic research and by the advocates themselves? The definition and scope of the problem has undergone some subtle transformations since the advent of widely available information technology and the coincident concern about personal privacy in the 1960s. This chapter traces the literature from the initial concerns about the "databank society," to the "new surveillance" characteristic of the network society, to more contemporary concerns about the monitoring of location and mobility within the ubiquitous "Internet of things." Along with other analysts, I contend that surveillance is a condition of modern societies, but also that the agents, subjects, and practices have broadened from the early days when the concerns were largely confined to the actions of the omniscient state operating large mainframe databanks. Another dimension of this story, however, is how the actors themselves see the problem. Do contemporary privacy advocates proceed with fixed definitions of "privacy" or deeper philosophical understandings about how to judge when a line has been crossed from the acceptable to the unacceptable, or the ethical to the unethical? Or do they rely more on the "gut instinct"—on the deeper sense that, regardless of technology, institution, and location, some practices are simply wrong and deserve resistance.

Chapter 2 provides a broad overview of the civil society groups through which privacy advocates work. In every advanced industrial society, there exist one or more groups whose self-defined mission is to raise alarm bells about practices that entail unacceptably high levels of surveillance. Sometimes these advocates operate within self-contained groups whose chief mission is to promote privacy. Others are located within larger organizations that try to promote a fuller range of civil liberties or human rights interests. Others are closely related to the consumer movement. Still others have emerged to defend the broad range of digital rights within cyberspace. Many focus on the "single issue." One of the preliminary tasks of the research is to paint a general and contemporary profile of the privacy advocacy network. A listing of the privacy advocacy groups referenced later is provided at the end of this Introduction.

The groups tell one story. The actors within them tell another. Chapter 3 analyzes the various roles played by contemporary privacy advocates. The network is comprised of Advocate-Activists, Advocate-Researchers, Advocate-Consultants, Advocate-Technologists, Advocate-Journalists, and Advocate-Artists. These categories are, of course, flexible and over-lapping. Most advocates tend to play multiple roles with sometimes conflicting commitments. Advocates also tend to move from one role to another with speed and ease. And how individuals self-define their roles is often inconsistent with the perceptions that others in the network have of them. The advocacy role is, for most, mediated by other identities—researcher, consultant, technology developer, journalist, or artist.

Chapter 4 discusses the strategies adopted by privacy advocates. Using the framework developed by Margaret Keck and Kathryn Sikkink (1998), this chapter explores how the privacy advocates have engaged in a combination of information, symbolic, accountability, and leverage politics. Much of their activity involves generating politically relevant information about privacy protection and moving it to where it will have the most impact. Thus many privacy advocates perform a range of fairly traditional advocacy functions in relation to the official agencies of the state. They give testimony. They comment on legislative and administrative proposals for new uses of personal information. They generate research and analysis. Privacy advocates also attempt to advance the cause in less public ways, by working with organizations to assist them to improve their practices. Privacy advocates also have to call upon symbols that make sense of these issues within the wider culture. This chapter, therefore, examines the relationship between privacy advocates and the media. On occasion advocates can also attempt to hold powerful governmental and corporate institutions to account, through official complaints or litigation. Standards for privacy protection are inherent in domestic law, international agreements, corporate privacy policies, and other standards. Advocates can, and have, tried to get organizations to live up to their regulatory obligations and public commitments. On occasion they can also exert leverage, mainly through the threat of bad publicity. "Naming and shaming" has a tradition within other areas of social, environmental, and human rights policy. It is increasingly apparent within this area as well.

Chapter 5 examines the dynamics of a number of key conflicts over privacy. The early disputes over the collection of information through the census in certain European countries were the first real examples of highly publicized conflicts over the erosion of privacy. The attempted introduction of identity cards (especially in Australia and the United Kingdom) has also been extremely contentious. Certain marketing schemes, especially over the Lotus Marketplace product, aroused considerable interest in the early 1990s. More recently, conflicts have occurred with respect to intrusive practices on the Internet, such as the development of key-escrow encryption, online advertising through third party cookies, and online authentication mechanisms such as the Microsoft passport. Highly publicized disputes over privacy are rare, but they are increasing in frequency and intensity. I explore the various reasons for this, and I try to establish the common conditions that have accompanied these cases and resulted in apparent victories for privacy advocates and their allies.

Chapter 6 examines the ways in which these various actors do, or do not, network—both online and offline. How do they connect, through privacy conferences and privacy campaigns and privacy coalitions? There is no "umbrella group." When privacy conflicts arise, they tend to be waged by a loose coalition of relatively small groups who come together for specific causes and then disband. An underlining and concluding theme in this chapter is the ways in which the Internet facilitates advocacy networks. Privacy advocacy provides a useful case study of the phenomenon of "net activism." Given the technological sophistication of many privacy activists, the Internet became the locus of some quite early conflicts over issues such as encryption, third-party cookies, and the construction of online databases (Gurak 1997). The Internet has been, therefore, both the object of contention and the means through which intrusive practices could be denounced. The question remains, however, whether the Internet has ushered in a new form of privacy advocacy, unrestrained by traditional constraints of membership, geographic space, and time, or whether it has just introduced a pattern of misinformed and chaotic "electronic panics." This chapter will speak directly to these questions.

The level of activism and media coverage about privacy has clearly risen in the last decade. But it cannot yet be argued that the greater salience of the issue is attributable to the rise of a global social movement devoted exclusively to the advancement of the privacy value. There has been an enormous amount of policy activity: law, codes of practice, international agreements, privacy-enhancing technologies, and so on, contributing to a "trading-up" of international regulation (Bennett and Raab 2006). However, little of this has occurred as a result of concerted grassroots campaigning. There is clearly no worldwide privacy movement that has anything like the scale, resources, or public recognition of organizations in the environmental, feminist, or human rights fields. Rather, the privacy protection issue has yielded a loose, fragmented, and open-ended network of individuals and organizations, most of which have responsibilities beyond this issue.

Is this the way it has to be? The aim of the final chapter is to understand the conditions under which a more coherent international social movement for privacy (and against surveillance) might develop. Is the absence of such a movement inevitable and explicable because of the inherent properties of this issue? Or is it something that might very well arise given the correct agents and strategic choices? It is hoped that the scholarly literature on interest groups and resource mobilization, as well as theories of social movements and transnational activism, will provide some insights into these questions.

Privacy is often considered a highly abstract and subjective issue. Whereas it is possible to observe and measure the direct results of much environmental pollution, arguments against excessive levels of surveillance often have to be pitched in terms of abstract rights, personal perceptions and fears of hypothetical consequences. To be sure, many horror stories about the inappropriate collection and use of personal information can be marshaled to the cause. But still, after over thirty years of advocacy, the privacy movement in every country hears the familiar and quite bogus argument: "If you have nothing to hide, you have nothing to fear." The chapters that follow will give the lie to that argument. The collection, processing, and dissemination of personal data, without the individual's knowledge and consent, are profoundly and increasingly worrying to the individuals concerned. Furthermore, the ability to control the circulation of that information is being eroded with deep consequences for the relationships among the state, the market, and civil society. Surveillance has become a condition of modern societies. Some have tried to challenge and resist these developments. This is their story.

The Methodology

"*Their* story" or "*my* story"? The question is not easy to answer. I do regard myself as a privacy advocate. I appear in the media. I give testimony, and I comment on government and private-sector proposals. I have been a part of the privacy advocacy network both in Canada and internationally for over twenty years. The relationship, therefore, between myself and the people I am studying is not one of the researcher studying his "subjects." Neither, obviously, is it one about which I can be detached, objective, and dispassionate. I believe in this cause, and I am generally sympathetic when privacy advocates succeed and disappointed when they fail. I am also aware that their efforts have been marginalized and regarded as "extreme," "unrealistic," even "lunatic." Those views have occasionally translated into puzzled questions to me about why I am bothering to devote my time and resources to studying a set of actors, perceived by some to be at most an irrelevant irritant on the fringe of the more significant policy community. Obviously, I hope the pages that follow convince these skeptics.

My aim is to hold a mirror up to this privacy advocacy network in a way that has not been attempted before. Thus, I have tried as far as possible to allow these men and women to speak for themselves. I do not agree with everything that the people described in this book do or say; but that is not the point. In presenting the views and voices of privacy advocates, I do so not necessarily because they are correct according to any objective standard. The point is that they hold these views and that they provide a distinctive set of viewpoints on a critically important issue of the day.

One of my respondents, whose anonymity I will protect, offered the insight that "privacy advocates are not normal people." Normal people seek secure paying jobs in government, business, or academia. They do not sacrifice income to work in the nonprofit sector fighting powerful state and corporate interests. Many privacy advocates are euphemistically described as "characters." They are highly visible, somewhat egotistical, very smart, generally unconventional, and extremely interesting. With few exceptions, and paradoxically, they do not lead "private lives." They are extremely social, and they network an enormous amount. Many in this community also joke that the privacy advocates are the biggest gossips out there. So I am not studying here the anonymous foot-soldiers that comprise other social movements. Many of these advocates are "out there" actively trying to shape elite and mass opinion.

All of these realities have had some implications for how I have collected my data and presented my findings. I have to a significant extent relied on "key-informant" interviews with around thirty respondents in the United States, Canada, Australia, and several European countries. The full list of respondents, as well as my interview schedule, is included in the appendixes. The main criteria for selection is current, or former, affiliation with a group one of whose principal missions is to promote privacy protection or to resist excessive surveillance. The vast majority of these individuals are within "not-for-profit" groups, although as we will see, that distinction is sometimes difficult to sustain. I am also not confining my analysis to groups conventionally considered "privacy advocacy groups." More revealing, I have found, is to commence with the simple question: when surveillance practices emerge within a particular society, who resists and in what ways? In most countries, this question leads to some "usual suspects," but not always. As a participant in this network for over twenty years, I was at the outset quite familiar with the various advocates in different countries and naturally tended to commence my research with them. Throughout the initial interviews, others were then suggested and the network, as well as my list of respondents, expanded in ways typical of the "snowball-sampling" methods used within the social sciences.

What is less typical is that most of these interviews have been conducted on an attributed basis. I am aware that this technique is not common within research on social movement politics. Many studies (e.g., Luker 1984) find it important to quote the participants in their own words, but do so anonymously to encourage candor. Furthermore, in many studies, it simply is not important to know the name of the speaker, just that the respondent has a particular identity (national, ethnic, gender, and so on), and that a person with these attributes holds these views. For me, it makes no sense to quote my respondents as, for instance, a "prominent American privacy advocate." In the first place, most informed readers would probably guess the identity from the views expressed and the language used. But second, I make no pretense here that these views are representative of anybody except the person speaking. Hence, the narrative is sprinkled with attributed quotations from my interviews that are simply designed to exemplify or reinforce a larger point that I wish to make. Each of these quotations has been approved by the respondent in question.

I have been able to interview most respondents in person, although travel and resource constraints did necessitate a certain number of telephone conversations. In some cases, the context did not permit formal interviewing techniques. For example, many advocates do not have office space, necessitating more informal meetings in coffee shops and other locations; I have used these interviews more as background information. In a couple of instances, I have been able to engage the groups as a "participant observer." In all cases, I have been able to supplement the interview data with views and opinions expressed in the traditional media, on Web sites and in blogs. By and large, it has not been difficult to find out what privacy advocates think about the questions I am posing in this book.

Time and resource limitations obviously have meant that some individuals and groups have had to be left out. Some of those included might question my categories and my characterization of their roles. I can only plead the perennial scholarly defense that I had to draw the lines some-where. Many will wonder about my selective presentation of evidence about their views and strategies. Others will see bias. However, and as explained earlier, this project is very much a pioneering study. At the very least, I do hope that this analysis convinces the reader that the pri-vacy advocacy network has been important, that it is becoming more im-portant, and that it deserves to be taken very seriously by policymakers in government and industry, as well as by academics.

Acknowledgments

My first acknowledgment, therefore, is to the men and women who granted me interviews for this project. I am part of their network, and this probably gained me a certain level of trust. But as I proceeded with the research, I began to realize how privileged I have been not only to study this important subject throughout my entire scholarly career but also to be associated with such an extraordinary group of individuals. I am also very grateful to an indeterminate number of advocates whom time and resources did not permit me to interview, including many within the community of international privacy and data protection commis-sioners. Numerous informal conversations and e-mail correspondence with others within the privacy community—in particular, Ann Cavou-kian, Andrew Clement, David Flaherty, Bob Gellman, Ian Kerr, David Lyon, Gary Marx, and Stephanie Perrin—have influenced my views and indirectly found their way into these pages.

As we will see below, privacy advocates attend a lot of conferences. The formal presentations at these events, as well as informal networking, also contributed to my understandings and insights. The annual Com-puters, Freedom and Privacy (CFP) conference has been particularly val-uable. I was also fortunate to participate in two research workshops dedicated to privacy advocacy: the Information Rights Workshop orga-nized by Andrew Clement at the University of Toronto in June 2006; and the Privacy Workshop held at the University of California, Berkeley, School of Law in June 2007.

I am particularly indebted to these colleagues at the University of Cal-ifornia, Berkeley. From January to July 2007, I was incredibly fortunate to enjoy a sabbatical leave at the Center for the Study of Law and Society (CSLS) at the UC Berkeley School of Law. The remarkable intellectual and cultural environment of Berkeley permitted me to draft this book, as well as to interact with some of the privacy scholars now there: Paul

Schwartz, Deidre Mulligan, Pamela Samuelson, James Rule, and Chris Hoofnagle. I am also grateful to Rosann Greenspan and Lauren Edelman who currently run the very successful Visiting Scholars program at the CSLS.

The work for this project has been funded by a grant from the Social Sciences and Humanities Research Council of Canada (Award 410–2004–0868). This grant allowed not only travel for research purposes but also the employment of hardworking and talented graduate research assistants from the MA program in the Department of Political Science at the University of Victoria: Meghan McCeachern, Sanda Farcas, and Ben Gonzales. I am especially appreciative of Meghan's transcription of my interviews. Also close to home, I would like to thank the man that runs an indispensable privacy press-clipping service through his Institute for the Study of Privacy Issues (ISPI), Mark Hughes. Charles Raab, Jim Rule, Paul Schwartz, and Warren Magnusson, each read various chapters and gave me valuable and critical feedback. Bob Prior and Alyssa Larose of MIT Press ensured that the publication process was timely and straightforward. And as ever, my lifelong gratitude to my wife, Robin Bayley, for support, encouragement, and tolerance of my moods when the writer's block hit.

The views of many privacy advocates are recorded in the pages that follow. There are many voices, but there is only one responsibility—my own. The book is dedicated to privacy advocates—anywhere and everywhere—however you want to define them.

List of Privacy Advocacy Organizations

Organization	Abbreviation	Country
Alfa-Redi		Peru
American Civil Liberties Union	ACLU	United States
Amnesty International	AI	International
Arbeitskreis Vorratsdatenspeicherung (Working Group on Data Retention)		Germany
Arge Daten		Austria
Association Electronique Libre (Electronic Freedom Association)	AEL	Belgium
Association for Technology and Internet	APTI	Romania
Australian Privacy Foundation	APF	Australia
Bits of Freedom	BoF	Netherlands
British Columbia Civil Liberties Association	BCCLA	Canada
Buro Jansen and Janssen		Netherlands
Californians against Telephone Solicitations	CATS	United States
Campaign for Digital Rights	CDR	United Kingdom
Canadian Civil Liberties Association	CCLA	Canada
Canadian Internet Public Policy Clinic	CIPPIC	Canada
CATO Institute	CATO	United States
Center for Digital Democracy	CDD	United States
Center for Democracy and Technology	CDT	United States
Chaos Computer Club	CCC	Germany
Coalition Against Unsolicited Commercial Email	CAUCE	United States
Computer Professionals for Social Responsibility	CPSR	United States (chapters in Canada, Spain, Peru, Africa, Japan)
Consumer Action	CA	United States
Consumer Association		United Kingdom
Consumers Against Supermarket Privacy Invasion and Numbering	CASPIAN	United States

Organization	Abbreviation	Country
Cyber-Rights and Cyber-Liberties		United Kingdom
Derechos Digitales (Digital Rights)		Chile
Deutsche Vereinigung für Datenschutz (German Association for Data Protection)	DVD	Germany
Die Humanistische Union (The Humanist Union)	HU	Germany
Digital Rights Denmark		Denmark
Digital Rights Ireland		Ireland
Electronic Frontier Finland	EFFI	Finland
Electronic Frontier Foundation	EFF	United States
Electronic Privacy Information Center	EPIC	United States
European Civil Liberties Network	ECLN	Europe
European Digital Rights Initiative	EDRI	Europe
FoeBuD		Germany
Förderverein Informationstechnik und Gesellschaft (Association for Information Technology and Society)	FITUG	Germany
Forum Informatikerinnen für Frieden and gesellschaftliche Verandwortung (Forum of Computer Professionals for Peace and Social Responsibility)	FIFF	Germany
Foundation for Information Policy Research	FIPR	United Kingdom
Foundation for Taxpayer and Consumer Rights	FTCR	United States
Frontline		Canada
Fundacion via Libre (Open Source Foundation)		Argentina
Global Internet Liberty Campaign	GILC	International
Health Privacy	HP	United States
ID Theft Resource Center	ITRC	United States
Imaginons un Réseau Internet Solidaire	IRIS	France
International Civil Liberties Monitoring Group	ICLMG	Canada
Internet Society		Bulgaria
Iuridicum Remedium		Czech Republic
Junkbusters		United States
La Ligue des Droits et Libertés (League of Rights and Liberties)		Quebec, Canada
Leave Those Kids Alone	LTKA	United Kingdom
Liberty Coalition		United States
Medical Privacy Coalition	MPC	United States
Motorists Against Detection	MAD	United Kingdom
National Association of State Public Interest Research Groups	US PIRG	United States
National Consumers League	NCL	United States
National Council for Civil Liberties	NCCL	United Kingdom
Netjus		Italy
Netzwerk Neue Medien (Network New Media)	NNM	Germany

Organization	Abbreviation	Country
New York Surveillance Camera Players	SCP	United States
NO2ID		United Kingdom
Patient Privacy Rights Coalition		United States
Privacy International	PI	United Kingdom
Privacy Rights Clearinghouse	PRC	United States
Privacy Ukraine		Ukraine
Privacy Activism		United States
Privacy Journal		United States
Privacy Mongolia		Mongolia
Privacy Times		United States
Private Citizen, Inc.		United States
Privaterra		Canada
Public Interest Advocacy Center	PIAC	Canada
Public Interest Computing Association	PICA	United States
Quintessenz		Austria
Seguridad en Democracia (Security and Democracy)	SEDEM	Guatemala
Statewatch		Europe
Stichting Waakzaamheid Persoonregistratiie (Privacy Alert)		Netherlands
Swiss Internet User Group	SIUG	Switzerland
Transatlantic Consumer Dialogue	TCD	Europe
UK National Consumer Council	NCC	United Kingdom
Utilities Commission Action Network	UCAN	United States
Verbraucherzentrale Bundesverband (Federation of German Consumer Organizations)	VBV	Germany
Verein für Internet-Benutzer Österreichs (Association for Austrian Internet Users)	Vibe AT!	Austria
World Privacy Forum	WPF	United States

1 Framing the Problem

I give the fight up: let there be an end, a privacy, an obscure nook for me. I want to be forgotten even by God.
—Robert Browning, *Paracelsus* (1835)

We need an electronic bill of rights for this electronic age. . . . You should have the right to choose whether your personal information is disclosed; you should have the right to know how, when, and how much of that information is being used; and you should have the right to see it yourself, to know if it's accurate.
—Vice-President Al Gore, July 31, 1998

We are moving to a Google that knows more about you.
—Eric Schmidt, Google CEO, February 9, 2005

So what is the social problem, and how has it been defined and framed by privacy advocates? The answer is by no means clear as definitions and concerns about privacy have varied over time and according to national, cultural, and academic perspectives. "Privacy" is not a self-defining phenomenon, but a deeply contested concept that frames not one but a series of interrelated social and policy issues. The concept and the discourse can be, and are, molded to suit varying interests and agendas.

For any group that seeks to change public policy, or indeed the structural conditions that give rise to that policy, how issues get "framed" is crucial. Deriving originally from the work of sociologist Erving Goffman (1974), the concept of frames or framing is used to mean patterns of perception or methods of interpretation employed by social movement participants and organizations. A frame might be imagined as a kind of template or filter that organizes how one processes new information. For Sydney Tarrow, issue framing can define the crucial moment when politics expands into sustained interaction with opponents, and creates a social movement. Hence, for Tarrow, social movements should be based on "collective action frames that justify, dignify, and animate collective action." For "framing not only relates to the generalization of grievance, but defines the 'us' and 'them' in a movement's conflict structure" (1998, 21). David Snow has emphasized the importance of "frame alignment," the ability to render problems and events meaningful to a larger audience. There needs to be a resonance, therefore, between a network's interpretive work and the experiences of the broader political culture (Snow 1986, 464).

This chapter tries to trace the various ways that this cluster of issues has been framed in the academic literature and in social and political discourse. There is a framing of the issue around "privacy" and the attempts to draw ethical lines between the realm of the private and that of the social. There is a somewhat narrower framing of the issue around "information privacy," specifically focusing on the processing of personal data. There is also a framing of the problems around the concept of "surveillance" and the collective challenges that are posed when organizational imperatives combine with advanced information technology.

I trace these shifting conceptions in the academic literature, and then in various articulations by privacy advocacy groups. These frames are undoubtedly motivated by technological developments. However, they also reflect some interesting strategic choices about which messages "work" and which don't. For some, their arguments are influenced by the academic debate. Others have an aversion to theorization, preferring to base their activism on a set of basic and visceral instincts, and perhaps a moral authority, that can distinguish the intrusive from the nonintrusive, the acceptable from the unacceptable, and the just from the unjust. Lines therefore get negotiated and drawn—by scholars, by those with economic and political power, and by the advocates themselves.

The Privacy Frame

Although there is no consensus on how to define privacy, even in English-speaking nations, there is common agreement that privacy is something that every human being needs at some level and in some degree. This point is substantiated by a wealth of social psychological and anthropological evidence that has suggested that every society adopts mechanisms and structures (even as simple as the building of walls) that allow individuals to resist encroachment from other individuals or groups (Moore 1984).

As a clear organizational principle to frame political struggle, however, the concept leaves a lot to be desired. Scholars cannot make up their minds whether the problem stems from the fact that it is too narrowly focused on a conception of the individual subject or that it is too broad, vague, and protean. There have been many attempts to carve through the conceptual morass with definitions, taxonomies, and analytical frameworks. Yet after over thirty years of analysis, according to Daniel Solove, the concept is still in disarray: "Privacy seems to be about everything, and therefore it appears to be nothing" (2006, 479).

Let us begin with two sets of distinctions to help focus the analysis and summarize a very complicated and sprawling literature. The first relates to how one might draw the boundary between the public and the private; the second relates to the reasons or motives behind asserting a privacy claim, or why one might want to draw that boundary in the first place. The classic American definition of privacy offered at the end of the last century by Samuel Warren and Louis Brandeis ("the right to be let alone") embodies some subtle and important distinctions concerning what aspects of personal life should, in fact, be "let alone" (1890, 193). Further analysis suggests that there might be privacy of space, privacy of behavior, privacy of decisions, and privacy of information.

Many formulations and discussions of privacy adopt an explicit or implicit spatial dimension, and rest on the assumption that there is a "zone" or "realm" into which other individuals or organizations may not encroach—an "obscure nook" to quote Robert Browning in the epigraph to this chapter. The term "an Englishman's home is his castle" or the principle that the "state has no business in the bedrooms of the nation" (attributed to Pierre Trudeau, among others) are based on a conception of a spatial distinction, or a physical boundary between what is public and what is private. Contemporary concerns about the privacy of the physical person and its protection from various biometric devices are also centered on a notion of a physical or spatial boundary.

For others, the boundary is more properly drawn in terms of the specific behaviors, matters, or actions that should be shielded from intrusion. Take this justification by Charles Fried: "To respect, love, trust, feel affection for others, and to regard ourselves as the objects of love, trust and affection is at the heart of our notion of ourselves as persons among persons, and privacy is the necessary atmosphere for these attitudes and actions, as oxygen is for combustion" (1968, 477). Privacy is, therefore, essential for intimate behavior.

A third way to draw the line is in terms of individual decisions and choices. Privacy is essential for preventing coercive interference with decision making affecting intimate and personal affairs. This concept of decisional privacy has been relied upon, especially in American constitutional law, to protect decision making surrounding abortion, contraception, "lifestyle" choices, the right to choose one's spouse, the right to follow one's own sexual orientation and the right to rear one's children in accordance with one's own religious convictions (Allen 1988).

Finally, the boundary can be drawn in terms of information. Here the important point is not that certain information is perennially and inherently sensitive and therefore private, but that the individual should have a right to control its circulation. A number of definitions have centered on this informational aspect of the privacy question: "the control we have over information about ourselves" (Fried 1970, 140); "the individual's ability to control the circulation of information relating to him" (Miller 1971, 25); the "claim of individuals, groups, or institutions to determine for themselves when, how and to what extent information about them is communicated to others" (Westin 1967, 7); and the "interest an individual has in controlling, or at least significantly influencing, the handling of data about themselves" (Clarke 1997). Definitions surrounding the concept of information tend therefore to emphasize the importance of "control" or "choice"—as in the quotation from Al Gore in the epigraph to this chapter.

It is clear that there is no single essential characteristic that all privacy violations share. Moreover, none of these spatial, behavioral, decisional, or informational distinctions can be absolute. Thus the state should have no interest in sexual relations between consenting adults in the privacy of their home, but it may have a significant interest in regulating such behavior in a public place. Decision making on intimate issues can never be wholly private. Neither can the control of personal information. Whether drawn in spatial, behavioral, decisional, or informational terms, each of these boundaries is inherently flexible, contestable, and dependent on context (Nissenbaum 2004). Privacy is not about isolation or removal from society, but about social relations. Social norms about privacy not only protect individuals but also regulate what can and should be done in the public domain (Schoeman 1992).

It is therefore useful to reflect on the purposes for the assertion of privacy claims. In previous work, I have distinguished among three overlapping dimensions of the problem: humanistic, political, and instrumental (Bennett 1992, 22–37). Fundamentally, privacy claims are made for humanistic reasons. Here the essential concern is to protect the dignity, individuality, integrity, or private personality of each and every one of us, regardless of wider implications or consequences. This notion corresponds broadly to what James Rule and his colleagues mean by an "aesthetic" conception of privacy or "the restriction of personal information as an end in itself" (Rule et al. 1980, 22). The fundamental issue is the loss of human dignity, respect, and autonomy that results when one loses control over the circumstances under which one's space, behavior, decisions, or personal information is intruded upon. These conceptions are at the heart of the privacy movement in virtually every democratic state.

A second dimension, however, is explicitly political. Privacy plays important functions within liberal democratic societies by preventing the total politicizing of life; it promotes the freedom of association; it shields scholarship and science from unnecessary interference by government; it permits and protects the use of a secret ballot; it restrains improper police conduct such as compulsory self-incrimination and "unreasonable searches and seizures"; and it serves also to shield those institutions, such as the press, that operate to keep government accountable (Westin 1967, 25). In a similar vein, Paul Schwartz (1999) has advanced a similar theory of "constitutive privacy" to protect the ability of individuals to speak freely and participate in public life on the Internet.

A third, and somewhat different, purpose is an instrumental, functional, or strategic one. The promotion of privacy may also serve to ensure that, in Paul Sieghart's terms, "the right people use the right data for the right purposes" (1976, 76). When anyone of those conditions is absent, critical rights, interests, and services might be jeopardized. This is an explicit concern about information, but it expresses a fundamental assumption that if you can protect the information on which decisions are made about individuals, you can also protect the fairness, integrity, and effectiveness of that decision-making process. In contrast to the first two concerns, this aspect of the problem stems not so much from the collection of personal data as from its use and dissemination. In this view, organizations can collect as much personal information as they like, provided there are adequate procedures in place to make sure that the "right people use it for the right purposes."

Privacy concerns go back centuries. And specific problems about how certain types of personal information in certain contexts, particularly medical contexts, have been the subject of claim and counterclaim, and regulatory and judicial decision making for a very long time. Privacy protection as a public policy question, however, is of more recent vintage. The issue came to the agenda of advanced industrial states in the late 1960s because of two main characteristics of post-industrialism —bureaucratization and information technology. When those forces reached a critical point in the 1960s and 1970s with the expansion of the state and the computerization of state functions, many Western societies then attempted to develop a coordinated public policy approach.

As a public policy question, governments tended to define the problem in informational, rather than in spatial, decisional, or behavioral terms. Even though some laws (such as in Canada, Australia, and the United States) are entitled "privacy acts," statutory protections have historically focused on the informational dimension of the problem, on the assumption that other aspects of the privacy question can be dealt with by the courts, or can be redefined or reduced to informational terms. And in general, policymakers have been more influenced by arguments of instrumental damage, than of aesthetic appeal. The argument that we all deserve privacy on a humanistic level is abstract. The position that individual interests can be harmed when personal information is processed inappropriately, especially if that position is supported by well-chosen horror stories, can have a more direct political appeal. The history of privacy, as a public policy (rather than a legal or ethical) issue has been dominated by a quite particular understanding of how the issue should be framed. Since the 1960s and 1970s, for better or worse, this informational and instrumental conception of privacy has tended to drive policy debate and has set national and international policy choices on a particular trajectory.

The Information Privacy Frame

The concept of informational privacy (sometimes referred to as data privacy) arose in the 1960s and 1970s at about the same time that "data protection" (derived from the German *Datenschutz*) entered the vocabulary of European experts. The notion is closely connected to the information processing capabilities of computers, and to the need to build protective safeguards at a time when large national data integration projects were being contemplated in different advanced industrial states. These projects raised the fears of an omniscient "Big Brother" government with unprecedented surveillance power.

The overall policy goal in every country has been to provide individuals greater control of the information that is collected, stored, processed, and disseminated about them by public and private organizations. This goal was prominent in English-speaking countries, as well as in continental Europe. The concept of *Informationsselbstbestimmung* (informational self-determination) was later developed and given constitutional status in Germany. Control over personal information means rights for the individual, as well as obligations for organizations. It therefore yields a number of basic principles for personal information management. These "fair information principles" can be briefly traced to policy analysis in Europe and the United States in the late 1960s and early 1970s (Bennett 1992, 95–115), and were soon regarded as a logical regime for the protection of information privacy rights. Those experts who were attempting to resolve this issue in national arenas shared a strong desire to draw lessons from their counterparts overseas and produced an international consensus on how best to resolve the privacy problem through public policy. These analytical efforts led to the world's first "data protection" or "information privacy" statutes (Bennett 1992).

The fair information principles (FIPs) can be distilled to the following: An organization (public or private):

• must be accountable for all the personal information in its possession

• should identify the purposes for which the information is processed at or before the time of collection

• should only collect personal information with the knowledge and consent of the individual (except under specified circumstances)

• should limit the collection of personal information to that which is necessary for pursuing the identified purposes

• should not use or disclose personal information for purposes other than those identified, except with the consent of the individual (the finality principle)

• should retain information only as long as necessary

• should ensure that personal information is kept accurate, complete, and up-to-date

• should protect personal information with appropriate security safeguards

• should be open about its policies and practices and maintain no secret information system

• should allow data subjects access to their personal information, with an ability to amend it, if inaccurate, incomplete, or obsolete (Bennett and Grant 1999, 6).

These principles are also conceived in relative terms. Each must be balanced against correlative rights and obligations to the community.

The fair information principles appear either explicitly or implicitly within all national data protection laws, including those in the United States, Australia, New Zealand, and Canada that are called privacy acts, as well as in self-regulatory codes and standards. They have also spread as a result of international agreements. The increasing ease with which personal data might be transmitted outside the borders of the country of origin has produced an interesting history of international harmonization efforts, and a concomitant effort to regulate transborder data flows. In the 1980s, these harmonization efforts were reflected in two international agreements, the 1981 Guidelines from the Organization for Economic Cooperation and Development (OECD 1981), and the 1981 Convention from the Council of Europe. In the 1990s, these initiatives were extended through the 1995 European Union Data Protection Directive, which tries to harmonize European data protection law according to a higher standard of protection and to impose that standard on any country within which personal data on European citizens might be processed.[1] In this decade, there have also been attempts to extend their reach to the Asia-Pacific region (Greenleaf 2005).

Despite this harmonization there are, of course, continuing debates about how the FIPs doctrine should be translated into statutory language (Bygrave 2002). There are disputes for example: about how to regulate the secondary uses of personal data—through a standard of relevance, or through specific provisions about the legitimate custodians of those data; about the limitation on collection principle and to what extent the organization should be obliged to justify the relevance of the data for specific purposes; about the circumstances under which "express" rather than "implied" consent should be required; and about the distinction among collection, use, and disclosure of information, and whether indeed these distinctions make sense and should not be subsumed under the overarching concept of "processing." How these and other statutory issues are dealt with will, of course, have profound implications for the implementation of privacy protection standards within any one jurisdiction.

The laws have also differed on the extent of organizational coverage—those in North America and Australia have historically mainly regulated public-sector agencies plus selected sectors of private industry, whereas those elsewhere (especially in Europe) encompass all organizations. In recent years this distinction has all but disappeared as countries like Canada, Australia, and Japan have introduced information privacy statutes for the private sector. In most countries (with the notable exception of the United States) these laws are overseen by small privacy or data protection agencies with varying oversight, advisory, or regulatory powers. Some of these agencies have strong enforcement and regulatory authority; others act as more advisory "ombudsman-like" bodies. Some are headed by a collective commission (such as in France), others (such as in Canada and Australia) by a single "privacy commissioner" or "data protection commissioner." One of the effects of the 1995 EU Data Protection Directive has been to extend the process of policy convergence beyond the level of basic statutory principles. This directive also pushes for greater conformity in how these principles are enforced through a "supervisory authority." Moreover, the principle of independent oversight is also regarded as a test of the "adequacy" of data protection in non-European countries. The process of convergence of data protection norms is extending geographically and deepening in meaning and content (Bennett 1997).

Thus, in just forty years, there exists a broad and diverse policy sector embracing a very large number of government officials, lawyers, independent consultants, chief privacy officers, technology providers, academics, and nongovernmental organizations. The "governance of privacy" is a responsibility of many actors operating at different international, national, and local levels. The issue has become institutionalized. As a policy sector, it is not going away. Too many people have a stake in its continuation.

The Surveillance Frame

According to some, however, just as laws are not going to go away, neither are the institutions and technologies of surveillance. At the same time as there has been an undeniable expansion of the policy sector and a "trading-up" of laws and regulations, there has also been a growing body of criticism about whether the concept of privacy, and the policies it generates, are equal to the scale of the social problem (Lyon 2001; Rule et al. 1980; Gandy 1993). For some, privacy is simply not the "antidote to surveillance" (Stalder 2002).

There are several intertwined elements to this critique pitched at different conceptual and practical levels. Philosophically, privacy has its roots in liberal individualism and is perhaps not reflective of the complex subjectivities and identities characteristic of the modern world. Privacy tends to reinforce individuation, rather than community, sociability, trust, and so on. It therefore never challenges the larger questions of categorical discrimination. Individuals are arguably placed at risk because of their membership in certain groups, rather than on the basis of their individual identities and the personal information it generates (Gandy 1993).

As a legal right, some have also pointed out that privacy is plagued with some of the same problems associated with the rights discourse more generally (Haggerty and Erickson 2006, 9). As a legal concept it pushes debate toward experts and authorities and fails to serve the people most at risk (Gilliom 2006, 123). At root, privacy claims tend not to see surveillance as a social question, but as a problem that can be addressed by properly implementing the fair information principles doctrine in relation to the personal data on discrete individuals. Thus contemporary information privacy legislation is designed to manage the processing of personal data, rather than to limit it. From the perspective of those interested in understanding and curtailing excessive surveillance, the formulation of the privacy problem in terms of trying to strike the right "balance" between privacy and organizational demands for personal information does not address the deeper issue and cannot halt surveillance. Information privacy policies may produce a fairer and more efficient use and management of personal data, but they cannot control the voracious and inherent appetite of modern organizations for more and more increasingly refined personal information (Rule et al. 1980).

There have been attempts to realign, rather than abandon, the privacy concept. Priscilla Regan, for instance, has argued that privacy should be seen as a common value, "in that all individuals value some degree of privacy and have some common conceptions about privacy." It is a public value, "in that it has value not just to the individual...but also to the democratic political system." And it is a collective value, "in that technology and market forces are making it hard for any one person to have privacy without all persons having a similar minimum level of privacy" (Regan 1995, 213). She contends that an individualistic conceptualization of privacy does not serve the privacy advocate well. Her analysis suggests that privacy, framed in individualistic terms, is always on the defensive against arguments for the social benefits of surveillance. Privacy will always be in conflict with those social and collective issues, which tend to motivate general publics and their representatives. We must, therefore, frame the question in social terms. Society is better off if individuals have higher levels of privacy.

For others, however, the way to frame the problem is not in terms of protecting privacy, but of curtailing excessive surveillance. In popular parlance, surveillance has historically been associated with the notion of observing, normally by visual means, people under "suspicion."[2] More scholarly definitions tend to be more inclusive. Rule and his colleagues, for instance, suggest that surveillance is "any systematic attention to a person's life aimed at exerting influence over it" (Rule et al. 1983, 223). David Lyon states that surveillance is "any collection and processing of personal data, whether identifiable or not, for the purposes of influencing or managing those whose data have been garnered" (2001, 2). In later work he adds that surveillance is the "focused, systematic and routine attention to personal details for purposes of influence, management, protection or direction" (Lyon 2007, 14).

It has also become evident that surveillance is often as much about classification or "social sorting" as about monitoring (Lyon 2003a). Surveillance therefore discriminates, in both passive and negative senses of that term. It is "Janus-faced"; the same process both empowers individuals but also constrains them. It gives us a variety of advantages (security, convenience, ease of communication, and so on). It also enhances the power of the modern organization to the detriment of individual liberties and to the disadvantage of marginalized groups. Lyon demonstrates how surveillance systems have grown up to compensate for the weakening of face-to-face social relationships in which mechanisms for social integration are increasingly removed and abstract. Surveillance, then, is the necessary glue that builds trust throughout a "society of strangers." The "Invisible Frameworks" of integrated information and communications networks contribute to the "orchestration" of this society of strangers. These same trends have been reinforced in the wake of 9/11 and the global "war on terror" (Lyon 2003b).

For modern sociology, surveillance is a condition of modernity, integral to the development of disciplinary power and new forms of governance (Haggerty and Erickson 2006, 4). It is integral to the development of the nation state, and to the decentered forms of disciplinary power and "governmentalities" inherent within modern neo-liberal societies (Foucault 1991). It is also central to the new order of global capitalism (Deleuze 1992). It is *that* important.

Surveillance therefore now embraces a far broader recognition of the agents and subjects of monitoring. It is not only about powerful organizations controlling hapless subjects. Figure 1.1 attempts to convey the more routine or everyday forms of surveillance in modern societies. It displays a simple four-cell typology distinguishing between the watchers and the watched, and organizations (public and private) and individuals.

THE
WATCHERS

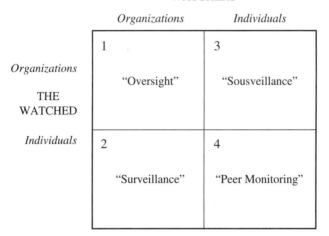

Figure 1.1
A typology of surveillance practices.

Box 1, where the watchers and the watched are both organizations captures an admittedly broad range of practices where organizational accountability is at stake. Surveillance can then occur through a range of
oversight mechanisms: auditing, legislative investigation, regulatory accountability, safety inspections, and so on. The word is increasingly used
in this sense, particularly within the context of laboratory surveillance by
governmental health or environmental protection agencies to enhance
safety.[3] The quality assurance inspections conducted in the course of ob-
taining registration to the ISO 9000 standards are also sometimes called
"surveillance audits."

Box 3 embraces a range of practices where the individual monitors
the organization. This practice is consistent with what Steve Mann, researcher at the University of Toronto and pioneer of "wearable computing," calls "sousveillance," stemming from the contrasting French words
sur, meaning above, and *sous*, meaning below. Surveillance connotes a
kind of omniscient eye-in-the-sky. It is often equated with the notion of
"panopticism" whereby the very possibility of observation constructs a
set of power relations between the watched and the watchers such that
the latter are self-disciplined to conform even though they may not be
observed constantly at every hour of the day. Conversely, sousveillance
involves the recording of the activities of the observers by the observed.

Sousveillance seeks to decentralize the observation, thus inverting the panopticon and achieving ultimately a state of "equiveillance."[4]

Mann provides several contemporary examples of sousveillance: a taxicab passenger photographs the driver to keep tabs on his behavior; a 1-800 number with "Am I driving OK?" on a truck so citizens can report the behavior of the driver to the trucking company; student evaluations of professors;[5] shoppers keeping tabs on shopkeepers (reporting misleading advertising, unsafe fire exits, etc.).[6] "Sousveillance" is also deeply integrated into Mann's own aesthetic critique of surveillance through the development of "wearable computing" devices.[7] His methods are controversial, especially when they involve the photographing of low-level clerks, security personnel, and others not directly responsible for organizational policy. Other attempts to subvert surveillance technology include, most notably, the New York Surveillance Camera Players (SCP), who have gained a notoriety for their regular performances of such classics as Samuel Beckett's *Waiting for Godot*, Edgar Allen Poe's "The Raven," and, of course, George Orwell's *1984* in front of the video-surveillance cameras on the Manhattan subway.[8]

"Peer monitoring" (included in Box 4) has been the subject of some very interesting recent analysis of how ordinary individuals are increasingly encouraged to keep tabs on their fellow citizens. These forms of surveillance tend to find the most chilling examples in more authoritarian regimes through accounts, in particular, of the reliance on informants of the secret police in Eastern Europe (Ash 1997; Funder 2003). But there also seems to be a trend in more democratic states toward individual-individual monitoring. Voyeurism, of course, is one aspect of this form of monitoring—a practice so brilliantly critiqued in Gary Marx's fictional description of the behavior of his Thomas I. Voire (Marx 2003). Voyeurism has also, of course, reached new levels of intrusiveness with the ready availability of camera phones, and other mobile surveillance toys, used to satisfy the prurient interest.

More interesting perhaps are the ways in which individuals become the watchers, either through a subtle process of cooptation or through clever marketing. Recent empirical work suggests that there are a host of "peer-monitoring" or "lateral surveillance" examples from neighborhood watch schemes, to landlord/tenant monitoring, to citizens groups that publicize the vehicle license nos. of those suspected of soliciting prostitutes, to Web cams for the surveillance of children, teenagers, domestic employees, to the locational devices that can be embedded in automobiles to monitor speed, safety procedures, drug/alcohol use, and so on (Wood 2004). Peer-to-peer monitoring was also institutionalized in the United States after 9/11 through Operation TIPS, a program that allows ordinary Americans, such as mail carriers, meter readers, and repair service persons, to act as informants about any suspicious terrorist activity that they might encounter in their professional capacities. Inevitably, somebody then set up a Web site for "Operation TIPS-TIPS" through which people could report on the alleged informants.[9] There is nothing new about this kind of peer-to-peer monitoring in the United States. From 1915 to 1917, the American Protective League boasted around a quarter million badge-wearing members, who proudly informed the Justice Department about any suspicious activity, especially among those citizens of German origin.

Despite these interesting examples, the vast majority of surveillance literature has centered on the monitoring of individuals by organizations (Box 2), and this is the meaning most commonly understood in the literature and implied in the various definitions. Lyon stresses the systematic and the routine, but he also concedes that "surveillance in the end directs its attention to individuals" (Lyon 2007, 14). It is also about how ordinary people in their roles as citizens, workers, travelers, consumers, and so on, interact with surveillance—how they comply, negotiate, and perhaps resist.

This idea that advanced industrial societies are creeping inexorably toward an unacceptable level of surveillance has influenced writers from a number of disciplinary and national backgrounds. David Flaherty, a Canadian scholar of legal history, ended up calling his comparative analysis of the operation of data protection laws in Germany, Sweden, the United States, France, and Canada, "Protecting Privacy in Surveillance Societies." He begins: "The central theme of this volume is that individuals in the Western world are increasingly subject to surveillance through the use of databases in the public and private sectors, and that these developments have negative implications for the quality of life in our societies and for the protection of human rights" (1989, 1).

In the 1970s and early 1980s, the general assumption was that privacy problems stemmed from the centralized and coordinated control of personal information held by governments in discrete, mainframe "databanks." To the extent that private-sector organizations were a matter of concern, advocates tended to focus on the most visible and monopolistic corporations and on the subject of the majority of complaints—namely, the consumer credit industry. This industry was also the first to be subject to regulation for its personal data processing practices. Throughout the 1980s and 1990s, however, it was either obvious that the private sector deserved as much attention as the public, or that it was increasingly difficult to tell the difference between the two.

The notion of "monitoring" also comes under critical scrutiny in the 1990s. These and other trends lead Philip Agre (1994) to the conclusion that a "capture" model is just as evocative as a "surveillance model" to represent the new commodification of personal information. This model is built upon linguistic rather than visual metaphors and has its roots in the disciplinary practices of applied computing rather than in the historical experiences of the "surveillance state." Others have written about "surveillance by design" and how the capacity to capture personal information can become embedded within the architecture of information systems (Samarajiva 1996). More recently, however, Haggerty and Erickson have pointed out that this "capture model" also has its shortcomings because the ongoing politics of surveillance more often involves the provision of "inducements and enticements at the precise threshold where individuals will willingly surrender their information" (2006, 12). Thus privacy is not "invaded," "breached," or "violated"; it is surrendered within the many transactions and relationships that constitute modern life.

Roger Clarke (1988, 1997) found it necessary to coin a new word—"dataveillance"—to describe these new forms of surveillance that are facilitated, not by direct visual or audio monitoring, but by the manipulation of personal data. He contends that the "Big Brother" scenario has not arrived because it is unnecessary. Besides, dataveillance, according to Clarke, is more efficient, whether from a technical, economic, or political standpoint. There is a wide, and imperfectly understood, range of practices for the analysis of personal data currently used by modern institutions. Dataveillance practices vary along five different dimensions: (1) whether personal or mass dataveillance is being conducted; the former involves the analysis of the records of individuals who have already attracted attention, the latter begins with no a priori knowledge of the subjects who may warrant attention; (2) whether the dataveillance is internal or external to the agency that initially collected the data; (3) whether the analysis is upfront or post facto, that is whether the check is made before or after an individual receives a government benefit of service; (4) whether the analysis is conducted on a single variable, or a multiple number of variables (such as when profiling occurs); and (5) whether the practices have a negative or positive impact on individuals (Bennett 1996). Dataveillance, therefore, facilitates the integration of surveillance capabilities across institutional, technological, and national boundaries.

As technology has become smaller, less expensive, and more decentralized, analysts have argued that a "new surveillance" is at work that transcends distance, darkness, and physical barriers: "The awesome power of the new surveillance," Marx summarizes, "lies partly in the paradoxical, never-before-possible combination of decentralized and centralized forms" (1988, 217). Philip Agre and Marc Rotenberg observed a "new landscape" for privacy and technology "that is more variegated, more dangerous, and more hopeful than before" (1997, 1). Haggerty and Ericson (2000) coined the term the "surveillant assemblage" to capture the ability of various institutional actors to integrate, combine, and coordinate various personal information systems to extend and intensify processes of social control. They paint a picture of complex and intertwining flows of personal data that are abstracted from humans and their territorial locations. These flows are then reassembled in different locations as discrete and virtual "data doubles." They emerge to the surface in rather the same way that a rhizomatic root structure produces different manifestations above the surface of the earth.

Hence, when we observe the nature of surveillance in the first decade of the twenty-first century, a number of trends have been at work producing the many and various practices that in turn have animated the actions of privacy advocates. First, surveillance trends have completely eroded traditional distinctions between public and private sectors. The flows of personal data now percolate through systems that are more porous, and less discrete. Second, it is also commonly agreed that we need to concentrate on a further dimension of the privacy problem—not only who we are and what we are doing but also where we are doing it. We are now a "mobile" society, and there is extraordinary potential for "mobile" surveillance (Bennett and Regan 2004). Third, surveillance targets not only "suspects" but everyone. It is about the "monitoring of everyday life" (Lyon 2001). Contemporary surveillance has developed largely through the uncontrolled decisions of thousands of decentralized organizations and individuals, all making supposedly rational decisions that one more incremental invasion of privacy is a price worth paying for greater efficiency, security, profit, and so on. Surveillance has become everyday, routine, and mundane. Finally, the tools of surveillance are becoming more decentralized, culminating in the visions of ubiquitous computing, and the Internet of things, realized through the spread of radio frequency identification devices (RFIDs). Each of these themes will resurface during our later discussion of privacy advocacy.

In summary, the literature on surveillance leaves us with the overwhelming message that the quantity and quality of monitoring have changed. It is not just that we have less "privacy" but that these new surveillance practices have produced qualitative changes in how we subjectively experience our interactions with institutions and technologies. As Haggerty and Erickson put it: "Privacy invasions now often *feel* different than they did in the past" (2006, 11).

Perhaps all these trends suggest that the lines articulated in the heuristic framework of figure 1.1 have all but broken down. However, there is now some critical debate about the breadth and inclusiveness to the concept of surveillance, which has been expanded to embrace any capture of personal information, whether identifiable or not, and whether having positive or negative implications for the individual. It too, therefore, is a concept that carries a lot of theoretical baggage, and is in danger of being stretched so far that it, like "privacy," might mean everything and nothing.

In particular, there is arguably an important distinction between the collection of personal data and the subsequent analysis of that data for the purposes of making a decision about that person. The routine capture of personal data is a feature of modern societies whenever we book an airline ticket, make a credit card purchase, reserve a hotel room, surf the Internet, or make a cellular phone call. But, as I have contended elsewhere (Bennett 2005), the everyday capture and storage of such data is qualitatively different from the use of that data to determine whether the person should or should not fly, would or would not be a credit risk, will or will not be able to pay his hotel bill, may or may not be downloading child pornography, or is or is not a terrorist threat. The analysis of the risks of surveillance needs to be sensitive to the distinction between the routine capture of data and the subsequent use of that data. The concept of "surveillance" conflates many processes and motivations.

Framing Dilemmas

Hence, surveillance is everywhere and it is getting more complex, latent, and subtle. It is a central feature of modern life. It is challenged by a value that has also been impossible to define and that many scholars regard as inadequate—conceptually, legally, and practically. This incomplete sketch of a sprawling literature suggests, therefore, that the people who might want to challenge these developments face some profound dilemmas about how the social and political problem (or problems) might be "framed." It is one thing for academics to analyze and frame understandings of how these issues have developed, and how they should be framed. It is another thing for those who actively press for social change.

The last portion of this chapter looks at the way these various themes have played out in the stated motivations and goals of contemporary privacy advocates. For the social and political activist, the breadth and complexity of the problems produce a number of tricky strategic dilemmas, through which they have to navigate. These dilemmas are manifested on two levels, within the formally stated mission statements of the various organizations, as well as in the more informal perceptions of the individual activists.

Very few people within the privacy advocacy network operate within any fixed and guiding definition of what privacy means. Organizations have tended not to waste valuable time parsing the many definitions, and arguing about concepts and doctrine. The term "privacy" is used over and again, but it is rarely given a clear definition within the various mission statements of privacy organizations. There does tend to be a pervasive "I don't know what it is, but I know it when I see it" assumption. At the same time, there are some different approaches to issue framing.

First, there is a dilemma about whether to regard privacy in its fullest manifestations, and thus broader than information privacy or data protection. When Privacy International (PI) was founded in 1990, the founder, and current director general, Simon Davies, argued forcefully for the need for a broader approach:

Privacy should not be regarded merely as data protection. Data protection appears to be quite clearly a sub set of privacy, and for the sake of maintaining clarity of the issues it should remain so. If all privacy matters were interpreted as data protection, solutions would generally be juridical and legal rather than being subjected to the broader range of influences. In addition, data protection surely cannot exist where there is no obtainable data, and those familiar with Foucault's principle of the panopticon representing the surveillance state will understand that privacy must surely have wider parameters.[10]

In a similar vein, British Columbia's Freedom of Information and Protection of Privacy Association (FIPA) defines privacy as "the ability or right to have a 'private life'—to be left alone, free from illegal or unwanted scrutiny and intrusions. Privacy rights include informational privacy—the right to control or limit the collection, use, and disclosure of one's own personal information by other agencies, whether they are part of government or the private sector."[11]

Yet others seem to be more comfortable with focusing on the information privacy aspects, and thus mirroring and overshadowing the work of the official data protection agencies. For example, there is an Austrian organization called ArgenDaten, and a Deutsche Vereinigung for Datenschutz (German Association for Data Protection). A focus on digital technology also tends to be accompanied by an emphasis on the informational dimensions of the issue. The Center for Digital Democracy's (CDD) specific reference to the fair information principles and its attempt to justify privacy as a necessary condition for the enjoyment of other democratic rights resonates with some of the themes discussed earlier:

Information privacy is the right to control the collection and use of personal information. And Fair Information Practices provide that control. A concept developed in the 1970s, Fair Information Practices provide individuals with the right to have information collected only with consent, updated and maintained accurately, collected for a specific purpose, secured from unauthorized access or alteration, used only with knowledge of what will be done with the data, provided with the ability to view and correct data after collection, and ensured a means to hold the data collector accountable.[12]

Similarly, the Global Internet Liberty Campaign advocates: "Ensuring that personal information generated on the GII [global information infrastructure] for one purpose is not used for an unrelated purpose or disclosed without the person's informed consent and enabling individuals to review personal information on the Internet and to correct inaccurate Information."[13]

A second dilemma relates to whether or not privacy is justified in universal or national terms. Many American groups, for example, take pains to stress how the value is rooted in their own constitutional traditions. The Electronic Privacy Information Center (EPIC), for example, contextualizes its goals in terms of bedrock American principles: "[EPIC] was established in 1994 to focus public attention on emerging civil liberties issues and to protect privacy, the First Amendment, and constitutional values."[14] As does the Privacy Coalition (coordinated through EPIC): "Privacy is one of America's most fundamental values. The Fourth Amendment states that 'The right of the people to be secure in their persons, houses, papers, and effects, against unreasonable searches and seizures, shall not be violated.' In addition, the U.S. has adopted many laws protecting Americans from privacy invasive practices by both the public and private sectors."[15] One of the strongest national privacy groups exists in Australia. The Australian Privacy Foundation (APF) "is the primary association dedicated to protecting the privacy rights of Australians. The Foundation aims to focus public attention on emerging issues that pose a threat to the freedom and privacy of Australians. The Foundation has led the fight to defend the right of individuals to control their personal information and to be free of excessive intrusions."[16]

A third tension exists with respect to the relationship between privacy and related human rights and civil liberties. For some groups, privacy protection is justified and contextualized within a broader suite of civil liberties, especially in relation to the Internet and a wider conception of "digital rights." The Center for Democracy and Technology (CDT), for instance, "works to promote democratic values and constitutional liberties in the digital age. . . . Our mission is to conceptualize, develop, and implement public policies to preserve and enhance free expression, privacy, open access, and other democratic values in the new and increasingly integrated communications medium."[17] The Electronic Frontier Foundation (EFF) has a similar identity: "EFF continues to confront cutting-edge issues defending free speech, privacy, innovation, and consumer rights today. From the beginning, EFF has championed the public interest in every critical battle affecting digital rights."[18]

A fourth tension is also observed over the question of whether privacy is a fundamental or an instrumental value. The Center for Digital Democracy explains how "privacy is important to enhance other rights such as free speech or freedom of association. By withholding identity, some may be more willing to voice political or controversial speech—thus promoting diversity in civil discourse."[19] Similarly, and in the case of the Health Privacy Project: "A substantial barrier to improving the quality of care and access to care is the lack of enforceable privacy rules. Individuals share a great deal of sensitive, personal information with their doctors. . . . Without adequate privacy protections, individuals take steps to shield themselves from what they consider harmful and intrusive uses of their health information often at significant cost to their health.[20]

Yet other groups frame the issues in larger sociological terms about surveillance. The American Civil Liberties Union (ACLU), for instance, notes the "the tremendous explosion in surveillance-enabling technologies, combined with the ongoing weakening in legal restraints that protect our privacy have us drifting toward a surveillance society. The ACLU's Technology and Liberty Project fights this trend and works to preserve the American tradition that the government not track individuals or violate privacy unless it has evidence of wrongdoing."[21]

A Dutch group, Bits of Freedom (BoF), gets a little more specific:

During the past 6 years both governments and companies have initiated many measures and activities that have endangered civil rights. Governments have extended their powers in many ways. Instead of dedicated investigations into the activities of people suspected of serious crimes, law enforcement authorities silently but massively revert to data-mining techniques to examine the daily behaviour of innocent citizens.... But besides government, industry also plays a very important role in the increasing control of the behaviour of citizens and consumers. This tendency is illustrated by developments such as mandatory data retention, the proposed central storage of biometric passport data and the central storage of travel-data created by the new national public transport chip card.[22]

And then there are groups that take a more radical posture, regarding the advancement of privacy rights as a way to control, perhaps dismantle, the "surveillance state." The Surveillance Camera Players, for instance, are: "completely distrustful of all government.... We protest against the use of surveillance cameras in public places because our cameras violate our constitutionally protected right to privacy.[23] The International Campaign Against Mass Surveillance argues:

This new "security" paradigm is being used to roll back freedom and increase police powers in order to exercise increasing control over individuals and populations. Under the public's radar screen, a registration and surveillance infrastructure of global reach is quietly being constructed. It includes the convergence of national and international databases, the creation of data profiles for whole populations, the creation of a global ID system, the global surveillance of movement, and the global surveillance of electronic communications.... Governments around the world must abandon the intrusive and discriminatory measures inherent in the practice of mass registration and surveillance, and put the genuine protection and development of citizens—in the fullest sense, including the protection of our rights—at the centre of any approach to "security."[24]

For some groups, therefore, privacy is simply not the issue, but the nexus among the state, capitalism, and new information technology producing unprecedented surveillance capabilities. The issue is simply about power.

Conclusion: Privacy, Surveillance, and Power

I will paint a more comprehensive picture of the entire range of groups that advocate for privacy in the next chapter. The above statements, strategies, purposes, and rhetoric simply offer a preface to the groups and themes discussed in this book.

Earlier, I drew a distinction among humanistic, political, and instrumental motivations behind privacy protection, each of which is expressed in the quotations above. Some groups see the issue in terms of promoting and protecting an essential human dignity. Others emphasize political dimensions, seeing privacy as one value that can be advanced to control the worst effects of power (public and private). Others view it in instrumental terms—to advance better health care, to promote a free and unregulated Internet, to advance consumer protection, and so on.

It is also instructive how some advocates stress individual protection, while others see the value in a social framework. The word "surveillance" is explicit in the framing of the issue by some groups, thus posing the question in more collective terms: "is this the kind of society we wish to live in?" The distinction is important, and we will return to it. New technologies—video surveillance, for instance—can be used in ways that are detrimental to individual privacy rights; tapes can be inappropriately accessed, individuals might be victims of mistaken identity, they might be recognized in contexts that they would rather keep confidential, and so on. At an individual level, we have plenty of evidence that informational privacy rights can be violated by this technology, occasionally inspiring complaints and litigation. But the issue can also be framed in social terms: "do we wish to live in a society in which cameras are monitoring our every move?" Some groups tend to see the issue in this broader framework; others are directed by the desire and need to resolve the individual grievance.

Some groups see the issues in international, perhaps global, terms. Others tend to be more focused on specific countries. Some have a very broad technological span. Others prefer to concentrate their efforts on a selection of the more intrusive practices. Some see their mandate as to protect individuals as "citizens"; others focus on "consumers." For some groups, privacy is the central focus. For others it is one of a suite of civil liberties and rights necessary for the protection of liberal democracy. For some, whether surveillance is offline or online is immaterial. For others it is crucial; privacy rights are one frontier over which the essential structure of the Internet is being fought.

These are merely tendencies, and we should not read too much into differences of emphasis, nor of course infer that these statements have been carefully considered, debated, and ratified as accurate expressions of organizational purpose. Nor should it be inferred that these various justifications actually motivate the individual activists. One very powerful theme that animates privacy advocates is the abuse of power. Many, as we will see, get their batteries recharged when they force a powerful organization on the defensive, or embarrass an arrogant minister or CEO, or catch those organizations in a lie. Privacy is one vehicle, among many, for redressing the balance between the powerful and the powerless.

After we have examined the organization, networking, and strategies of privacy advocacy groups in the pages that follow, it will be possible to address in a more sustained manner the central question about whether, in Tarrow's terms, there is a "generalization of grievance" that defines the "us and them" in the conflict structure. It is clear that privacy is a multidimensional and often subjective value. It can mean a lot of things, and it can mean different things to different people. But, despite the conceptual confusion, for better or worse, privacy is still the concept around which the major policy issues have been framed (at least in the English-speaking world) for more than forty years. And "privacy advocates" have learned to live with it.

2 The Groups

The desire for privacy is not an admission of guilt.
—Individual-I.com

Nos Libertés sont notre sécurité.
—The Ligue des Droits et Libertés of Quebec

The spontaneous emergence of numerous "voluntary associations" that can advance the multiple interests of complex societies and influence social attitudes and government policy has long been regarded as one crucial test of liberal democracy. Over the years, the concepts have been refined and different models have been developed to explain the rise of groups and to describe the patterns of "group-government intermediation" in different societies. In some countries, there are tendencies toward more clientilist or corporatist relations, where government officially sanctions certain groups over others and proactively brings them into the policymaking process. In others—notably, the United States—the patterns are more unpredictable, spontaneous, fragmented, and "pluralistic." In every country, it is commonly assumed that the understanding of law and policy must reside in some measure in the activities of groups that operate outside the formal institutions of the state.

The aim of this chapter is to describe the community of groups that has emerged to promote the cause of personal privacy protection. The approach is not unlike that pursued in sociological studies of organizational ecology, which investigate how organizations arise, adapt, and disband as a result of changes in the wider environmental conditions (Hannan and Freeman 1989). This landscape is necessarily viewed as if from a high-flying aircraft; I leave more detailed exploration to later chapters. It is also necessarily global in scope. Personal information knows no national or cultural attachments. Neither do the policy issues surrounding privacy.

Some groups obviously focus on their own national governments, but many have to operate on a wider stage.

At the associational level, many groups eschew the word privacy in their names. I cannot rely on titles or self-descriptions. Rather, my approach is driven by the question: when important issues surrounding the collection, processing, and distribution of personal information—surveillance issues—arise, who objects, resists, perhaps mobilizes? When framed in these terms, the list of groups is a very long one, and the landscape impossibly complicated. I need, therefore, a useful classification that captures both the breadth and complexity of privacy advocacy, is suggestive of the different emphases, and indicates the various reasons why the major groups have entered this terrain.

I also need to draw some lines of exclusion. As noted in the introduction, this book does not analyze the official data protection authorities established under national data protection or privacy laws. Most countries (with the notable exception of the United States) have set up small privacy or data protection agencies with varying oversight, advisory, investigative, educational, and regulatory powers. Some of these agencies have strong enforcement and regulatory powers; others act as more advisory, "ombudsman-like" bodies. Some are headed by a collective commission (such as in France), others by a single "privacy commissioner" or "data protection commissioner" (as in Canada, Australia, and Germany).

There is no doubt that privacy and data protection commissioners can be strong advocates. Indeed, in Europe, Canada, Australia, and other states, these are the primary agencies expected to resist excessive surveillance and promote the cause of privacy. However, the fact that these authorities do have official status and a statutory mandate makes their roles less interesting from the point of view of this study. There is plenty written by, and about, the official "data protectors" (Flaherty 1989; Bygrave 2002; Bennett and Raab 2006). Their activities do enter this analysis, but not as a central focus.

Privacy advocates also work with great effect within large corporations. Most major companies have now appointed chief privacy officers (CPOs) who can play an important role within their organizations and on the broader national and international stage. In some countries, such as Canada and Germany, every organization that processes personal information is statutorily expected to appoint a responsible official who can oversee the implementation of privacy protection principles within the organization. In other countries, these offices have been established out of recognition that privacy makes "good business sense." Again, however, these individuals operate with an official organizational mandate and have to be sidelined.

The exclusion of the state and the market then leaves those groups that have arisen more spontaneously from "civil society" defined by the London School of Economics Center for Civil Society as follows:

> Civil society refers to the arena of uncoerced collective action around shared interests, purposes and values. In theory, its institutional forms are distinct from those of the state, family and market, though in practice, the boundaries between state, civil society, family and market are often complex, blurred and negotiated. Civil society commonly embraces a diversity of spaces, actors and institutional forms, varying in their degree of formality, autonomy and power.[1]

This conception refers more to a space than to the structures that might operate within that space. Civil society implies a sphere of social action wherein groups can spontaneously arise, grow, split, merge, disband, coalesce, and generally compete for attention (Keane 2003). These groups are distinct from both government and market, but they interpenetrate each in ways that affect both.

This broad conception only gets us so far. Privacy related groups can be located within civil society without playing any kind of advocacy role. Some, for example, may solely be engaged in research or journalism. Others might work as for-profit consultancies; I have tried as far as possible to focus on the nonprofit sector.[2] Others have a primary mandate to offer training and education for organizations. Blogs also complicate the picture. As do organizations whose sole purpose is to provide privacy-enhancing technologies.

Another way to view the distinctions within this community is in terms of motivations. There are those groups with essentially instrumental goals—such as the multinational corporations, labor unions, or trade associations. There are also those motivated principally by shared expertise, such as scientific groups, or "epistemic communities." And then there are those driven principally by common principled ideas or values. These are the groups that seek collective goods, the achievement of which benefit everyone, and not just the membership or the activists within the organization. Privacy advocacy groups tend to fall into this last category.

As chapter 1 demonstrated, privacy is a value of extraordinary breadth and flexibility that frames a number of interrelated social and political issues. The organizational ecology also tends to reflect this multiplicity of discourses and aims. The following typology is neither jointly exhaustive not mutually exclusive; overlaps, contradictions, and inconsistencies are observed at every juncture. Nevertheless emphases and tendencies are apparent, depending on whether privacy is viewed (1) as a separate issue in its own right, (2) as one of a broader suite of civil liberties, (3) as a human right, (4) as an issue of consumer protection, (5) as one of several associated digital rights related to the development of the Internet, or (6) as an issue that needs to be disaggregated into a plethora of "single issues." With this categorization in mind, we can observe certain national and international tendencies in the global phenomenon of privacy advocacy.

Privacy-centric Advocacy Groups

Which groups and associations focus exclusively, or almost exclusively, on privacy and data protection issues? Which take their very identity and raison d'être from the issue itself, regardless of technology and regardless of whether the privacy invasions are perpetrated by the state or by business? Which tend to leave advocacy on related issues, such as freedom of information, freedom of speech, intellectual property, and so on, to others? With these parameters, the list is not long.

Let us begin with Privacy International (PI), founded in 1990 as a "watchdog on surveillance and privacy invasions by governments and corporations." PI was the brainchild of Simon Davies, who earlier had worked on the Australia Card campaign and was a leading figure in the Australian Privacy Foundation. It arose as a result of informal conversations among disparate individuals about the need for international coordination, especially as surveillance issues and privacy instruments were becoming transnational in scope. At that time, there was no Internet and few conference opportunities for networking. Davies had to engage in a lot of international travel and also apparently spent many months based at the New South Wales Law School building a network and running up a huge fax bill.[3]

PI was originally conceived as an umbrella organization, on the model of Amnesty International, linking the various national organizations and experts interested in the issue. PI was to facilitate the strengthening of privacy advocacy groups where they existed and the creation of such groups where they did not. Davies conceived of himself as a kind of international troubleshooter, flying in and helping out the national activists when intrusive surveillance schemes were being contemplated. Originally the network embraced representatives from around forty countries. In the words of the first chairman, Jan Holvast, this cooperation "is a necessity in a world in which technology generally is used for one purpose: namely, to strengthen the power of those who have it, and almost never for the purpose of strengthening people's rights and freedoms." Holvast also stressed the central motivation to view privacy as "primarily, a political problem, although in most countries with a data protection law the emphasis is on jurisdictional measures."[4] Davies also echoed the need for a broader approach:

Many members in countries ruled by totalitarian and military regimes know that invasions of privacy often intersect with violations of other fundamental rights and freedoms. The link between the traditional and modern hemispheres of privacy is vital to ensure that privacy protection remains a vital and pro-active issue for the people, and not simply the domain of technocrats. If privacy is indeed a reflection of the power relationships in society, then the pursuit of its protection must surely be groundbreaking and energetic. Such countries as Germany, the Netherlands and Australia which have witnessed extensive campaigns to protect privacy have learned that protection of these rights requires a constant testing of political limits.[5]

Over the years, PI has waged a number of campaigns on diverse issues in many countries. Indeed over the last sixteen years, there have been few privacy-related issues with which PI has not, at some level, been involved. But it ceased any pretense of being an "umbrella organization" long ago. It has never embraced a mass membership, nor received any consistent source of funding. In the words of Gus Hosein, who joined PI in 1996: "It's a small fish trying to pretend it's a big one. It is in reality just three people and we all do our own thing trying to keep up on all the battles that are going on."[6] And in the words of Davies, "We never wanted this to be an umbrella in the classic sense because it meant we wouldn't be able to perform activism so easily. We would have been hamstrung by constant reference to the membership's wishes."[7]

Today, therefore, PI is small, but very visible. Davies describes the organization as "panther-like"—quickly springing into action with analysis, press releases, media commentary, and public complaints to commissioners, when the time and issue is right. Hosein describes its role in these terms:

The term we use on our Web site is a "watchdog organization" but really we like to think of ourselves also as a sniper organization where we see an issue and we try to find the most effective way of hitting it down and then we pull back and move on to the next because there are so many issues out there. We tried for a while long-term research on a specific area, such as terrorism policy. But that just went on and on. We were never able to follow through with advocacy in time, before the given policy moved on. Now we are going back to the sniper shots where we just aim, shoot and move on to the next target.[8]

Later chapters review some of the cases where these tactics have sometimes been very effective.

As mentioned previously, the inspiration for PI came in part from the successful opposition to the Australia Card and subsequent formation of the Australian Privacy Foundation. APF remains one of the only national organizations dedicated solely to the protection of privacy rights. And it too has always been a small organization with a big reputation. It was started in 1988 during the Australia Card campaign by a few experts who had been involved in the issue, either in academic capacities, through legal or journalistic work or through their association with the New South Wales Privacy Committee. APF continued after the defeat of the Australia Card, initially to ensure the passage of effective privacy legislation for the public sector.

Since then, a core and relatively stable group of advocates has consistently and expertly advanced the cause and gained a respect with business and government. They were particularly influential in securing effective credit reporting legislation in 1990, and leading the opposition to a self-regulatory option for privacy protection in the private sector in the late 1990s. In 1993, a parallel and broader organization, the Australian Privacy Charter Council, launched the Australian Privacy Charter, a strong statement of privacy principles, which influenced the later development of national privacy principles for the private sector and was later adopted as APF's policy constitution. More recently, APF has played a key role in the opposition to the government's proposals for Australia Card II, the "Access Card."

However, APF has never had a mass membership to speak of, and it really operates on the voluntary efforts of a few key people. It has remained, nevertheless, the main NGO voice for privacy protection in Australia. In its own words: "The Privacy Foundation plays a unique role as a nongovernment organization active on a wide range of privacy issues. It works with consumer organizations, civil liberties councils, professional associations, and other community groups on specific privacy issues. The Privacy Foundation is also a participant in Privacy International, the worldwide privacy protection network. Where possible, it cooperates with and supports official agencies, but it is entirely independent—and often critical—of the performance of agencies set up to protect our privacy."[9]

Most privacy advocacy groups are located in the United States, and one of the most prominent is the Electronic Privacy Information Center

(EPIC). EPIC is described as "a public interest research center in Washington, D.C. It was established in 1994 to focus public attention on emerging civil liberties issues and to protect privacy, the First Amendment, and constitutional values." The founder, and current executive director, is Marc Rotenberg, who had been an intern at the ACLU, executive director of an early organization called the Public Interest Computing Association (PICA), counsel to Senator Patrick Leahy of Vermont, and staff counsel to the Senate subcommittee on Law and Technology. In 1988, Rotenberg joined the staff of Computer Professionals for Social Responsibility (CPSR) as the National Program Director for its Computing and Civil Liberties project, inaugurated to provide research support to Washington organizations that knew little or nothing about computing.[10] It was from CPSR that Rotenberg launched in 1990 one of the first privacy campaigns against the Lotus Marketplace product, discussed in chapter 5.

EPIC has its roots in Rotenberg's recognition of the importance of institutionalizing public interest advocacy in the field of privacy and civil liberties.[11] By the early 1990s, when networked communications were proliferating, he was convinced that a separate and privacy-focused advocacy group in Washington, D.C., was necessary. EPIC has had considerable success in attracting donations from major foundations, including the Ford Foundation, the Open Society Institute, and the Fund for Constitutional Government. Other support comes from individual contributions, attorneys' fees, *cy pres* funds,[12] and the sale of its publications. Over the last decade or so, it has been able to employ a permanent staff, including a staff counsel, and run a fellows program. It also has a nine-person board of directors, as well as an advisory board, that has included some of the most prominent privacy and security experts in the world, and has proven an invaluable resource for advice and guidance, especially on complicated technical privacy questions. But it does not maintain a membership base, reducing the maintenance costs of the organization and allowing it a greater freedom to pursue its priorities (Kuerbis 2005).

In policy terms, EPIC has been involved in issues concerning free speech, open government, electronic voting, and privacy. It is fair to say, however, that its primary focus has been toward privacy issues, and the name itself implies that emphasis. EPIC's work is also not confined to Internet-related issues. Over the years, it has conducted research and waged campaigns on an extraordinary range of privacy-related issues in both government and business, regardless of technology.[13] The only

possible exceptions are the larger privacy questions associated with repro-
ductive freedoms, or sexual identity, that at least in the United States
have been constitutionalized as privacy rights.

EPIC's activities and campaigns will appear regularly throughout this
study. A prior case study of EPIC's work (Kuerbis 2005) has also emphasized its "commitment to movement-building" through activities such
as the Public Voice Project, which provides for civil society leaders to
engage directly with officials of government and international organizations for "constructive engagement about current policy issues" (EPIC
2006, 6). It is also important to note EPIC's international reach through
organizations such as the World Summit on the Information Society
(WSIS) and the Internet Corporation for Assigned Names and Numbers
(ICANN). Together with Privacy International, it has published a comprehensive annual report on privacy and human rights around the world
since 1999, now coordinating the work of over three hundred contributors
(EPIC 2007). It also distributes a weekly update on privacy developments
entitled, EPIC-ALERT.

The Privacy Rights Clearinghouse (PRC), founded in 1992 and based
in San Diego, is another American advocacy group that deserves early
mention. It was originally set up under a cy pres award resulting from a
class action suit by the Utilities Commission Action Network (UCAN)
against the then Pacific Bell, and a consequent decision to establish a consumer education program around privacy. It now principally receives
funds from the Rose Foundation. PRC's goals are to raise consumers'
awareness, empower consumers to take action to control their own personal information, respond to specific privacy-related complaints from
consumers, document the nature of consumers' complaints and questions
about privacy, and advocate for consumers' privacy rights in local, state,
and federal public policy proceedings.[14]

In the American context, PRC is the only privacy NGO that actually
receives individual complaints. Beth Givens, the founder and director,
explains why it was established: "When we started in July 1992, I was
not able to find any information resources on how to protect your privacy, except for, say, *Privacy Journal* and Bob Ellis Smith. So, I guess I
felt we were filling a niche. There was just nothing out there on how to
protect your privacy except for Bob's work. We wanted to publish real
'nuts and bolts' information."[15]

PRC operates with a very small staff and receives inquiries by phone or
e-mail from all manner of people. It documents these inquiries, which
might be anonymous, and refer inquirers either to their own fact sheets

or to the resources of other organizations. It also issues regular alerts on key consumer issues at key times—telemarketing, phishing, ID theft, privacy tips at tax time, and so on. It employs one part-time lobbyist in Sacramento who can advance privacy interests at the state level, and occasionally stop intrusive measures from being passed. But its primary mission as educational. Givens again: "I think we are unique. I see the other groups as really focusing on policy. I see us filling a great need in terms of developing information resources for individuals on ways they can protect their privacy.... We do get involved in policy, yes, but I would say our educational role is the stronger."[16] No other advocacy group in the United States is set up to receive inquiries from ordinary citizens, even though most other groups do try to assist and refer. Yet, PRC is explicitly a "clearinghouse" and takes that role very seriously.

The various issues addressed by PRC also demonstrate the difficulty of considering "consumer" privacy rights in isolation from other civil liberties or human rights issues. In fact, Givens does not particularly like the term. Nevertheless, a consumer orientation does suggest an emphasis on private-sector practices, and indeed most of its focus on identity theft, direct marketing, consumer credit, financial privacy, background checks in the workplace, Internet, and telecommunications suggests that they do try to leave some of the larger state surveillance, or Fourth Amendment, issues to other groups. Nevertheless, they also do work on the uses of public records, medical records, the uses of the social security number, and other explicitly government-related privacy questions. The distinction between public and private sectors, and therefore between the individual as a "citizen" and the individual as a "consumer" is impossible to draw.

Beyond those mentioned, it is difficult to find organizations that share the same focus on privacy per se. A relatively new group is Privacy Activism, a "non-profit organization whose goal is to enable people to make well-informed decisions about the importance of privacy on both a personal and societal level." Its emphasis is upon the "real-world implications of privacy losses or invasions" because privacy is too often discussed in technical and legal jargon that makes the issues seem abstract. According to its volunteers: "We intend to make the discussion more concrete and relevant by helping people understand the ramifications of the choices that they make in everyday life." To accomplish this, they make use of graphics, videos, games, and stories to communicate the issues. The volunteers include not only lawyers and technologists but also graphic designers, artists, and writers. The emphasis is very much on grassroots activism and organization as opposed to advocacy or lobbying of governments.[17] Their work to date has been limited to a few high-profile issues related to surveillance and airline profiling. They have also organized a grassroots campaign to file one hundred thousand comments on the Real ID initiative, the effort to harmonize U.S. drivers' licenses.[18]

Again within the United States, the World Privacy Forum (WPF) is another recent organization that focuses on "conducting in-depth research and consumer education in the intersecting areas of technology and privacy." The WPF has conducted research on consumer data privacy, workplace privacy, job applicant rights and privacy, background checks and public records, identity issues, communications privacy, financial privacy, and especially medical privacy. The focus is on "informing the public about their privacy rights and the short- and long-term consequences of losing them—either inadvertently, or by explicitly trading them away for the perception of security or convenience."[19]

The group was founded and led by Pam Dixon, a former journalist for the *San Diego Tribune*. It is more or less a small consortium of researchers, with different legal, policy, and technical expertise, who contract to conduct research and write reports on critical privacy issues of the day. Funding is, therefore, project related and is typically provided through independent foundation grants. Dixon explains the rationale: "I felt that there were many groups that were doing lobbying on legislative activities. There were also a number of groups that were doing victim advocacy, where they would say: "here's how to fix your files".... But what I felt was missing was the investigative piece. Who was looking at privacy and innovating? I felt that was completely lacking and so that's really the niche."[20] The WPF also attempts to forge links in areas of the world where there is not a solid NGO tradition, and has been trying to advance the issue in areas such as Asia and Latin America.

Even in countries where there is a "solid NGO tradition" the number of groups dedicated principally to privacy advocacy is few and far between. For example, there is no equivalent to EPIC or APF in Canada where privacy advocacy has traditionally been advanced through a network of individuals drawn from other consumer and civil liberties organizations as well as academia. There is a Freedom of Information and Privacy Association (FIPA) in British Columbia that over the years has concentrated more and more on privacy questions, but all attempts to form a more coherent coalition have been thwarted by lack of funds as well as by the difficulty of face-to-face meetings within such a huge country. Thus, the only current manifestation of a national privacy movement is the National Privacy Coalition LISTSERV.

In countries in which privacy and data protection legislation is quite advanced, and in which official data protection agencies have a lengthy history, often privacy advocacy groups can be crowded out of the policy space. So when we look to European countries for equivalents for dedicated groups of this kind, there are few current examples. An important group of historic importance, however, is the Dutch organization Privacy Alert (Stichtung Waakzaamheid Persoonregistratiie), which was established in 1970 as a result of controversy over the Dutch census, and which has conducted research, worked for citizens, and lobbied successfully on a range of issues. By the late 1980s it was probably the best-staffed nongovernmental privacy watchdog in the world (Davies 1999, 154). But it ran out of funds in 1993 and was disbanded a year later.

One explanation for the demise is the institutionalization of the privacy watchdog function in Dutch society. At around this time, the Dutch data protection authority (then called the Registratiekammer), established in 1988, was assuming an official role as the protector of privacy rights and interests in the Netherlands. The growth of official data protection authorities can have the effect of crowding out the policy space for nongovernmental advocacy groups. An early organization in (West) Germany, the German Association for Data Protection (Deutsche Vereinigung für Datenschutz) declined in importance as the network of German data protection commissioners (Datenschutzbeauftragte) became institutionalized throughout the 1980s and 1990s. There is also a small Austrian equivalent (Arge Daten), which maintains an active membership, a LIST-SERV, a complaints resolution process, and an active lobbying presence in Austria.[21]

The broad conclusion at this stage is that the modern policy issue, defined as privacy in the United States and data protection in Europe, has sustained few advocacy groups whose principal interests are in these issues. In most countries, the privacy advocacy role is inextricably linked to broader civil liberties, human rights, consumer, or Internet freedom questions. Most groups have arisen, therefore, for reasons beyond those of advocating for privacy rights.

Privacy Advocacy and Civil Liberties

The protection of privacy has always featured prominently within the agendas of civil liberties organizations, historically concerned with the legitimate boundaries between the individual and state and with the protection of citizens from abuses of power. For these groups, therefore, privacy advocacy tends to be focused on the protection of individuals from intrusions by the instruments of the state, and most especially by law enforcement agencies. Further, the political cultures of many countries do not readily embrace a "civil liberties tradition" that tends to be associated with countries with written constitutions and enumerated rights therein. It also tends to connote individual, rather than group (or civil) rights. However defined, in most advanced industrial societies we find civil society groups that have long sought to protect individuals from abuses of power by the state. Privacy advocacy, while often not described as such, is a significant component of that tradition.

By far the oldest, biggest, and most well-funded civil liberties group in the world is the American Civil Liberties Union. It was begun in 1920 and now boasts more than half a million supporters and members, five hundred staff members in Washington, D.C., alone, as well as offices in every U.S. state. With an annual budget of $100 million, raised through subscriptions, foundation grants and donations, the ACLU, in contrast with all other groups in this network, is gargantuan. It therefore has a unique ability to mobilize a vast network throughout the United States and to use its unequaled experience in legislative lobbying and "impact litigation."

Of course, the ACLU's raison d'être is to protect all the rights (and especially minority rights) protected by the U.S. Constitution. Privacy protection, therefore, is generally not treated as a question with a profile distinct from the broader civil liberties agenda. Privacy advocacy within the ACLU must, as all other advocacy, conform to the policies, decided by its Board of Directors, and to its established decision-making procedures. Privacy advocacy must also compete for time and resources within this large and complex organization. The ACLU is also based on a quite decentralized, perhaps confederal, model. All its local affiliates are independent. So national campaigns require active support and buy-in across the country, especially where there are state and local implications. Affiliates are also free to act and campaign alone, so long as they do not contradict national policies. Sometimes they will act in concert with other state affiliates, without the participation of the national office.[22]

The history and politics of the ACLU are matters of scholarly debate and controversy in their own right. Whether it is an organization driven by principle—"defending everybody" (Garey 1998)—or an inherently "political" organization whose leadership possesses distinct political agendas about the kind of society they would like to see (Donahue 1985), is not a matter that can be debated here. There is no doubt, however, that its espousal of privacy rights must be seen in this larger context. Unlike almost any other organization discussed in his book, the ACLU is a household name. It is an organization that inspires passionate feelings in support and opposition, as a result of the famous cases it has fought over the decades. In its principled attempt to defend the rights of minorities regardless of political affiliation, it has attracted vehement attacks for being "pro-criminal," "pro-communist," "pro-Nazi" and in current circumstances, "pro-terrorist."[23]

Privacy issues tend to span ideological divides and have generally been less controversial for the ACLU—perhaps "the most widely accepted civil liberties principle and the most systematically threatened" (Walker 1999, 309). These issues were propelled onto the U.S. national agenda in the post-Watergate climate of the 1970s, which offered a window of opportunity to provide some legislative protections against abuses of personal databanks, most notably the 1974 Privacy Act. It had become apparent that governmental power was being expanded and deepened and that the other constitutional rights and liberties were profoundly dependent on giving individuals better control over their personal information.

The work of the director, Aryeh Neier (1974), was instrumental in pushing privacy as a separate topic to the ACLU's agenda. But perhaps the most influential figure in these years was Morton Halperin, who served as director of the Center for National Security Studies from 1975 to 1992, and was also the executive director of the ACLU's Washington office from 1984 to 1992. A dedicated Privacy Project was begun in these years, first headed by Jerry Berman and then by Janlori Goldman. Later in the 1990s, and certainly since 9/11, the issue has been regarded as inseparable from the broader civil liberties agenda. It currently tends to fit within the Technology and Liberty Project, established in 2002 to "monitor the interplay between cutting-edge technology and civil liberties, actively promoting responsible uses of technology that enhance privacy and freedom, while opposing those that undermine our freedoms and move us closer to a surveillance society."[24]

Throughout the 1980s and 1990s, the ACLU has been prominent in most privacy-related debates within the United States and beyond. It tends to focus on governmental surveillance programs, which have Bill of Rights implications, rather than on private-sector issues. An examination of the ACLU's privacy agenda today reveals, however, a powerful belief that since 9/11 and the war on terror, the issue has been on the defensive. It also reveals that historic distinctions between government and private sector have broken down. The surveillance society now embraces a complicated and largely unfathomable web of governmental and non-governmental networks.[25] The organizational distinctions have been blurred, as have the traditional agendas for the ACLU. Its agenda today covers both consumer and workplace privacy questions, as well as the more traditional concerns over the behavior of U.S. law enforcement and national security agencies. There is now a "Bigger Monster" and "Weaker Chains."[26]

For other groups, however, the distinctions between public and private sectors remain crucial. The CATO Institute would not describe itself as a "civil liberties" organization. It is animated by a particular view of the American liberal tradition, which differs in many respects from that of the ACLU: "The Jeffersonian philosophy that animates CATO's work has increasingly come to be called "libertarianism" or "market liberalism." It combines an appreciation for entrepreneurship, the market process, and lower taxes with strict respect for civil liberties and skepticism about the benefits of both the welfare state and foreign military adventurism. The market-liberal vision brings the wisdom of the American Founders to bear on the problems of today."[27]

Privacy protection can sit easily within this ideological framework at least in so far as it constrains governmental actions. For CATO, threats from business are nowhere near as important as those from government. Jim Harper, director of Information Studies at the CATO Institute, has a particular reading of Orwell that is instructive: "George Orwell coined the term Big Brother as a warning against the invasive power of governments, not the private sector." For him, governments have a unique ability to compel the extraction of personal information through the force of law. Whereas "a web of laws and incentives constrain private sector use and misuse of data, government databases hang like a sword of Damocles over the privacy and civil liberties of citizens."[28] CATO is also very resistant to the idea that governmental agencies or agents can act as official protectors or overseers of individual privacy rights. In this vein, Solveig Singleton has argued that the "most effective rules for ameliorating federal threats to privacy are to limit the powers of the federal government overall and restrict the growth of federal programs. So long as such programs grow unchecked and taxes rise unchecked, government demands for more information will prove irresistible."[29]

Over the last few years, therefore, the CATO Institute has been critical of new technologies and methods of government identification, including biometrics. It has opposed ID cards vociferously as well as the expanding governmental surveillance programs inherent in the Bush administration's war on terror. Similar issues have been advanced by a more recent group with similar ideology called the Liberty Coalition, whose mission is to "help organize, support, and coordinate transpartisan public policy activities related to civil liberties and human rights." They too have discovered that one prominent area for "transpartisan activity" is privacy.[30]

There are civil liberties organizations in many other countries, but they are generally a lot smaller and poorer than the ACLU. Some also have not made privacy protection a priority. The Canadian Civil Liberties Association (CCLA), for instance, was established in 1964. Its mission is stated as the protection of the fundamental freedoms essential to the democratic system, the promotion of legal protections against unreasonable invasion by public authority of the freedom and dignity of the individual, and the promotion of fair procedures for the resolution and adjudication of conflicts and disputes. Historically, its work on privacy-related questions has tended to be confined to issues of search and seizure by police. Since 9/11, however, there has been a greater emphasis on issues such as the sharing of airline passenger information, video surveillance, cyber-snooping, and national identity cards.[31]

A more significant player on the Canadian and international stage has been the British Columbia Civil Liberties Association (BCCLA), which predates the CCLA, has a somewhat different vision of civil liberties campaigning, and, indeed, has never been affiliated with the CCLA. It was born out of general dissatisfaction with the earlier Canadian Civil Liberties Union, which had grown up in the 1930s, as well as out of a desire to develop an organization that was less waspish, male, and intellectual. The organization was also the product of a particular abuse of police power over the Doukhabour organization called the "Sons of Freedom," labeled subversive by many British Columbians with, as the BCCLA notes, "disturbing parallels to current public debates about the rights of terrorists."[32]

The contemporary BCCLA is probably the most effective, and best funded, civil liberties organization in Canada. It has also been far more vocal in the major privacy debates in Canada, including national identification systems, video surveillance, and access to telephone and Internet traffic data, as well as in more local questions (Westwood 1999). It has also been prominent in the various efforts to develop and strengthen Canadian privacy law and in overseeing the work of Canada's federal and provincial privacy commissioners. Again, however, the BCCLA's mission is broadly defined, and privacy protection is one theme in the larger array of civil liberties and human rights interests on its agenda.

In a similar fashion, privacy advocacy appears with varying prominence within the agendas of other national civil liberties organizations. In Germany, the equivalent organization is probably *Die Humanistische Union*, established in 1961 to advance civil rights, explicitly in opposition to conservative and Catholic influences in German political parties at the time. Over the years, it has taken up certain privacy and data protection issues, and in recent times has been involved in questions of video surveillance and the retention of communications traffic data.[33]

In Britain, the major civil liberties organizations are Liberty and Statewatch. The aims of the former, which until 1991 was called the National Council for Civil Liberties (NCCL), are described broadly: "We believe in a society based on the democratic participation of all its members and the principles of justice, openness, the right to dissent, and respect for diversity. We aim to secure the equal rights of everyone (as long as they don't infringe on the rights and freedoms of others) and oppose any abuse or excessive power by the state against its people."[34] Like many of its counterparts in other countries, the NCCL has its origins in the conflicts and oppression prevalent during the 1930s, with the mass unemployment, hunger marches, and rise of Fascism.

Statewatch used to be a specific project of the NCCL. It broke away in 1991 and has a more explicit European focus as well as a stronger emphasis on questions of surveillance. It is now composed of "lawyers, academics, journalists, researchers, and community activists. Its European network of contributors is drawn from fifteen countries. Statewatch encourages the publication of investigative journalism and critical research in Europe in the fields of the state, justice and home affairs, civil liberties, accountability and openness."[35] It therefore has close affiliations with sister organizations in Europe.[36] A further effort at integration occurred in 2005 with the creation of the European Civil Liberties Network (ECLN), which aims to bring together "groups and individuals who share the common objectives of seeking to create a European society based on freedom and equality, of fundamental civil liberties and personal and political freedoms, of free movement and freedom of information, and equal rights for minorities."[37]

The ECLN, therefore, intends to campaign on children's rights, democratic standards, freedom of information, immigration and asylum questions, military questions, policing and public order, prisons, racism, security, and intelligence, as well as on surveillance and the war on terror. This breadth is typical and has some implications for privacy advocacy. For the civil liberties organization, privacy campaigning is inseparable from the larger attempt to extend democratic rights. It tends, therefore, to be seen in collective as well as individual terms where privacy advocacy is not only an issue of civil liberties but also one of discrimination. Some people simply get more surveillance (and less privacy) than others. The opposition to racism, sexism, and homophobia, prominent on the agendas of all civil liberties organizations, is deeply connected to societal practices concerning the collection and processing of personal information. Thus, the integration of surveillance questions into wider objectives for social justice and equality is inevitable and deliberate, and especially prominent within European civil liberties organizations, such as Statewatch, Liberty, or the Dutch organization, Buro Jansen and Janssen.[38]

When one drills down to more specific issue areas there is no question that inherent contradictions and conflicts emerge from time to time. Civil liberties organizations defend rights to free speech and the press, and occasionally the claim of certain individuals to anonymity clashes directly with demands for accountability. Similar conflicts can occur with respect to the criminal justice system. For instance, holding law enforcement agencies accountable sometimes requires detailed information about their activities (such as arrest patterns), with implications for the privacy of arrestees (Walker 1999, 308). Privacy conflicts with other public interests on an ethical level, as well as on a policy level. Any civil liberties organization also has to negotiate these competing claims.

Privacy Advocacy and Human Rights

Many would insist that privacy is fundamentally a human right. The claims of civil liberties advocates tend to be made with reference to specific national constitutional guarantees, such as the Bill of Rights in the United States. Claims about privacy as a "human right" tend to be made in more universalistic terms on the grounds that we possess certain inherent human rights by virtue of our humanity, rather than our citizenship. Thus the Universal Declaration of Human Rights (UDHR) states that "everyone has the right to life, liberty and security of person" (Article 3). It goes on to state that "no one shall be subjected to arbitrary interference with his privacy, family, home or correspondence, nor to attacks upon his honor and reputation. Everyone has the right to the protection of the law against such interference or attacks" (Article 12).

In societies with recent histories of extreme repression, issues of torture, imprisonment without trial, genocide (ethnic cleansing), and so on, obviously take priority over the kinds of privacy questions debated within advanced democratic states. An antisurveillance agenda has never entered the work of Amnesty International (AI) for example, an organization that has tended to shun theorization about problems in favor of practical and action-oriented activism based on a shared belief in the moral authority of its campaigns (Hopgood 2006, 19). Those campaigns are rarely addressed in terms of promoting "privacy" and yet there is a clear, if unstated, bond between the use of surveillance technology and the kinds of oppression documented by AI.

For example, in the context of supporting freedom of expression on the Internet, it has opposed the monitoring of Internet use and the companies that have been complicit with governments in providing information on their users, and in supporting censorship. These and other efforts are embraced by AI's general campaign on the Internet and Human Rights. It declares: "The internet is the new frontline in the fight for human rights. The initial grace period in which internet-users enjoyed complete freedom, while the authorities caught up with the technology, has ended. Governments are increasingly monitoring Web, email and blog use, censoring and prosecuting their citizens for expressing their opinions online."[39] Their very vision of a world in which everybody enjoys all the rights enshrined in the UDHR clearly embraces a world in which individuals are free from unnecessary intrusions into their private lives. In this sense, AI is also a privacy advocacy organization.

These issues have come to prominence with respect to very high profile cases concerning the relationship between certain Internet companies and the government of China. Most notably, in 2005, Yahoo, via its Chinese partner company, provided the authorities with private and confidential information about its users that has been used to convict and imprison journalists. In 2006, Google cooperated with Chinese officials to restrict search results for topics such as "human rights," "political reform," "Tiananmen Square" and "Falun Gong." A government-sponsored Canadian group, the International Centre for Human Rights and Democratic Development (now called Rights and Democracy) has been constantly pushing Western governments and companies to restrict sales of certain cyber-technology, which might be used for surveillance purposes, to Chinese agencies.[40]

There is evidence that many groups in democratizing countries see the close relationship between surveillance and other forms of repression and have embraced a pro-privacy agenda, even if it is not termed as such. Privacy issues are often brought to the fore as a result of the practical and inherent problems of campaigning for human rights in repressive regimes.

Human rights organizations face some agonizing dilemmas about the collection and confidentiality of extraordinarily sensitive information about rights abuses, dissidents, and so on. They are, themselves, subjected to surveillance, the interception of communications and sometimes more brutal treatment. Privaterra[41] works with human rights groups around the world offering training and advice about communications security and database privacy. It offers basic education as well as more technical assistance about various encryption tools. Robert Guerra, one of the founders of the organization in 2001, explains the importance of its work and the differences between privacy breaches in the developed world and those in some of the societies in which he has worked:

If I were to give you maybe some experience from either the fieldwork or actually some of the organizations that I've worked with, the breaches of information are far more serious in other parts of the world compared to here. And so whereas [in Canada], we see the instances of tapes going missing or medical records appearing in dumpsters, in other parts of world, it's been organizations having armed men come to their organizations and taking their computers. Then the people who are mentioned in the computers have things start happening to them.[42]

A related group, Frontline, has produced a manual of security and cryptography methods written in plain language for the human rights worker. They remind us that the lack of interest or capacity to learn about electronic security "has led to numerous arrests, attacks and misunderstandings in the human rights community. Electronic security and digital privacy should become not just an important area for comprehension and participation, but also a new battleground in the struggle for the worldwide adherence to the principles of the UDHR" (Vitaliev 2007, 8).

It is difficult, however, to find examples of NGOs in the developing world whose mission is focused on privacy and surveillance questions. Privaterra's main work has been in countries of Central and Latin America, where data protection law has been slow to develop.[43] There are some interesting provisions in some Latin American constitutions that provide rights to "habeas data." There is also a slow emergence of a network of experts and NGOs in some Latin American countries, as organizations with broader interests in human rights have begun to focus on privacy issues.[44]

In the newly democratizing societies of Eastern Europe, there is a sprinkling of small NGOs dedicated to the privacy cause. A small group named Privacy Ukraine was established in 1999 specializing in the "protection of right to privacy, freedom of expression and information regardless of frontiers."[45] For several years, its founder, Andriy Pazuk worked to pass personal data protection legislation in Ukraine based on the Council of Europe Convention. Certain other groups in Hungary, the Czech Republic and Bulgaria have also launched their own versions of Privacy International's Big Brother Awards.[46] In countries with very recent memories of authoritarianism, such efforts perhaps carry greater significance than those of their counterparts in more established democratic systems. Perhaps the most remarkable indication of the spread of privacy, as a human rights issue, was the establishment in 2007 of a group called Privacy Mongolia.[47]

It is also apparent that a human rights emphasis is more apparent in francophone societies. There is no exact equivalent for privacy in the French language. Thus, privacy questions tend to be framed in terms of a larger set of *droits et libertés*, which need to be protected in the context of *les informatiques*. The French data protection law, for instance, is termed *La loi sur l'informatique et libertés*, and is overseen by a Commission Nationale sur L'Informatique et Libertés (CNIL). In Quebec, La Ligue des Droits et Libertés has the mission of defending all the rights proclaimed in the UDHR. It has, therefore, a broader mission than the "civil liberties" groups in other parts of Canada and the United States. One of its self-proclaimed goals is to promote *la protection de la vie privée et des renseignements personnel* (the protection of privacy and personal information), and representatives from this organization have been very active in efforts to protect and promote privacy protection in Quebec as well as in Canada at large.

Also in English-speaking countries, there are many advocates who stress the importance of a broader conception of privacy, linked to the wider tradition of human rights advocacy and discourse. EPIC entitles its annual review of privacy law and developments *Privacy and Human Rights*. This view stands in some contrast to what are perceived as more technocratic concerns of data protection and data security. In the Canadian context, Val Steeves has emphasized this approach in her work: "My understanding of privacy is very far removed from data protection. I often find that data protection works against privacy protection. Sometimes it makes it look ridiculous.... In working with Members of Parliament, if you can create a dialogue and sensitize them to the issues and make the links between privacy and democratic freedom, then they pay attention, but if you don't do that then they're overwhelmed with the national security risk analysis that they get on a daily basis."[48]

A human rights perspective also stands in contrast to the idea that privacy is important as a "risk management" strategy to encourage consumers to "trust" new technologies and use them to order goods and services online. Attention to privacy issues has become a necessary condition for organizations, and countries, to participate within the international information economy. It is naturally, therefore, also a consumer issue, and some other groups orient themselves toward that dimension of the problem.

Privacy Advocacy and Consumer Protection

National and international consumer protection groups have a long involvement with privacy issues. They have assisted individuals with complaints about consumer credit, direct marketing, identity theft, as well as with the various consumer services on the Internet. They have lobbied for better privacy and data protection laws. They have researched and written reports on new and emerging consumer issues. The illegitimate capture, collection, use, and disclosure of personal information are issues of deceptive trading. Good privacy protection is also deemed to be good business practice. Many consumer advocates have no difficulty also being privacy advocates.

So most national consumer organizations have historic origins and have been able to embrace privacy and data protection within their programs. The U.K. National Consumer Council (2005), for example, has lobbied for better data protection in Britain, often supporting the work of the Information Commissioner, and has warned about the creeping tide of surveillance over the "glass consumer." Its sister organization, the Consumer Association, which publishes the magazine *Which?* also gives consumer advice about data protection issues.[49] In Germany, the *Verbraucherzentrale Bundesverband* (Federation of German Consumer Organizations) has used similar imagery to give useful tips about protecting one's data.[50] The Consumers Association of Canada was heavily involved with the early stages in the preparation of the Canadian private-sector privacy law, and continues to monitor privacy issues through its Privacy Advisory Group.[51] Japan also provides an interesting case. Consumer organizations, including the national Housewives Federation, were very active in pressing for the 2005 Personal Information Protection Act. Indeed, one can find advice and reports on consumer privacy issues on the Web sites, and in the publications, of most, if not all, established consumer associations.[52] Each of them has a "privacy slice."

Most national consumer associations are, however, constantly engaged in the full range of consumer-related issues: product safety, fair pricing, monopoly practices, intellectual property, responsible consumption and sustainability, and so on. Some organizations do not confine their attentions to the private sector, and also lobby on access to social services, health care, housing, and so on. Privacy protection is, of course, closely linked to each of these questions, but it can be overwhelmed by the more material questions faced by underfunded organizations with overworked staff. It can also conflict with other consumer issues. Direct marketing, for instance, can be viewed as an intrusion. It can also be seen as an efficient and more reliable vehicle by which to provide accurate and relevant information about products and services to interested consumers. Often it takes a single individual within a larger consumer organization to carry the torch for the privacy interest within such organizations. Ed Mierzwinski, of the National Association of State Public Interest Research Groups (US PIRG) is an example within the United States. Since the 1980s, Mierzwinski has been a forceful advocate on issues such as credit reporting, social security numbers, and, more recently, identity theft.[53]

Certain privacy advocacy groups have also focused on the consumer angle. Consumers Against Supermarket Privacy Invasion and Numbering (CASPIAN), for instance, tries to keep a more explicit focus on the consumer issues encountered in the retail industry and has lead the fight against invasive uses of customer loyalty cards, consumer profiling, and especially the use of RFIDs.[54] It was established in 1999 as an explicitly "grassroots organization" that has now grown up to an organization of over fifteen thousand members in all fifty U.S. states and over thirty countries (Albrecht and McIntyre 2005). The founder, Katherine Albrecht explains how and why CASPIAN emerged:

I found myself with a wallet full of shopper cards ... and one day it occurred to me that every one of those cards, every plastic card in my wallet, represented a database and information about me, everything from my library privileges (what books I had read), to my bus pass. And the ones that I found the most offensive were the ones that were actually keeping track of the food that I needed to live on, because to decide not to participate would have meant spending a lot more for my groceries. So in a pretty intense week ... I just said I am going to put together a web site and I am going to learn everything there is to learn about this—I am going to dive in with both feet. And I put together the website at nocards.org, which was the founding website of CASPIAN.[55]

She goes on to explain the current motivation behind CASPIAN's membership: "And all you had to do, and even to this day all you have to do to be a member of CASPIAN, is say that you agree that it is wrong to spy on people through the things and services they buy. That's it—there is no political affiliation, there is no philosophical belief, there's nothing—I mean that's all you have to do."[56]

CASPIAN, therefore, does have an explicit focus on consumers. Although, through the subsequent campaigns about RFIDs, certain governmental programs became a target, it still tries to direct its energies to the protection of the ordinary shopper and the retail industry. This focus is deliberate: "I learned early on, maybe from watching other people, that the more narrow you are the more effective you can be. I did not want to be an EPIC or an EFF that had the broad-based "we tackle everything" approach. I wanted to find a specific niche and be the best at that.... I was the supermarket woman, I did just supermarket cards and if you wanted to talk supermarket cards you'd talk to me and if you wanted to talk about anything else, I would send you to some other colleague."[57] CASPIAN's strategies, and its links to certain Christian organizations, will be discussed later. It stands, however, as a quite unique example of a consumer-focused organization that stresses the importance of grassroots organization, including protests and boycotts, in lieu of networking and lobbying at elite levels.

CASPIAN's influence in other countries also highlights the importance of international collaboration on consumer-related privacy issues. The Transatlantic Consumer Dialogue (TACD) is a very effective forum launched in 1995 to promote consumer interests in EU and U.S. policymaking. It now brings together forty-five European and twenty U.S. consumer organizations, some of which have been discussed earlier, and analyzes and makes recommendations about a range of issues through an international working group structure. It has been particularly active on data privacy issues, including RFIDs, passenger name records (PNRs), unsolicited electronic mail, children's privacy issues, and so on.[58] Again, however, it is impossible to judge where consumer privacy issues begin and end, as exemplified by the discussion of the Privacy Rights Clearinghouse above. Many groups with a civil liberties or human rights emphasis participate alongside national consumer organizations within national and international coalitions, even though they might lament the associated implication that privacy has been commodified as something of benefit or cost to the consumer within the free market (Davies 1997).

Privacy Advocacy and Digital Rights

Virtually every group mentioned so far has been involved in Internet privacy questions. Some, however, would not have emerged *but for* the Internet and the desire to create an open medium based on sound democratic principles. Here is the rallying call of the Electronic Frontier Foundation:

From the Internet to the iPod, technologies are transforming our society and empowering us as speakers, citizens, creators, and consumers. When our freedoms in the networked world come under attack, the Electronic Frontier Foundation (EFF) is the first line of defense. EFF broke new ground when it was founded in 1990—well before the Internet was on most people's radar—and continues to confront cutting-edge issues defending free speech, privacy, innovation, and consumer rights today. From the beginning, EFF has championed the public interest in every critical battle affecting digital rights.[59]

That there is a separate set of "digital rights," which are an extension of more fundamental civil rights and liberties, is controversial. The belief, however, frames the work of a number of national and international organizations, of which EFF is probably the most important.

EFF was born out of a general belief that the emerging decentralized networks based on server/client rather than mainframe technology were ushering in an enormous potential for different forms of communication and social relations. At the same time, it saw threats from powerful interests as well as a practical need to defend the rights of young people in particular who were beginning to use these technologies in creative and innovative ways. Its spirit was, and in some respects, remains very libertarian, and its very name is redolent of the "frontier spirit" through which the American land was "settled." The electronic frontier was, and is, a new space of creativity and innovation, and had to be left alone rather than regulated and protected.

The proximate reason for EFF's creation was outrage on the part of three men: Mitch Kapor, the former president of Lotus Development Corporation, John Perry Barlow, Wyoming cattle rancher and lyricist for the Grateful Dead, and John Gilmore, an early programmer with Sun Microsystems, at the arrest of one Steve Jackson. The Secret Service had executed a warrant against Jackson and seized all electronic equipment from his premises allegedly on the grounds that he had illegally copied a document describing the operation of the E-911 emergency response system. The Secret Service did not press charges and returned his computers, having accessed and deleted much of the e-mail from the company's electronic bulletin board. Jackson could not find an existing civil liberties group to assist him that had the technical expertise. On the same day in July 1990, Kapor, Barlow, and Gilmore announced that they would file suit against the U.S. Secret Service, and also announced the creation of EFF.

Barlow's "A Declaration of the Independence of Cyberspace" became a rallying call for a generation of young computer enthusiasts, hackers, and cypherpunks:

Governments of the Industrial World, you weary giants of flesh and steel, I come from Cyberspace, the new home of Mind. On behalf of the future, I ask you of the past to leave us alone. You are not welcome among us. You have no sovereignty where we gather. . . . You have not engaged in our great and gathering conversation, nor did you create the wealth of our marketplaces. You do not know our culture, our ethics, or the unwritten codes that already provide our society more order than could be obtained by any of your impositions. . . . Cyberspace consists of transactions, relationships, and thought itself, arrayed like a standing wave in the web of our communications. Ours is a world that is both everywhere and nowhere, but it is not where bodies live. We are creating a world that all may enter without privilege or prejudice accorded by race, economic power, military force, or station of birth. We are creating a world where anyone, anywhere may express his or her beliefs, no matter how singular, without fear of being coerced into silence or conformity.[60]

Though newly expressed, this philosophy is deeply rooted in a particular interpretation of the American political tradition and an absolutist reading of the First Amendment to the U.S. Constitution. Indeed, EFF's early campaigns were nothing more than reminders about the timelessness of those principles and of the importance of applying them to the new frontiers of cyberspace.[61] And as the early and cumbersome network protocols of the early 1990s transformed into the World Wide Web, and as the Internet spread into a medium for e-commerce and e-government, so the EFF has tried to remain faithful to these principles.

Privacy protection has always had an uneasy relationship with this "I am going to do and say as I wish" ethos. Early conferences on Computers, Freedom and Privacy (CFP) brought these tensions to the fore as those in favor of individual choice and self-regulation confronted more traditional privacy advocates insisting that government regulation of personal data processing on the Internet was essential. The EFF has therefore had to pick and choose its privacy fights. Fortunately, the huge privacy issue of the 1990s, the availability and distribution of free cryptographic products and services, provided the issue around which free speech and privacy advocates could easily converge. The right to anonymous communication promotes both values, and it was threatened by various key-management and key-escrow schemes (notably the Clipper chip), and by export controls over cryptographic products (Diffie and Landau 1998).

The EFF also has experienced tensions over its strategic direction. Within two years of EFF's debut, it opened an office in Washington, D.C., under the direction of Jerry Berman, with the intention of being a major player in the policy debates surrounding the Internet. Some saw this move as a signal that it was abandoning the "quasi-bohemian counterculture of Harvard square for the power-obsessed and insincere atmosphere of Capitol Hill" (Li 2003, 70). This philosophical divide reached its height during the passage of the Communications Assistance for Law Enforcement Act (CALEA) in 1994, and the decision by EFF's board to collaborate with legislators over this legislation in the hope of influencing the outcome, rather than to oppose it in principle. The passage of this law created much distrust, further suspicion of Washington politics, and an ultimate decision to move to California, with the intent of trying to influence business decisions in Silicon Valley, rather than political decisions in the corridors of power.

Given the current pervasiveness of the Internet, it is today very unclear what is, and what is not, a "digital rights issue." Thus, EFF's privacy agenda today embraces a full range of topics including surveillance by law enforcement and national security organizations, the sharing of air passenger data, travel screening at airports, national identification schemes such as Real ID, data mining, RFID technology, surveillance cameras, and biometrics. These issues seem to sit very easily alongside EFF's advocacy on free speech, intellectual property, digital rights management, electronic voting, and so on. EFF now has smaller offshoots in a number of other countries, including Canada and Australia.[62]

To this day, EFF stands out for its high level of technical acumen, as well as for its emphasis on litigation.[63] It still does not have a permanent presence in Washington, D.C. It has never seen itself, therefore, as a group that could effectively engage with the legislative process in a deep and sustained way. This was one of the reasons why Jerry Berman, former executive director of EFF, decided to found the Center for Democracy and Technology (CDT) in 1994. Its mission is also "to promote democratic values and constitutional liberties in the digital age."[64] As Berman explains:

The Center for Democracy and Technology was founded almost a decade ago in the belief that the Internet could be a revolutionary force, not only for commerce but also for the democratic values of free expression, creativity and civic participation. Yet almost from the moment the Internet emerged as a mass medium, it has faced a barrage of challenges from lawmakers and regulators seeking to limit the breadth of content available online. At the same time security vulnerabilities, spam, spyware, fraud and a lack of trust in the privacy of personal information disclosed online have threatened the Internet's potential.[65]

CDT's work on privacy is seen as largely compatible with its other missions to promote free speech, access, and democratic participation.[66] It is also explicitly in favor of "the development of public policies and technology tools that give people the ability to take control of their personal information online and make informed, meaningful choices about the collection, use and disclosure of personal information."[67] CDT places, therefore, an emphasis on "practical solutions to enhance free expression and privacy in global communications technologies. CDT is dedicated to building consensus among all parties interested in the future of the Internet and other new communications media."[68] It prides itself on being able to work through the complexities of the technology, the dynamic market and the relevant case law to develop practical solutions, in the form of industry guidelines ("soft-law") and ultimately legislative language that might be presented to Congress.

CDT tries to work toward these solutions by playing a convening role within a series of working groups on various subjects, including Internet Privacy, Digital Privacy and Security, User Empowerment, and Spyware. It is this model that sustains CDT's work, for the groups comprise the companies and associations, which have to pay to be at the table, as well as representatives from a variety of public interest groups. Reports are then written and fed into the policy process. Sometimes guidelines are produced to which companies can commit. Obviously, it is easier to build a consensus around some issues, such as spyware, where there is a common consensus on a wrong that needs to be corrected. Other questions that require balancing of law enforcement or capitalist interests against the rights of consumers are more difficult to negotiate.

In the American context, CDT is controversial because of the funding model. The majority of its funding comes from foundations, but a significant proportion in any one year comes from high-tech companies, who are essentially paying for a "seat at the table." This raises suspicions from other privacy advocacy groups. CDT counters by arguing that you cannot develop public policy without understanding the technology, and that requires close cooperation with hardware and software vendors, Internet Service Providers, and telecommunication companies. Washington Privacy Consultant, Robert Gellman, offers the following assessment: "CDT does not always do a good job in defining its role for any given project, and that fuels disquiet in the privacy community. It also contributes to the frequent identification of CDT with its funding sources, something that is pervasive and somewhat unfair."[69] We will return to the differences between "insider" and "outsider" advocacy in chapter 4.

Privacy advocacy also finds its way onto the agendas of certain groups interested in open access to the new media. An example is the Center for Digital Democracy (CDD), begun in 2001 by Jeff Chester, a long-term opponent of monopolistic media practices, and advocate for public interest media policies (Chester 2007). Privacy converges with the interests of CDD to the extent that it is threatened by monopolistic ownership and control practices. Thus, for example, it has teamed up with other privacy groups to oppose the proposed takeover by Google of the online advertising firm, DoubleClick.[70]

Similar digital rights groups have grown up in Europe. An example is Bits of Freedom (BoF), established in 2000 to lobby for digital rights within the Netherlands. With few employees and meager funding, it was forced to cease its operations in 2006. Other European examples include the Italian group Netjus; the French group Imaginons un Réseau Internet Solidaire (IRIS); Digital Rights Denmark; and Digital Rights Ireland.[71] These, and other organizations, have close associations with their respective hacker communities, and their interests in rights to free cryptography.[72]

The British equivalent is probably the Foundation for Information Policy Research (FIPR). Established in 1998, and funded initially by Microsoft and subsequently by other corporate and foundation grants, FIPR gained a reputation in a short time as the most important think tank in the United Kingdom for Internet policy, including e-commerce and e-government, copyright, cryptography, as well as privacy and data protection. The original vision was for a small organization that could inject informed research on Internet-related issues into the political process. According to its founder, Caspar Bowden, FIPR was also informed by a desire to represent the "heady techno-utopianism that was around in the early 1990s in ways that were more palatable and acceptable to the British body politic."[73] After a short time, however, legislative events, and especially the promotion of the government's Regulation of Investigative Powers Act, a controversial piece of legislation that tried to update the rules for the interception of communications for the Internet age, forced FIPR into the world of advocacy and lobbying, and Bowden into a set of activities for which he had little preparation.[74] Another example of a one-person advocacy organization from the United Kingdom is Cyber-Rights and Cyber-Liberties, formed in 1996 by Yaman Akdeniz and dedicated to the protection of free speech and privacy in cyberspace.[75]

More controversial is the German Chaos Computer Club (CCC), a household name in Germany and certainly the most influential hacker community in Europe, through its highly public exposure of security breaches.[76] The "hacker ethic," that system cracking for fun and exploration is a powerful social good, flies in the face of many information privacy principles. There can be no question that public displays of security vulnerabilities sensitize corporations and governments to the risks and, in an indirect way, contribute to the larger cause of privacy and data protection. Furthermore, there is a strong antistatist and anticorporatist ideology within the hacker community, which can translate also into an antisurveillance ideology. Witness the CCC's activities in opposition to data retention initiatives, biometric technologies and smart cards.[77] A less controversial German group is the Forum Informatikerinnen für Frieden und gesellschaftliche Verandwortung (Forum of Computer Professionals for Peace and Social Responsibility), begun in 1984 in association with the peace movement. Its members are mainly computer professionals interested in public interest issues, such as intellectual property, IT in the workplace, computers and war, and of course data protection.[78]

In 2002, many of the European digital rights groups banded together to form the European Digital Rights Initiative (EDRI). There were two incentives; the need to coordinate European groups at the European level, and to establish a counter to the American dominance of privacy advocacy groups. It currently coordinates the work of twenty-five privacy and digital rights organizations from around sixteen countries.[79] Among the issues EDRI has worked on are traffic data retention, spam, telecommunications interception, copyright and fair use restrictions, and the cybercrime treaty.[80] In 2006, however, it ceased to operate a central office in Brussels. Its activities now concentrate on the publication of the very successful bi-weekly newsletter, the Edrigram.

Privacy advocacy for the range of digital rights must also embrace those who actively promote and market a range of privacy-enhancing technologies. Thus, the providers of tools for anonymous (or pseudonymous) browsing, for the management of cookies and spyware, for e-mail encryption products, for electronic cash, and so on, also play crucial roles as privacy advocates.[81] Privacy-enhancing technologies (PETs) are now embraced and marketed by some of the biggest corporations on the Internet. They have ceased to be the concerns of a few dedicated advocates. Technological solutions to privacy problems are now widely regarded as a crucial policy instrument within the toolbox of the contemporary regulator. Even though few of the early start-ups are still in existence, many of the individuals are, however, still active as digital rights advocates. Their roles will be discussed further in chapter 3.

Privacy Advocacy and the "Single Issue"

Our final category embraces a sprawling number of single-issue groups that have decided for various reasons to concentrate their efforts on a particular technology or practice, on a type of information, on a set of vulnerable people (such as children), or on a particular business sector.

Some of the more intrusive surveillance technologies have in themselves motivated group formation. National identity card schemes are a very visible manifestation of governmental surveillance and have inspired some of the strongest opposition, especially in countries like Australia and the United Kingdom whose citizens have only had to carry identity cards in times of war.[82] The British dispute propelled a number of protest groups into existence, most notably NO2ID, formed to "bring together individuals and organizations from all sections of the community and seek to ensure that the case against ID cards and the database state is forcefully put forward in the media, in the corridors of power and at grassroots level." Although the 2006 Identity Cards Act was eventually passed, the group continues to campaign for its repeal.[83] Similar local groups have been established throughout the United Kingdom. The "loyalty cards" of certain grocery chains have also been targeted: "A free people do not show identity papers to buy bread" declares a group calling itself the No-Cards Shoppers.[84]

A number of groups have also sprung up in opposition to unsolicited marketing. Californians against Telephone Solicitations (CATS) gives advice about how to deal with telemarketing calls, and assists with registering on the National Do Not Call Registry.[85] CATS is an example of one of the many "organizations" that is probably no more than one person with a Web site, a bulletin board, and a post office box number. The Coalition Against Unsolicited Commercial Email (CAUCE) has a membership that grew out of a discussion group (SPAM-LAW) and is solely directed toward the elimination of spam e-mail. It also has sister organizations in Canada, Europe, India, Australia, and the Asia-Pacific.[86] They proudly declare: "We have no money, we have no office. CAUCE is a creation of the Internet—it exists on this web site, in newsgroups, discussion lists, and in the ideas and dedication of those who oppose the damaging, costly, and unfair practice of unsolicited commercial email." Private Citizen, Inc., claims to be the "largest and most effective organization of its type to cut your junk calls and junk mail." For a small fee, anybody can be listed in its Private Citizen Directory, which it then sends to over fifteen hundred national telemarketing firms together with a warning of a $500 fee for commercial use of one's name: "Use of my offered property or service without payment may be construed as your intent to unjustly enrich yourself at my expense and/or maintain a nuisance in my premises and/or invade my privacy. Such wrongful acts may result in my seeking an exemplary amount in addition to my fee." Most companies simply choose to remove the customer's name from the database.[87]

Other groups have focused on public surveillance camera systems. The New York Surveillance Camera Players publish maps of video camera systems, organize guided tours of facilities, and perform specially written plays before the cameras in selected venues (New York Surveillance Camera Players 2006). In May 1997 a group of revelers in the United Kingdom danced around one camera as if it were a maypole, dressing it in ribbons. Other cameras have been covered up with bags, balloons, stickers, and other efforts to ridicule the technology (Davies 1998). Other groups have focused on the speed camera. In the United Kingdom, Speed Cameras Dot Org provides a forum for discussion and protest, not so much because of their privacy invasiveness but because of their ineffectiveness in reducing accidents and saving lives.[88] More controversial is a group that calls itself Motorists Against Detection. It too publishes maps of speed camera locations, and keeps track of the evolving technologies. It also advocates vandalism and since 2000 has been destroying speed cameras to make its point against "money-grabbing local authorities." Its Web site proclaims that there is a hardcore group of about two hundred supporters who plan their campaigns through encrypted e-mail and payphones, and who have destroyed about a thousand cameras throughout the United Kingdom.[89]

Other groups have formed in order to defend privacy rights with respect to certain types of information, and most notably health information. There is a general presumption that these data are among the most sensitive and requiring of the most stringent protections. There is also a presumption that doctor-patient confidentiality is inviolable. As the Patient Privacy Rights Coalition in the United States explains: "Americans and their doctors have always kept a pact of privacy. What doctors saw and what we told them behind the closed doors of exam rooms and offices would remain forever private. Privacy is a shared assumption, a contract, and a core ethical principle in medicine, dating back to Hippocrates. Though your doctors are sworn to keeping your information private, once information is sent out of their offices, they have no control over how the information is used."[90] A particular target for this group are the regulations under the Health Insurance Portability and Accountability Act.

Another important U.S. group is the Health Privacy Project, dedicated to "raising public awareness of the importance of ensuring health privacy in order to improve health care access and quality, both on an individual and a community level." The group was established at George Washington University by Janlori Goldman, formerly of the ACLU and CDT. The project was particularly instrumental in securing the passage of the federal privacy regulations made pursuant to the 1996 Health Insurance Portability and Accountability Act. It also convenes the Consumer Coalition for Health Privacy designed to give health-care consumers a prominent and informed voice on health privacy issues at the federal, state, and local levels.[91] The Medical Privacy Coalition (MPC) has a similar mission to uphold "the long-standing and fundamental confidentiality right of individuals to decide when and to whom their personal health information is disclosed." To accomplish this mission, the MPC "seeks to restore, maintain, and improve individuals' right to give their informed consent before their personal health information is shared with others, including for purposes related to health-care treatment, payment, and health-care operations. The MPC is seeking to obtain administrative, legislative and/ or judicial action to ensure that individuals' consent is obtained prior to the release of their personal health information."[92] In Britain, a National Health Service Confidentiality Campaign has been set up in opposition to recent efforts to develop electronic health record systems without adequate provisions for patient consent.[93]

Since the atrocities of 9/11, the issue of airline travel and security has been more prominent. A range of measures from security screening, to biometric passports, to the transfer of passenger name records (PNRs) has prompted larger questions about our rights to travel freely and anonymously. These issues have been taken up by groups such as the ACLU and EPIC. They have also motivated the creation of the Identity Project, specifically designed to provide advice to travelers about the circumstances under which they do, and do not, have to surrender their identification and to conduct education and research on new travel-related identification measures.[94] The leading figure in the group is the travel expert and author, Ed Hasbrouck, known for his Practical Nomad guides on how to travel the world.[95]

A final category of group has emerged as a result of the privacy challenges to particularly vulnerable categories of people. Children's privacy rights groups have been especially effective in raising awareness and challenging surveillance measures in schools. Leave Those Kids Alone (LTKA) is a British group formed to protest the use of computerized fingerprinting systems in elementary schools without parents' consent.[96] Fingerprinting was introduced as part of a subsidized library package called "Junior Librarian" purchased by the U.K. government. Instead of using a library card, children place their thumbs on a scanner when taking out a library book. The group says that schools are not the place for developing and using biometric systems, simply because the systems are expensive and the schools do not have the funds or technical staff to ensure that the system is up-to-date. And as with other technologies, this one is also susceptible to a process of "function creep" as fingerprints become general identifiers for access to other services—lunches, sporting facilities, and so on. In the United States, privacy advocates have so far successfully resisted plans in some schools to force children to wear mandatory ID badges containing RFID chips.[97] The surveillance of children is sensitive and can mobilize parents who otherwise might not have considered the privacy issue.

Single issue privacy advocacy groups can focus their scarce energies and resources on a technology, a practice, a set of organizations, and a type of information. They can also make common cause with other advocacy groups from that sector. LTKA, for example, has sought support from UNESCO, Save the Children, and the National Society for the Prevention of Cruelty to Children (NSPCC). Medical privacy rights groups often have close links with professional groups and associations. They are, however, dependent on the continued salience of the issue in public consciousness. There is a high rate of atrophy as attention shifts and the media spotlight falls on other issues.

The Privacy Advocacy Network

The aim of this chapter has been primarily descriptive, but can we reach any conclusions about the multitude of various groups, associations, coalitions, centers, campaigns, and so on, which have lobbied for privacy (or against surveillance) in their respective societies? A listing has been provided at the outset of the book, but it is not comprehensive and was probably out-of-date as soon as it was put to paper. Any kind of "network analysis" performed through the analysis of Web site links is also of little value. The pattern of group formation tends to reflect the issue itself—constantly changing, very diverse and almost infinitely flexible. A definitive "mapping" of the landscape is impossible. Nevertheless, some conclusions can be reached.

First, it is readily apparent that the number of groups engaged in privacy advocacy has increased dramatically during the last ten to fifteen years. Further, privacy is on the agendas of an increasing number of more established groups. The reasons are quite obvious: the advent of the Internet, both as a means of communication and as a medium that needed to be defended as a free space; the variety and pervasiveness of surveillance technologies; and the globalization of personal information flows.

Second, it is also obvious that privacy advocacy spans the ideological spectrum. It is probably the case that most of the groups share a somewhat center-left, civil libertarian political perspective. Others, however, would be positioned on the radical left, and would find sympathies with an anticapitalist or antiglobalization agenda. Some spring from a libertarian philosophy of minimal governmental intervention. Others find favor with those on the Christian right. Privacy advocacy has no conventional ideology. It can be promoted and opposed by those from all political and partisan positions.

Third, it is probably the case that most privacy advocacy groups have sprung from the American political culture. Certainly those that are the best funded are American. This seems to support the thesis that the more pluralistic atmosphere for group formation in the United States, as well as the relatively open and fragmented political system, is conducive to the proliferation of many voluntary associations. Legislative processes at state and federal levels tend to be based on open hearings at which outside groups are invited to testify. Where legislatures fail, the courts may also be avenues for redress and policy change. The multiple access points to the political system encourage a culture of group formation. Any U.S. privacy advocate would testify to the uphill battle and the powerful state and corporate forces weighed against them. Nevertheless, the political culture does provide multiple opportunities for voices to be heard. But it is also instructive how quickly the groups in the United States have proliferated. Within the space of a few years, the American landscape shifted from one in which the principal activity was centered within the Privacy and Technology project of the ACLU to one in which, by the mid-1990s, there was a multiple set of actors, jostling for a position within the American privacy space.

Fourth, and contrary to many assumptions, it is not true that privacy advocacy is primarily a U.S. phenomenon. There is an extraordinary variety of groups in other parts of the world that have taken up this issue, only a fraction of whom could be described above. It is true that most of this advocacy is embedded within other groups with broader civil liberties, human rights, consumer protection, or digital rights agendas. It is also true that in most other democratic societies, the privacy advocacy role has been institutionalized through the institutions of privacy and data protection authorities, which then gain the reputation as being the "official" voice of the issue. These agencies then have the unintended effect of crowding the policy space. They tend to be the first agencies to be listened to in legislative hearings, the first with whom the media makes contact, and the first to whom the public goes for advice. That there is no privacy commissioner in the United States allows privacy advocacy groups to bloom, and simulate the role of the official data protectors elsewhere. But is also the case that this survey has unearthed a range of advocacy activity outside the United States that is rarely recognized within the United States.

Finally, it is not clear that the word "group" adequately captures all the advocacy behavior documented in this chapter. Some are indeed voluntary associations in the classic mold—nonprofit groups registered under their respective statutes with membership lists and subscription dues. Many, however, have no membership base, though they might operate with boards of advisors. Some can have grandiose titles that describe nothing more than a Web site, and perhaps a bulletin board, blog, or LISTSERV. When these groups atrophy, they still tend to maintain a well-publicized Web presence.[98] There is deceptiveness in the numbers. The Internet provides many false fronts, behind which are the same cast of characters.

Traditional concepts do not adequately capture the dynamic, volatile, overlapping, fragmented, and somewhat illusive nature of privacy advocacy. There is certainly no clear structure. Neither is there a social movement with an identifiable base. Perhaps the closest is that of the "advocacy network," which can be conceptualized not as a fixed structure, but as a series of concentric circles. Those at the center possess a set of core beliefs about the importance of privacy, and as one passes to the outer edges, the issue becomes more and more peripheral. Policy change occurs, according to some hypotheses, when those on the periphery begin to share the core beliefs of those at the center (Sabatier and Jenkins-Smith 1988).

With respect to privacy protection, the advocacy network might look something like that depicted in figure 2.1. At the center are a number

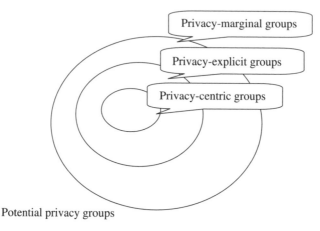

Potential privacy groups

Figure 2.1
The Privacy Advocacy Network.

of *privacy-centric* groups such as EPIC, PI, the Australian Privacy Foundation, Privacy Rights Clearinghouse, and CASPIAN. Other issues are peripheral, and, if addressed, have to be entirely consistent with a pro-privacy (antisurveillance) message. As we move out of the center of the circle, we then encounter a number of *privacy-explicit* groups for whom privacy protection is one prominent goal among several. Many of the civil liberties and digital rights organizations, such as the ACLU, the EFF, BoF, and Statewatch, fall into this category. In these organizations, privacy has to compete within the group's agenda for attention and resources. Sometimes ethical and policy conflicts occur and need to be resolved. Within the outer circle, there are an almost indefinite number of *privacy-marginal* groups, for whom privacy is a peripheral goal. Rarely does one find the word on their Web sites, or in publicity materials. Their goals are defined in very different terms—promoting human rights in the case of AI, defending the rights of women, gays and lesbians, the homeless, children, ethnic minorities, or journalists, advancing the ethical use of genetic technologies,[99] and so on. And yet the protection of personal information and the restriction of government surveillance can be central to that group's purpose and instrumental in promoting its core aims. There is therefore a vast range of groups for whom privacy is a marginal purpose, and for whom it might become a central goal with the right motivation.

Beyond the outer edge of the third circle are, therefore, a huge number of *potential groups* whose support could be mobilized given the correct circumstance, the right issue, or the correct case of intrusive governmental or corporate behavior. Privacy is an implicit or potential goal for these groups. The notion of "potential groups" is an important one within democratic theory (Truman 1951). The ability to mobilize and to redress individual or social grievances is considered a central test of pluralism. That ability is supposed to ensure that particular interests cannot get too far out of hand, before opposing interests mobilize to redress the balance.

Although groups come and go from the scene with great rapidity, and although they may enter the third circle as issues arise, it is extraordinary how permanent the stated missions of groups have become. By and large they do not tend to cross these boundaries. So a group in the second category would rarely, if ever, decide that it is going to abandon its other goals to focus entirely on privacy. A group in the third circle would rarely, if ever, pronounce privacy to be an explicit goal and move to the second circle. It is perhaps easier to fragment and splinter and form new groups than to change established goals and practices. Thus, while it is impossible to provide a definitive listing of the groups within each category at any one time, the categories provide a useful framework in the abstract.

The volatility and fragmentation of this landscape also expose the importance of the individual actors. The analysis of groups and associations tells one story about the place of privacy advocacy in civil society, the individual actors tell another. Who are these individuals? How did they become "privacy advocates"? What roles do they play? How do *they* see the landscape depicted in this chapter?

3 The Actors

We are all privacy advocates about something in our personal lives.
—Marc Rotenberg

We should all be our own privacy advocates.
—David H. Flaherty

He's a privacy kind of guy.
—from the *Wall Street Journal*, regarding President George W. Bush

Chapter 2 readily demonstrated that the formality of group identity and structure provides only a partial and deceptive glimpse into the phenomenon of privacy advocacy. We need also to ask questions at an individual level. Most of the groups discussed above have been sustained by the energy, commitment, knowledge, and skill of specific men and women—the actors and the entrepreneurs. So who are the "privacy advocates"? How did they become such? How do they see their roles in championing this cause?

The term "privacy advocate" is used in a very loose way in the media, as the 580,000 Google hits on the phrase clearly demonstrate. The media often frames stories in confrontational terms. Privacy advocates are those called upon to comment, critique, and offer the opposing perspective when controversial government and business schemes for the processing of personal data are proposed, or when scandals erupt. But the designation is often externally imposed and constructed. So how do the "advocates" describe themselves? This chapter addresses that question and then proceeds to offer a more refined classification, and a more subtle description of the range of roles played within this community, and of the tensions that often exist within those roles.

What Is a Privacy Advocate?

There is a plausible argument that everybody is, or should be, a privacy advocate. Rotenberg's words in the epigraph to this chapter suggest that. Personal information is collected, stored, processed, and disseminated about each and every one of us. We all have a subjective interest in ensuring that the right information is handled by the right people for the right purposes. At some point, we may all declare that our information should not be provided to this or that organization, on the grounds that it is "none of their business." We all have a subjective, if largely unrecognized, interest in these values, regardless of gender, race, class, or any other ascriptive characteristic. We are all privacy advocates—even President George W. Bush.

David Flaherty, when he was the Information and Privacy Commissioner of British Columbia, used to add a prescriptive flavor to this argument, arguing that we *should* all be our own privacy advocates. His interest, as a regulator, was to ensure a vigilant population, a citizenry that cared about how its data were being used and that questioned organizational practices. From the point of view of many official data protection authorities, a privacy-aware citizenry is an enormous assistance in increasing organizational awareness and, indirectly, reducing the numbers of privacy problems that arrive on their desks.

Advocates are supposed to do what they do to promote a cause, a principle, or a norm. They advocate changes in policy and practice because they believe it is right, not because it is linked to a rationalist understanding of their interests. This interpretation is not necessarily consistent with the way the term is used in the legal world. The role of the legal advocate is to represent the client, regardless of the principles of the lawyer. Many lawyers take the position that their commitment is to advance the client's rights whether or not they have sympathy with that person's views and behavior.

The term "advocate," however, not only implies a normative commitment to a set of principles or values but also a desire and ability to speak on behalf of others. That meaning is also implied in terms like "animal rights advocates" or "child protection advocates." Advocacy suggests an assumption that it is necessary to speak on behalf of others, precisely because few of us have the time and energy to be our own advocates. We therefore need a set of informed and interested individuals to act as the "gatekeepers" between a concerned but poorly informed citizenry and the governments and corporations that process our information.

That is Valerie Steeves's take on the phenomenon: "To me an advocate is someone who voices concerns on behalf of a broader population and seeks to effect some kind of positive change. So it's bridging a potential gap between the public sphere and discourses within the public sphere and concerns from citizens in that democratic space, and what happens at a policy level ... So I don't think it's solely a matter of lobbying. I think it's more attempting to understand the various concerns that are raised in civil society and to articulate them in ways that create a more informed public debate around the issues."[1] For Pippa Lawson of the Canadian Internet Public Policy Clinic (CIPPIC), "advocacy means being proactive not just reactive ... The advocacy part of it means actually taking positions and pursuing those positions in one way or another with the goal of influencing policy."[2] And for Graham Greenleaf of APF, "a privacy advocate is someone who plays an active role in the public disputes related to privacy issues—on the side of the protection of individual privacy."[3]

The designation is used in the media in indiscriminate ways and without the necessary consent of the subject. When Ari Schwartz of CDT was asked whether he regarded himself as a privacy advocate, he responded: "I think it is hard not to because people call me that all the time anyway."[4] And Simon Davies believes that "privacy advocacy is just a short-hand. It is a convenient label to apply to a person who believes in the autonomy and dignity of the individual.... I think privacy advocacy as a label is becoming counter-productive. It has not served our best interests as a sector. It has now become almost a term that is abused. It's narrow in its application. In reality, we're fighting for a core value, the right of the individual that to me maximizes independence, choice and personal power."[5]

The term *has* become a shorthand term for those who raise challenges to every kind of intrusive technology or practice. It designates specific individuals as well as a community. It is also a term used to describe certain individuals in an official capacity. As Lee Tien of the EFF observes, "privacy advocates can be anywhere. Sometimes you find very effective privacy advocates embedded within private-sector companies or in government agencies."[6] The privacy protection policies of the U.S. Internal Revenue Service, for example, used to be administered by a Privacy Advocate.[7] A company called Network Technologies Inc. (NTI) has appointed a Privacy Advocate to administer its privacy and security policies.[8]

Self-identified privacy advocates come from many walks of life—government, private sector, education, nonprofit, and so on. They have a wide range of training—in law, social sciences, computer technology, librarianship, even medicine. In fact, the only common characteristic of the men and women interviewed in this study is higher levels of education. Most have postgraduate degrees of one sort or another. That education is essential because it establishes some broad intellectual interests that can provide the empirical and philosophical underpinnings of their work. But many arrive at the issue circuitously. A good number of advocates with legal training, for instance, made a relatively early decision to concentrate on public interest advocacy, and sooner or later found a niche in privacy. In the 1970s and 1980s, privacy was seen as a hot and up-and-coming issue, about which little had been written, and within which reputations could be made. Some advocates with legal training also made early decisions to gain some education in computer science. Rotenberg is a good example.

For others the attraction has been more personal and comes from perhaps a family tradition of activism and progressive politics. Rich Neumeister has been a privacy and civil rights advocate in Minnesota for over thirty years: "I think you have to take a look at where one comes from and what shapes a person. For me I was born, one of four boys, four years difference between myself and my younger brother. My dad was a disabled vet; we lived in low-income housing. We saw differences of where you lived and where someone else lived. You were the project kid; government coming to inspect your apartment—those are things that you start to see when you grow up."[9]

Some have experienced personal intrusions that have animated their interests in political and social change. Gus Hosein of Privacy International gave me the following advice:

I think if you really want to do a study of privacy advocates, you should meet their mothers. I think that has an effect on you.... My mother was always very careful with personal information. Whenever she'd go shopping and someone would ask for our telephone number, she'd say it's unlisted. I had no idea what she was talking about but she was very good about that and I think that made me aware. And from my first degree I was very good friends with a woman who had discovered, that three years prior, she had sexual intercourse with a guy and he filmed the entire thing and he circulated that film to a lot of his friends. But she only found about this event three years later and I took her to the police and asked what could be done and was told that essentially nothing could be done. It just left an awful feeling in my stomach for days, the frustration of it happening, the powerlessness of knowing it had happened and being unable to do anything about it.

He goes on to explain his subsequent motivations: "I am fanatical about privacy. It is a gut feeling. It really is all about what is in the gut."[10]

Chris Hoofnagle, formerly of EPIC, would agree about the importance of family influence: "First of all, my family is fairly antiauthoritarian, in terms of being skeptical of authority.... My parents would tell me things like 'don't talk to the police.'" He too had an early lesson about the ways that personal information can be abused:

While I was in school I ran a student group that was very progressive. It was a free speech group and my campus[11] had banned sidewalk chalk—a staple expressive tool on any campus. So we would repeatedly chalk the campus—the entire campus, essentially bating them to charge us with a violation of rules because we would win.... What happened was that the officials at the university obtained our membership list and started retaliating against the younger individuals in the group.... They went after the freshmen because they were most vulnerable to authority and to pressure. Some of them lost their positions in other student groups as a result of this. So the consequences were somewhat severe for some of these students. I actually used the Freedom of Information Act to determine that this had happened. I used it on the Dean of students to determine that they had an e-mail colloquy where they were discussing targeting our group and getting our membership list. This wasn't speculation; we actually documented it. I've always been interested in the way in which society shapes people into what they become.[12]

The fact that an advocate has not suffered personal harm, should not minimize their commitment to the issue. As Jim Dempsey of CDT reminds us: "My definition of 'liberal' is the ability to place oneself in the shoes of others. So the fact that I have never suffered discrimination does not make me any less strong in opposing it."[13]

For others, the motivations come from a general desire to stem the abuse of power. Here's Robert Ellis Smith, founder and current editor of *Privacy Journal*: "It's more the distaste for bureaucracy and the pomposity and arrogance that propels me. I think it was Abbie Hoffman who said I don't pretend that I change the world with what I do, but when I can get a bureaucracy upset that is really what gets the juices flowing. So I went after the credit bureaus. That was more enlightening for me than a pure approach to privacy. As a journalist, I was outraged that there were these organizations in the American economy that reported on people and didn't care about accuracy in the least—that really got me irritated."[14] These motivations are pervasive. Many advocates do get a rush from embarrassing the top official or CEO, or from exposing deception, or from convincing a public audience of the ineffectiveness and intrusiveness of certain measures. For some advocates, those are the things that "get the juices flowing."

Others have a more measured approach. The name of Alan Westin has been associated with the privacy protection issue since the late 1950s. His 1967 book, *Privacy and Freedom*, is regarded as one of the classic texts in the entire field. When asked whether he considers himself a "privacy advocate," however, he responded:

I'm a balance person. I identify dangers to privacy, but my solutions are much more about recognizing the competing values that need to be brought into some kind of harmony. I appreciate the roles of the American Civil Liberties Union, the Electronic Privacy Information Center and the Center for Democracy and Technology in always being the advocates of the total privacy solution, but I would never want to live under their regimes—not that I mind their pointing out dangers in various kinds of new anti-surveillance proposals. I'm a Libra, which are the scales. On one hand this; on the other hand that. If you're a Libra, balance is what the stars have given you—or cursed you to.[15]

There are no easy generalizations about what makes and motivates privacy advocates, because the term conflates a number of different roles and identities. We need, therefore, to think in terms not of one role, but of several. The following typology is not intended as a mechanism through which to stereotype complex individuals, all of whom have many motivations and characteristics. It is presented as a way to understand overlapping roles, to gain some insights into the complexity of the advocacy community, as well as the many conflicts and contradictions encountered. There are some individuals whose primary identity is defined as a privacy advocate or activist. They are, however, a clear minority. Most privacy advocates play at least one other role—and they have to do so in order to make a living. For most, therefore, advocacy is mediated through other identities—academic, journalist, software developer, consultant, or artist. For most advocates those identities are malleable and negotiated.

Advocacy Types

The Advocate/Activist

Smith, editor of *Privacy Journal* since the 1970s and one of the longest serving observers of the privacy movement, has some problems with the word "privacy advocate":

I prefer the term activist. I picked that up about ten years ago because I think advocates do nothing but say what they think from the armchair. It doesn't have to be informed; it doesn't have to be based on knowledge. Anybody can be an advocate. An activist, I think, does things about injustices.... Being interviewed in the press a lot I get really irritated when what I call "armchair advocates" would be quoted. It's just so easy, especially in this business. You can always view from the armchair and get your name in the paper. So I want to distinguish between the two.[16]

Katherine Albrecht of CASPIAN adopts a similar distinction: "In my mind, a privacy advocate is someone who advocates philosophically, intellectually and in the abstract for the concept of privacy. And a privacy activist is someone who grasps a hold of the issues and actually tries to find leverage points to maneuver society away from privacy-invading initiatives and toward a more privacy-embracing type of culture."[17]

In April 2002, and funded through a grant from the settlement in the *Dennis v. Metromail* lawsuit, *Privacy Journal* convened a conference of "privacy activists" in Providence, Rhode Island.[18] The conference attracted around seventy attendees, most of whom were active in various U.S. state capitals. Professionally, however, the attendees represented a range of professions and organizations, from consumer groups to law firms to publishing to consulting to education. Only five of the attendees self-identified as "independent activists."

In the minds of others, privacy activists are identified not by their organizational affiliations but by the principles they espouse. They do not balance privacy against competing public interests, because they know that the opposing arguments will always be made with force and by people with far more resources than they have. For some advocates, the privacy argument requires uncompromising articulation rather than negotiation with competing social interests. The "balancer" is a "pragmatic advocate" (or "pragvocate"), according to Davies.[19] Greenleaf has written of the "pragvocates dilemma": "Is it better to have a valuable set of protections to ensure that surveillance will work more fairly when it occurs, even if by doing so you increase the likelihood that it will occur by providing a device which could legitimate it but which has little capacity to limit it?" (1996, 149). The privacy activist opposes surveillance on principle and lets others worry about the appropriate balance with governmental and corporate interests.[20]

Davies is often described in the media as the most widely known and cited privacy activist in the world, and he has cultivated the role of the activist/advocate perhaps more successfully than any other. He first emerged on the privacy scene during the conflict over the Australia Card in the late 1980s. Since then he has worked in many countries and written a number of books and articles. In the early 1990s, Privacy International was established under his guidance and leadership. He moved to London in the mid-1990s, and since 1997 has been affiliated with the London School of Economics.

He is steeped in a tradition of activism, and deeply influenced by the lessons of the past. In 1999, he declared his allegiance to the precepts of the American civil rights campaigner and organizer, Saul Alinsky. He drew the following lessons from Alinsky's famous book, *Rules for Radicals* (Davies 1999, 257–258):

· Power is not only what you have but what the enemy thinks you have.

· Wherever possible, go outside the experience of the enemy.

· Make the enemy live up to their own book of rules.

· A constructive alternative should always accompany a successful attack.

· Identify the target, isolate it, personalize it, and polarize it.

According to Davies, this is also a battle over language as well as over values: "Privacy tends to be whatever is left over after more pressing elements have been resolved. Whether through design or osmosis, information users employ a common set of terms that are hostile to privacy ... Thus privacy is seen as the bête noir of law enforcement, openness, progress, efficiency, and good government" (1999, 152).

But Davies also has an academic affiliation as a Visiting Fellow in the Computer Security Research Center at the London School of Economics, and the Department of Law at the University of Essex. His biography also states that he has advised a wide range of corporate, government, and professional bodies including UNESCO, the European Parliament, the British Medical Association, UNISYS, the RAND Corporation, IBM, and the U.K. government. He is also an author and journalist. Like other advocates, his roles are multiple and negotiated. He insists, however, that all these tasks are animated by a strong ethical compass. His message about privacy is not diluted by the fact that he takes money for giving a speech or for providing advice. Indeed, he would insist that he is expected to bring the tough, uncompromising message. Those who ask for his views do so in the knowledge that he is not a "pragvocate" but a strong voice for privacy. He always makes it clear that any kind of organizational relationship, whether money changes hands or not, would never insulate that organization from public criticism.[21]

Is there an ideal type of "privacy activist"—a person who is solely and uncompromisingly devoted to the cause of privacy, and who is rarely placed in a position of having to moderate those views because of financial or other commitments? This would be a person who can say what he/she thinks without fear of losing employment, income, or any other benefit. This person is unbeholden to any data user, and able without fear of repercussions to say, and act, as he or she thinks to promote the privacy value—with the general public, with business, and with government. Such a person is animated by the practice of activism, over and above anything else.

There are very few who fit this mold. One is Rich Neumeister of St. Paul, Minnesota. For nearly thirty years, and supported only by a series of part-time jobs, Neumeister has worked the corridors of the Minnesota legislature as a "citizen lobbyist." He describes himself as "just a plain old Joe Citizen"—"I'm just a lowly individual who is just trying to make a difference."[22] Politicized in the 1960s and 1970s, and sensitized to the intrusive practices of governments through growing up on welfare and food stamps in project housing, he has been working without compensation to advance the cause of civil liberties, freedom of information, and especially privacy protection in his state for nearly thirty years. Through sheer hard work, he has gained a reputation as a "superhero in the field of protecting individual privacy rights."[23] He rarely shows up to conferences. He does not teach. He writes very little. He has no e-mail address. He spends most of his spare time analyzing bills, poring over the official listings of Minnesota state and local government records, and talking with legislators, and occasionally the media. His advocacy is supported by a deep knowledge of the history and philosophy of his subject gained through reading books, articles, government reports, newspapers from all over the world, but rarely the Internet. Over the years, he has won many victories for the cause of privacy protection, with the result that his efforts are reflected in many state laws—on drivers' records, Internet privacy, medical records, transportation privacy, video surveillance, RFIDs, ID theft, and so on.

To some, Neumeister has a reputation in St. Paul as "just a pain."[24] For others he is the "weird guy."[25] But he has also earned an enormous respect for his integrity, knowledge, and commitment. He has eschewed working for lobbying firms and cashing in on his skills; that would involve shaving the long beard, getting a cell phone and losing his independence. Neither does he work with other civil liberties groups and advocates. His power comes from his independence, his historical knowledge, and his sheer persistence. He has been around these issues longer than anybody in the Minnesota legislature. It has come to the point that whenever Neumeister enters a committee room, legislators immediately know that there is a privacy concern with what they are doing. His rules of thumb are "1) Don't be intimidated—legislators are people, too; 2) find an issue that drives you and stick to it; and 3) find an old legislative hand to walk you through the process. Otherwise be prepared to spend a legislative session or two learning the intricate, age-old dance of the lawmakers."[26]

Kathleen Albrecht of CASPIAN does not have the same breadth of issue concern, but she does operate on the national, and international, stage. She is the activist most closely associated with RFID technology. In his forward to the book *Spychips*, Bruce Sterling describes her and her coauthor, Liz McIntyre, as follows:

The authors of this book lack big budgets, a power base, or an agenda. They are, however, energetic, clever, highly motivated, highly wired, and chock-full of feminine wiles. Thanks mostly to legwork, Google, and chatty e-mail from many like-minded souls; they have become a retailer's worst nightmare. They are as uncontainable and global as the industry they decry, for they are the Digitized Suburban Mom Shoppers from Hell: perceptive, well-connected, entirely self-educated, very American, highly skilled industry gurus; quotable, word-of-mouth branding killers with viral marketing voodoo; digital Cassandras who are second to none in downsides, dirty laundry, and doomsaying. Plus, they are witty and good-looking. (Albrecht and McIntyre 2005, xiii)

The second edition of *Spychips* is addressed more explicitly to Christians, in which arguments are made about intrusive technologies like RFIDs with explicit reference to the Book of Revelation (Albrecht and McIntyre 2006). Implanted chips are identified as a possible precursor to the "mark of the beast." According to the Bible, acceptance of the mark condemns individuals to eternal damnation.[27] Furthermore, many Conservative and Orthodox Jews believe that cutting, piercing, or marking the flesh is contrary to the Jewish notion that we were all made "in the image of God." For many orthodox Jews, any alteration of the body, including piercing or tattooing, is an alteration from its natural form and a blasphemy. Arguments about the creeping surveillance society are thus seen as harbingers of the apocalypse. The cost is not merely a loss of privacy or civil liberties; it becomes a contravention of God's will. According to Albrecht: "For millions of people around the globe, receiving a numbered mark is one of the most serious religious violations a person can commit."[28] In May 2007, CASPIAN organized an interfaith march and prayer vigil in West Palm Beach, Florida, to oppose the planned injection of VeriChip implants into two hundred Alzheimer's patients and their caregivers. At the same time they launched a new Web site to give special emphasis to the dehumanizing nature of chip implant technology.[29]

It is not only the bodily invasion that angers some Christian fundamentalists. The Mark of the Beast has been seen in more conventional forms of national identification, such as the Real ID proposals in the United States. Permanent forms of citizen identification, whether based on biometric measures or not, confront one basic precept of many religious faiths, that of the possibility of change through personal redemption. In 2002, an Ontario farmer by the name of George Bothwell challenged (unsuccessfully) the requirement that he submit a digital photo in order to obtain a drivers license. He too believed that such forms of identification are the work of the devil, and ultimately preferred not to drive rather than to submit to such surveillance and compromise his Christian beliefs.[30]

These examples suggest growing activism from "grassroots" organizations. Activism for some entails the education of the general public, such that they are more sensitive to the dangers of certain technologies, more aware of their rights, and more likely to put pressure on elected representatives. It is an activism rooted in the belief that real change can only arise from below, by changing public attitudes and behavior and thus altering the conditions that give rise to the perceived threats in the first place. Activism implies a transformation of ideas and beliefs, rather than a reform of instruments and mechanisms. Thus "grassroots activism" is contrasted with governmental "advocacy." The U.S. group Privacy Activism was established deliberately for these reasons.[31]

The ability to perform this role, however, is contingent not only on personality but also on the opportunities. There are few privacy advocates who are fortunate enough to enjoy sustained funding from foundations or individual contributions, rather than from governmental or private-sector sources. In many other cases, there is always the danger of "biting the hand that feeds you." Most advocates therefore have other roles and responsibilities, through which, against which, with which, privacy advocacy is filtered, negotiated, and mediated.

Whether the motivation to activism is in terms of behavior, principle, or concentration on the grassroots, there are probably a good number of individuals in a number of countries who would self-identify as such. At the same time, there would be a number who would not, because of the implication that activism is associated with more radical forms of resistance and protest. In a policy community dominated by legal and technical experts, an activist politics can sit uneasily. It is common, therefore, for the advocate/activists to be marginalized as extremists, and for their message to be denigrated. Terms like "privacy nuts"[32] or "privacy extremists"[33] have entered the rhetoric. In the wake of the 9/11 attacks, some conservative commentators considered opposition to national ID systems as tantamount to "giving comfort to terrorists."[34] In an article in the Wall Street Journal entitled "The Privacy Jihad," Heather Mac-Donald of the Manhattan Institute wrote:

The privacy advocates—who range from liberal groups focused on electronic privacy, such as the Electronic Privacy Information Center, to traditional conservative libertarians, such as Americans for Tax Reform—are fixated on a technique called "data mining." By now, however, they have killed enough different programs that their operating principle can only be formulated as this: No use of computer data or technology anywhere at any time for national defense, if there's the slightest possibility that a rogue use of that technology will offend someone's sense of privacy. They are pushing intelligence agencies back to a pre-9/11 mentality, when the mere potential for a privacy or civil liberties controversy trumped security concerns.

She went on to decry the "privacy vigilantes," or the "privacy zealots," and concluded that the "privocrats will rightly tell you that eternal vigilance is the price of liberty. Trouble is, they're aiming their vigilance at the wrong target."[35] She later decried the "escalating triumph of privacy advocacy over common sense."[36]

These attacks are extreme and unrepresentative, but they do remind us that there are high political and economic stakes associated with these issues. Furthermore, if privacy advocates did not carry some influence then they would be ignored, rather than denigrated. There are, therefore, many people who are not privacy advocates, who believe that the dangers are exaggerated, that the processing of personal information without the knowledge and consent of individuals is essential for law enforcement and national security, and that the advocacy/activism community is wrong and should be stopped. If such attitudes have the effect of drawing the battle lines, of defining an "us and them" and of radicalizing the resistance, then, for some advocates/activists, so be it.

This is how Davies sees the battle:

At any one moment, you will have clearly defined lines with a particular clearly defined enemy. That enemy may not be your enemy in three months time or three years—it's hard to tell. But for the moment, for the sake of the task at hand, you define the enemy and you have to see it in those terms. Now that doesn't necessarily negate the opportunity to work with potential enemies. It doesn't mean that there can't be a collaborative approach at a more general level. Remember the declaration of war is made by the other side not by the advocates. The advocates don't declare the war. The other side will declare war by imposing a radical technology or a radical law across the divide between citizen and state.[37]

For the advocate/activist this is an issue that is fundamental. Privacy cannot be compromised, commodified, or negotiated. There are clear rights and wrongs. The "wrongs" need to be resisted. There is an "us" and a "them."

The Advocate/Researcher

There are, of course, other perspectives. This second category of advocate believes that first and foremost privacy issues need to be researched, so that the dangers can be exposed. Privacy issues require a great deal of in-depth analysis—on the technical issues, the legal requirements, public attitudes, the costs of implementation, the philosophical underpinnings, and so on. The problems are not self-defining. They need to be unearthed and analyzed.

There is probably nobody in the privacy advocacy community who would not subscribe to this view. However, this category does include a wide variety of types of research and researcher. It includes tenured and untenured faculty with regular positions at universities; those in less permanent positions at universities employed through more temporary centers, programs, or projects; graduate students; and researchers in nongovernmental organizations, including those already cited. Some would self-identify as regular participants within the privacy advocacy network. Some come and go. Others perform their scholarship for other reasons, and it then gets picked up by privacy advocates without any necessary or express efforts on the part of the researcher. This is certainly one area of social policy where scholarly research and analysis cannot just be regarded as "academic." Privacy advocacy requires appropriate conceptual and theoretical articulation and empirical support. Many privacy advocates maintain strong connections to the scholarly research community, keep up with the literature, and use those insights to support and advance their work.

At one level, therefore, academic work provides the intellectual foundation for privacy advocacy by explaining and justifying the problems and challenges in larger historical, sociological, political, and philosophical terms. There is a number of overlapping scholarly traditions, covered in chapter 1. There is a legal tradition that continues to be very influential for privacy advocacy, and has accompanied the spread of data protection law in Europe and beyond.[38] There is also a very important social science tradition. The capture and processing of personal information indicates, to many sociological writers, a creeping surveillance, which constitutes a new and profound condition of modernity. New surveillance practices sort, categorize, and therefore discriminate, in positive and negative ways.[39] Another related tradition comes from the discipline of political science on the assumption that privacy is, at root, about power. As a policy issue that has risen to the agendas of advanced industrial states at roughly the same time, privacy offers interesting insights into the ways that different states have defined the problem, applied a range of policy instruments, and, in recent years, tried to balance this value against a more dominant security agenda.[40] Privacy protection also raises profound philosophical issues about the appropriate definitions of privacy and the ethical justifications for invasion—by the state and by other individuals. Philosophical writing has drawn spatial, behavioral, and informational distinctions and has suggested ways in which scholars and policymakers might better frame the question given different contexts.[41]

Work in the "physical sciences" also has some direct applicability to privacy advocacy. The work of cryptographers such as Ron Rivest and Whitfield Diffie is an example. Research on computer and information security, from people such as Bruce Schneier (2003), also finds direct and immediate resonance within the privacy advocacy community. A further academic research tradition centers on questions of anonymity. Latanya Sweeney runs the Data Privacy Lab at Carnegie Mellon University. She has made numerous discoveries related to the re-identification of individuals from so-called de-identified data. For Sweeney, there is a "science of privacy" and ways to construct "privacy technology" in such a way that personal information may be accessed only for legitimate purposes. Her pioneering work has received recognition among privacy advocates and regulators in many countries.[42]

When the privacy issue first arose to public and political attention, academic scholars had a very important impact on the development of privacy protection policy in their respective societies and have explicitly self-identified as privacy advocates. Indeed, one of the main explanations for the spread of data protection law in Europe in the 1970s was the influence of a fairly small group of primarily legal scholars and experts. The main example is Professor Spiros Simitis of the Goethe University's law school in Frankfurt, who became in 1970 the world's first Data Protection Commissioner in the German state of Hessen. Other examples include Herbert Burkert and Hans Peter Bull in Germany, Jan Freese and Peter Seipel in Sweden, Jon Bing in Norway, Stefano Rodota in Italy, and Paul Sieghart in the United Kingdom.[43] In the United States, both Alan Westin and Arthur Miller were very influential, as was David Flaherty in Canada, who later became the first Information and Privacy Commissioner of British Columbia.

Academics have continued to play a very significant role within the privacy policy community. There have been many opportunities for the privacy expert to contribute to the broader understanding of the issues. Many teach courses on these subjects and thus attempt to influence new generations. In addition to providing the intellectual analysis to support the privacy cause, many have engaged in other activities, such as giving testimony, being expert witnesses, lodging complaints, initiating litigation, commenting on government bills and documents, writing reports, and so on.

In addition to the full-time academic with a teaching position at an institution of higher education, there are a range of others who may be affiliated with universities and who also do important research and advocacy work. Some independently funded research centers have produced some very significant work. Some are devoted to privacy-related issues, while others have broader mandates.[44] In addition, there are a number of research and advocacy clinics, mainly associated with law schools, which do independent work on behalf of public interest groups. The students gain experience writing briefs and testimony and thus gain practical experience. The public interest groups thereby get the benefit of pro bono legal work.[45]

Deidre Mulligan has moved from an advocacy role with CDT to an academic position with the Samuelson Clinic at Berkeley. Her reflections on the different roles are instructive:

I can be much less reactive. I have a lot more of an opportunity to set my own agenda. It's part of the reason I don't talk to the press as much. I want to talk about what I want to talk about.... I've got my own agenda. Part of the reason why I came to academia was a feeling that there were some big gaps in research on privacy. I wanted to get aspiring academics engaged in research relevant to the policy dialogue. It's been nice because I've been able to get people who are doing economic research, or usability research, or system design research, or visual imaging research to think about the ways in which their research goals might actually incorporate understandings of privacy.... It means there is a richer base of intellectual material there to inform people in the advocacy or policy-making communities. I find that really rewarding.[46]

The role of academics within the privacy advocacy community raises larger questions about the responsibility of intellectuals within society. Should academic work be driven by the pressing social problems of the day? Should it be directed by the value preferences of the scholar? Many academics would insist that scholarly research agendas should only be directed by the curiosity of the researcher. If the principal responsibility of the scholar is to seek truth, then social and political agendas can get in the way. Here is Stanley Fish's advice to academics: "Do your job; don't try to do someone else's job, as you are unlikely to be qualified; and don't let anyone else do your job. In other words, don't confuse your academic obligations with the obligation so save the world; that's not your job as an academic; and don't surrender your academic obligations to the agenda of a non-academic constituency.... In short, don't cross the boundary between academic work and partisan advocacy, whether the advocacy is yours or someone else's."[47] If the resulting research becomes, at some point, relevant for those in politics, then so be it. But those agendas, and less still the research results, should never be governed by a criteria of social and political relevance. If scholarly work, on privacy or any other matter, is good then it should, sooner or later, get picked up by advocates and practitioners. The job of the academic is not to change the world, as Karl Marx said, but to interpret it.

In reality, scholarly research agendas are inevitably and increasingly directed by standards of political and social relevance because of the demands of granting agencies. Increasingly the research grants bodies, in North America and Europe, have stressed the need for researchers to direct their research agendas directly to pressing social and political problems and to engage with partners in their respective fields. There are few academics in the privacy field who have not, at some time and level, been motivated by the very topicality of these issues. It is impossible to measure, but it is probable that the "privacy academic" is more consistently engaged with the nonacademic constituencies than is his or her counterparts who research on other social issues. The topics are dynamic, rich, and replete with fascinating questions for academic research; they are also of deep concern to those who want to "change the world."

The tension is also exposed through methodology. For some academics, the adoption of a "critical" posture is essential for in-depth interrogation of the deeper social and political structures that give rise to violations of rights. Critical social scientists generally see no conflict between their value commitments to social change and the conduct of scholarly research. Indeed, for some scholars an understanding of the central place of surveillance within modern capitalist countries is central to an appropriate framing of the political and legal questions. Others, however, adopt a more empirical approach and are uncomfortable about drawing larger generalizations unless properly constructed hypotheses are derived from theory, and are then tested empirically against the most rigorous standards of the scientific method. For these academics, conflicts between advocacy and research are real and continuous.

The conduct and publication of public opinion surveys about privacy protection bring this tension into sharp relief. For those with a more critical orientation, survey research should be regarded with suspicion because responses to questionnaires about attitudes to privacy rarely tap the deeper processes by which power relations are constructed between data users and the average citizen. Surveys only gain a superficial snapshot of responses at particular times to particular questions. They rarely unearth deeper motivations and meanings. In the worst cases, they are designed to elicit particular responses in order to support specific policy conclusions. For others, however, the social survey is a crucial barometer of public attitudes, without which academics may make elitist assumptions about what ordinary people are thinking.[48] For the academic/ advocate, in most cases, public opinion surveys support the general assumption that privacy is an important social value, about which large majorities in many countries have strong concerns.

Opinion surveys are one prominent example, but there are countless others where tensions between the pursuit of "truth" and the desire to advance a cause arise. Academics cannot escape political commitments in an absolute sense, but crossing the boundary between academic and political work is fraught with risk. There is a distinction between academic and partisan labors. There is a difference between, for example, analyzing the costs of a new surveillance scheme, such as a national identity card, and working for its reversal.[49] The advocacy of academics is generally tempered, therefore, and it is expected to be so. Thus, when advocates move into the academic world to teach and research, they generally find that the adoption of an academic title, with the cachet that comes with it, carries a certain price. An expectation to be more scholarly, objective, removed, and nonpartisan means an expectation to see the competing public interests and to evaluate the risks on both sides of the debate.

The Advocate/Consultant

The boundary between research and advocacy is certainly crossed when advocates, including academics, take on clients. The term "consultant" is used in as many different ways as is the term advocate. It has different meanings and obligations dependent on profession. At root, it means being paid for services. Beyond that, there are a number of different consulting roles that privacy advocates can, and do, play.

Privacy protection is becoming a complex subject. Organizations find themselves having to comply with new privacy rules. They occasionally get media exposure. They receive pressure from their consumers and from regulators. When they develop new systems and services with privacy implications, they often have to conduct privacy impact assessments. Many organizations, therefore, need expertise—sometimes in a temporary capacity, and sometimes more continuously. A new profession has emerged—the "privacy consultant" with a new professional association, the International Association of Privacy Professionals.[50] Some privacy advocates find it difficult to resist the temptation to take money for advice, research, training, or education, and through those processes continue to advocate the privacy cause. Others resist that move, observing a slippery slope and believing that one can never be a privacy advocate and, at the same time, take money from data users. The tensions are real, and the lines need constant negotiation.

Some advocacy groups have explicit rules about the conditions under which money can be taken from clients. Some will not take any money from corporations for any reason. Others draw the line between general support and consulting for a fee or service. EPIC, for instance, does not "lobby for, consult or advise companies, nor do we endorse products or services. Contributions from companies are only accepted for general support."[51] Thus, if an organization came to EPIC wanting to know what it thought of a new product or service, or perhaps a self-regulatory initiative, EPIC would not assist because of the probability that such advice would never remain confidential, and the organization would then use the meeting to declare that EPIC approves of its intentions. Most privacy advocacy organizations have similar, if more implicit, rules.

We need to make some distinctions among forms of consulting. There are real differences among taking money first to advise clients, second to educate clients, third to represent clients, and fourth to do research for clients. The traditional image of a consultant is as someone who is hired by a public- or private-sector organization to give confidential advice and analysis to a public- or private-sector client. This is the traditional sense of the "management consultant," for example. Unlike the chief privacy officer, a role increasingly professionalized, the consultant is paid for temporary services. The fact that he or she is an outsider, rather than an in-house employee, provides the advantage of being able to offer candid and expert advice without fear of loss of employment. Also, clients have access to deeper levels of expertise than would be feasible for them to retain in-house, especially if the specialty is needed comparatively rarely. It is generally accepted good corporate governance to hire consultants on a range of issues—management, accountancy, human resources, public relations, environmental management, and so on.

In recent years, privacy has been added to that list and several experts have made lucrative livings by giving confidential advice on a range of privacy-related issues: legal compliance, policies and procedures, privacy impact assessments, technical security, as well as the management of publicity. Some operate primarily in an individual capacity; others work within consultancy firms.[52] For some privacy advocates, the consultancy role provides a deeper understanding of the practical difficulties of privacy management within complex organizations.[53] Some insist that they can remain strong proponents for privacy within the parameters of a confidential advising relationship. With the correct client, they can push the issue and improve organizational policies and internal practices. They can also play a valuable role in training employees and sensitizing management to the demands of the issue. The critical variable, however, is the attitude of the client, and whether it genuinely wishes to change its practices. Often consultants are approached to manage, rather than resolve, a problem—to give the appearance of privacy-friendliness without actually having to either make the tough choices or commit the necessary resources to change. Consultants naturally have to be very wary of being used, and they must be willing and able to walk away, a difficult move if income is dependent on keeping clients satisfied. Whereas some consultants will draw lines based on the anticipated posture of the client, others draw other distinctions. Some, for example, will refuse to represent clients before any other third party. They will not be a mouthpiece for the client before executive, legislative, and judicial agencies. They will not speak in the media on their behalf. They will not even accompany clients when, for example, clients represent themselves. They will also refuse the more private tactics—the word in the ear of a friendly privacy commissioner, for example. This line is also extremely difficult to maintain. Others will be proud of the advice that they have given and of its effects. If an organization has made a genuine and real attempt to change, then it will want to publicize those good practices, as an example to other organizations, as well as in the interests of self-promotion.

Others draw a line between an advisory function and a research function. In the latter, the consultant is hired to write a report on a particular problem, perhaps lay out options and recommendations, but will leave it at that. Some see this as a way of avoiding the problem of "capture." The client will outline what questions it wants addressed. The consultant will answer those questions and leave it up to the organization as to how to act. Many government consulting contracts are framed in this way and often then shield the consultant from further pressure for advice or representation.[54]

Others negotiate the roles by being very explicit. Roger Clarke was one of the founders of APF and continues to be a strong advocate. He also has a consultancy business and was, for a while, in an academic position:

So I have to be very distinct about my consultancy roles. My advocacy role therefore has to be declared left-right-and-center at conferences, in preliminary meetings with clients, and so on. So by an advocate I mean somebody who adopts a public interest perspective or possibly a sectoral perspective on behalf of some segment of the population.... So it's a conscious stepping aside from paid consulting work for a defined client, and it's also not sustaining a pretense of independence, overview, and rigor as is appropriate in the academic context.[55]

Clarke has learned with experience how to manage these different roles and relationships. Many others find it very difficult, and perhaps impossible.

How far can the advocacy/consultant go in advancing a more fundamental privacy argument? It is clear that there are constraints. Many contracts will include a confidentiality agreement that will prevent the consultant from outside comment. At the very least, and for most people, the consultancy role will tend to dull the edge of their criticism, and certainly make them more reluctant to speak in the media. The ability to play this role, therefore, is contingent on the ability to choose clients who genuinely want to change their practices and on the capacity of the consultant to walk away if they do not.

The Advocate/Technologist

This next category embraces a variety of advocates who have come to the issue through their computer expertise. Many privacy advocates are also developers of software products designed to enhance privacy protection. Pejoratively referred to as the "geeks," they are nevertheless a very important group within the network. Their contributions to the community come in three forms. First, they have successfully challenged the dominant and legalistic way of thinking about how to protect privacy. Second, they have developed and marketed software products, often in the face of considerable opposition from law enforcement and intelligence communities. And third, they have promoted the cause of security and privacy through working with governmental and business organizations, as advocacy/consultants.

It has been generally assumed that the contemporary privacy and data protection movement would not have arisen had it not been for the spread of increasingly sophisticated information and communications technologies. Laws have been designed, in large measure, to control the worst impacts that information technologies have on society. But is it appropriate to think of technology as having an "impact" on society, as if the two were conceptually and empirically separable? Some contend that technologies themselves are imbued with social and political values.[56] In this interpretation artifacts actually "contain" political and social biases and their very structure and architecture may be inextricably linked to particular patterns of power. Information technologies may carry, intentionally or unintentionally, a valence that may be pro-privacy, or pro-surveillance.

Hence, privacy experts have gradually embraced this notion that technologies can also be part of the solution as well as part of the problem. In a famous article, David Chaum claimed that the traditional data protection model, based on the fair information principles doctrine, can be radically altered if technologies can be designed in such a way that the default is the zero-collection of personal information. With the revolutionary discovery of "public-key" or "asymmetric" cryptography in the late 1970s, privacy, or perhaps more accurately anonymity, can be built into information systems in ways that do not compromise the ability of public and private organizations to authenticate transactions (Chaum 1992). A new concept—privacy-enhancing technologies—entered the vocabulary and began to complement other legal and self-regulatory measures (Bennett and Raab 2006, chap. 7).

This vision, together with challenges to the notion of anonymous communications and interactions from law enforcement interests, consolidated the community of mainly young technologists and turned them into privacy advocates. This community interacted through some of the earliest online networks. The principal example would be a group known as the Cypherpunks, the rise of which coincided with the first government attempts at cryptography regulation through key-escrow schemes such as the Clipper Chip. Its founder, Eric Hughes, wrote the group's manifesto in 1993:

We the Cypherpunks are dedicated to building anonymous systems. We are defending our privacy with cryptography, with anonymous mail forwarding systems, with digital signatures, and with electronic money.

Cypherpunks write code. We know that someone has to write software to defend privacy, and since we can't get privacy unless we all do, we're going to write it. We publish our code so that our fellow Cypherpunks may practice and play with it. Our code is free for all to use, worldwide. We don't much care if you don't approve of the software we write. We know that software can't be destroyed and that a widely dispersed system can't be shut down.

Cypherpunks deplore regulations on cryptography, for encryption is fundamentally a private act. The act of encryption, in fact, removes information from the public realm. Even laws against cryptography reach only so far as a nation's border and the arm of its violence. Cryptography will ineluctably spread over the whole globe, and with it the anonymous transaction systems that it makes possible.[57]

A similar spirit was invoked by John Gilmore, one of the original programmers at Sun Microsystems, at the first of the annual series of very influential Computers, Freedom and Privacy (CFP) conferences: "I want to guarantee—with physics and mathematics, not with laws—things like real privacy of personal communications... real privacy of personal records... real freedom of trade... real financial privacy... and real control of identification" (quoted in Levy 2001, 208). Gilmore went on also to make the case, post-9/11, for anonymous travel by challenging the airlines' practices of demanding identification on boarding an aircraft, and the Transportation Safety Administration's regulations that require it.[58]

The Cypherpunks also rose at the time that the e-mail program, Pretty Good Privacy (PGP), was being distributed by Phil Zimmerman in an effort to get free cryptography out to the general public before governments could wake up and regulate it (Levy 2001). Zimmerman was subsequently investigated and charged with violations of the U.S. Arms Export Control Act. The dispersal of PGP also raised questions about its possible infringement of the Rivest-Shamir-Adleman (RSA) patent, which had earlier developed a program called Mailsafe. But PGP spread uncontrollably outside the United States through users who were not vulnerable to investigation by U.S. law enforcement either for patent infringement or for export violations. In the end, the Department of Justice decided not to prosecute, but the perceived victimization of Zimmerman only served to increase PGP's popularity and its rapid spread throughout the world. Zimmerman subsequently founded a company and began to expand his product line.[59] PGP is now the global standard for e-mail encryption. He is now working to develop encrypted Internet telephony.[60]

Another advocate who stands out is Bruce Schneier, the security expert, author, and chief technology officer of BT Counterpane Internet Security Inc. Schneier's work has challenged governments, businesses and privacy advocates to think more critically and creatively about what we mean by security. His has contended that well-intentioned security measures, such as those introduced post-9/11, have actually made people more vulnerable rather than less (Schneier 2003, 2004). His work has tried to conceive of security in broader, nontechnical terms and in ways that are consistent with the beliefs, motivations, and limitations of fallible individuals and complex organizations. He believes that security needs to be malleable and pliable, so that when it breaks, it breaks in a predictable way. He also has a talent for the pithy one-liner such as those about privacy developed for the Individual-I.Com Web site (reproduced at the beginning of chapter 2), and for the clever insight that successfully exposes deep contradictions in government security measures: "Remember what the no-fly list is. It's a list of people who are so dangerous that they can't be allowed to board an airplane under any circumstances, yet so innocent that they can't be arrested—even under the provisions of the PATRIOT Act."[61]

Many other less well known and less controversial figures were part of this community, developing various privacy-enhancing tools throughout the 1990s. These included developers of anonymizing and pseudonymizing devices, tools for cookie and spyware filtering, instruments for the management of spam, and so on. However, the early enthusiasm about the privacy-enhancing potential of cryptographic tools gave way at the end of the decade to certain realism about the developing nature of the Internet. In the first place, the dominance of Microsoft forced a compliance with its operating systems, with the result that the Platform for Privacy Preferences (P3P) was developed, established as a standard by the World Wide Web consortium (W3C), and integrated into Microsoft Internet browsers. The crypto community also faced a stark realism about the extent to which ordinary consumers were actually interested in anonymous transactions. Most efforts to develop profit-making ventures from privacy-enhancing technologies failed, as encryption products became integrated into an increasingly corporate Internet.

The early advocates therefore dispersed: some to academic research work, others to major corporations, and others to the world of privacy and security consulting. For a while, however, privacy advocacy witnessed a relatively coherent movement, fueled by a genuine excitement about the potential of the Internet to foster private communications and transactions. The advocacy/technologists embraced a range of different characters, but they were all motivated by the belief that they could solve a problem that law and regulation had not solved, and by the vision that they were engaging in a crucial effort to shape this new medium de novo. Privacy became central to the debates about the character of the Internet, and privacy advocates assumed a pivotal role in a rapidly evolving story about the development of this revolutionary new medium of communication.

The Advocate/Journalist

A few others advocates have tried to carve out careers specifically as "privacy journalists" through the regular publication of newsletters about developments in the field. Perhaps the most notable is the *Privacy Journal*, published monthly by Robert Ellis Smith since 1974—"before there was an Internet, before there was e-mail, and before there was automated telemarketing. Thus, it's the oldest publication on privacy in the world." Smith covers privacy in all of its aspects—"the Internet, credit reporting, medical records, computer security, unwanted telephone calls, electronic surveillance, access to an individual's own records, the impact of European and Canadian practices on the U.S., biometric identification systems, the common law of privacy, the constitutional right to privacy, and much more."[62] Smith was steeped in civil rights and civil liberties politics and profoundly motivated by the various abuses of power during the Watergate scandal. He had a desire to combine his knowledge of law and journalism. *Privacy Journal* actually began as a newsletter for the ACLU. In 1974, he branched out on his own, thinking that *Privacy Journal* would only be a temporary activity. It is still going strong over thirty years later.

Smith engages in advocacy in a variety of ways. He gives congressional testimony. He appears as an expert witness and files amicus curiae briefs, and he gives speeches. But at heart he is a journalist and plays a vital role in trying to find out the facts of what government agencies and private companies are actually doing with personal data. Sometimes he breaks a story that is then taken up by the mainstream media. For example, *Privacy Journal* was the first publication to report on the lack of confidence in AIDS testing in the early 1980s because of the absence of confidentiality protocols. In 2006, it published the first cumulative list of laptop thefts and losses. Both stories were subsequently followed up in the mainstream media. At other times, he looks for the privacy angle on issues that are already being reported.

Over the years, he has developed the techniques of the journalist and adapted them to the particular challenges of reporting on privacy. In his words: "I am trying to get as much information as I possibly can. It's what I call triangulation. If I find it out from three different sources, I have acceptable proof that it is true. And the sources may be documents, they may be individuals. But it's not three people looking at it from the same direction but three different sources from a different perspective that satisfies me that I am accurate." He will also use another time-honored technique: "I say you can talk to me or not talk to me but I'm going to write the story anyway and then you're going to have to deal with it later. . . . So it's in your interest to tell me your side of the story. . . . I would say it's the exception not the rule when organizations refuse to talk to me."[63]

Evan Hendricks has published a similar newsletter since 1981 entitled Privacy Times. Like *Privacy Journal,* Privacy Times has not changed its format; both have the feel of the more low-tech and unglossy "broadsheet." Privacy Times is read largely by "attorneys and professionals who must stay abreast of the legislation, litigation, and executive branch activities, as well as consumer news, technology trends and business developments."[64] Over the years, Hendricks has played a similar role to Smith in the U.S. privacy advocacy community, though his background is somewhat different. In addition, there are other related journals that focus more on freedom of information but cover privacy developments as well.[65] In countries where there are more complete and established private-sector privacy laws, the privacy publications tend to report less on the current conflicts of the day, and more on legislative and policy developments, decisions by data protection agencies and courts, and self-regulatory initiatives. Examples include the online newsletter, *Privacy-Scan* in Canada, *Privacy Law and Policy Reporter* in Australia, as well as *Privacy Laws and Business* centered in the United Kingdom.

Other advocates have found privacy advocacy through their writings as journalists in the mainstream media. An example would be Pam Dixon who founded World Privacy Forum. As a reporter for the *San Diego Herald Tribune,* she became interested in the evolving online communications in the early 1990s, and particularly in their use for employment background checks. She realized the potentially pernicious use of the Internet, as it then was, to check up on employees and applicants, and wrote an award-winning book on the subject (Dixon 1995). She continued her interests in employment privacy throughout the 1990s, and ultimately joined the Privacy Foundation as a research fellow, working with

Richard Smith. When their funding ended, she founded the World Privacy Forum, where she continues to use her training as a journalist to do in-depth research reports on privacy questions.

There have been a number of reporters within the mainstream media within many countries who have, over the years, taken an interest in the subject and have provided a vehicle for privacy advocates to express their views. A fine example is David Burnham, formerly of the *New York Times*. Burnham's work has specialized in the critical examination of federal and state law enforcement. Privacy protection, therefore, became an obvious focus for his journalism as he documented and critiqued the "rise of the computer state" (Burnham 1983). In 1989, he founded the Transactional Records Access Clearinghouse (TRAC), a data gathering, research, and data distribution organization associated with Syracuse University, the goal of which is to provide the public and members of the oversight community—reporters, public interest groups, congressional committees, scholars, and others—with the "comprehensive performance data they need to hold federal investigative and regulatory agencies accountable."[66]

Another example is the British journalist, Duncan Campbell, who worked with the *New Statesman* from 1978–1991, and who now works as a freelance journalist TV producer. He has specialized in intelligence issues, and was prosecuted under the Official Secrets Act in 1978. More than any other journalist in Europe, he has tried to unearth some of the deeper secrets on the interception of communications by agencies of the state and to piece together the evolving international networks of intelligence collaboration—principally that called "Echelon." Others, like Jim Bronskill in Canada, have taken a close interest in workings of the post-9/11 antiterrorism measures, such as no-fly lists. Indeed, one could name a large number of journalists in many countries who have immersed themselves in law enforcement and intelligence issues, and who from time to time uncover information of great interest to the privacy advocate.

There is, however, a tension between the interests of the journalistic profession and privacy. These conflicts tend not to arise when the general story is one of the abuses of power by state or corporate agencies to the detriment of individuals. They do arise with respect to issues concerning the private lives of public figures. They do surface with respect to disputes over the "public" nature of certain government records systems. And they do emerge in full vigor when privacy protection laws are being proposed and developed, with the result that most laws contain blanket exemptions for personal information collected in the course of investigative journalistic activity. Whereas many journalists see value in exposing stories about privacy breaches and invasions, their representative lobby groups tend to err more on the side of disclosure and access. With few exceptions, therefore, advocate/journalists also face tensions and conflicts, and tend to work those out on a case-by-case basis.

The Advocate/Artist

The fact is often overlooked that an antisurveillance politics can be expressed through many art forms. Advocate/artists rarely participate in more conventional group politics, infrequently engage with government and business elites on these issues, and almost never turn up to conferences. For some, it may be a stretch to include them within the broad privacy advocacy community. By directing the public's attention to the capacities and dangers of new surveillance, however, they play a vital role. Art can set the conditions under which individuals might come to understand surveillance practices and the shifting boundaries between public and private space.

For many years, of course, privacy advocates have invoked fictional representations to support their case. A few famous works have even been elevated to the level of sociological debate and have provided more abstract frameworks for the appreciation of current trends. The Orwellian *1984* imagery is dominant, and the omnipresent "Big Brother" is now invoked to describe almost any form of technological capturing of personal information for purposes of social control. However, others have found inspiration in Aldous Huxley's *Brave New World*, for an understanding of how we become complicit to forms of power, or in Franz Kafka's *The Castle*, for a vision of the bizarre and opaque ways that power is exercised.[67] Less well known works include *Oath of Fealty*, a 1982 novel by Larry Niven and Jerry Pournelle describing a large "arcology" whose dwellers choose to live there because of extraordinary efficiencies and to be subjected to constant surveillance. The list of fiction, invoked by privacy advocates, could go on and on.

Movies can perhaps be more influential, and many have been invoked over the years. A 1974 Gene Hackman film, *The Conversation*, depicts the lonely and conflicted work of the private investigator, who, with 1974 technology, claims he can record any conversation between two people in any public space, but who gets so caught up in his work that the distinction between the "monitor" and the "monitored" becomes deeply intertwined. A more recent example exploring similar themes is *Enemy of the State*, a 1998 film about the use of surveillance and the powers it provides a corrupt politician who could track a person who has evidence of a politically motivated crime that would expose a murder. Other movies focus on the technology, such as the world's most advanced helicopter, nicknamed "Blue Thunder," in the film of the same name that is essentially a military style combat helicopter used as a surveillance platform and for large crowd control missions. Other films focus on the larger societal vision, such as *Brazil* by Terry Gilliam, depicting a kind of oppressive total surveillance, and *Minority Report*, a story about a society that arrests people for crimes they have yet to commit.[68] At writing, the inspiring German film, *Das Leben der Anderen* (The Lives of Others) about the Stasi monitoring of the East German cultural and artistic community in 1984, has captivated the attention of scholars and privacy advocates alike, raising larger questions about why state surveillance techniques seem oppressive in that time and context, but increasingly permissible in more "democratic" states today.

The depiction of themes of privacy and surveillance in popular culture has been analyzed by others in terms of the various reflections of social trends. The influence on public consciousness is, however, difficult to gauge. For the privacy advocate, fictional representations of technologies and practices of surveillance might serve as a crucial warning; for others, they might be read with fascination or glorification. This thematic offers stimulating material for the cultural studies experts, but the surveillance symbols within fiction, cinema, TV, popular music, and so on can operate as a two-edged sword. The popularity of the voyeuristic *Big Brother* reality shows are perhaps the best examples.

More interesting, perhaps, are the efforts of the individual visual artists who have tried for a more immediate and direct impact on the viewer. There are several surveillance themes that find expression in contemporary art. Visual art can directly engage the viewer with a number of questions about the boundaries between the public and private space, about the distinction between the person and the technology, about the problematic between the watched and the watchers, and so forth. The "do you look at art, or does the art watch you" question provides all kinds of opportunities to rouse consciousness about surveillance.

Surveillance related questions have increasingly become a major focus of contemporary cultural productions.[69] An online exhibition developed in Germany, for instance, entitled CTRL [SPACE] tried to map the various "rhetorics of surveillance from Bentham to Big Brother." In its exploration of the full range of cultural engagements with panoptic issues, it tried to offer "both a state of the art survey of the full range of panopticism—in architecture, digital culture, video, painting, photography, conceptual art, cinema, installation work, television, robotics and satellite imaging—and a largely unknown history of the various attempts to critically and creatively appropriate, refunction, expose and undermine these logics."[70] This Web site provides a very nice overview of some of the artists who have engaged with themes of surveillance: Andy Warhol's explorations of early closed-circuit video in the 1960s, Bruce Nauman's "video corridors," Dan Graham's "Time Delay Rooms," Rem Koolhas's "Project for the Renovation of a Panoptic Prison," Sophie Calle's documentation of a detective hired to spy on her, Thomas Ruff's night photographs, and various glass installations by Diller and Scofidio.

Some artists deliberately misuse technology to expose its hidden ideological mechanisms. Perhaps the best example is the series of perverse applications of new technologies dreamed up by an anonymous group called the Bureau of Inverse Technology.[71] One example is the miniature spy plane, released over the Silicon Valley to capture aerial portraits of the information age. Another is Super Vision, a multimedia piece presented by a group called the Builders Association about the way data surveillance is infiltrating our daily routines. It blends actors with several technologies: motion capture, panoramic video projection, custom-made biometric applications, and multiple rendering systems that let the video director synthesize prerecorded and real-time elements. In a series of vignettes, Super Vision introduces the audience to several people struggling with identity loss. For example, ticketholders' own data, assembled from box office receipts and public information, is integrated into the production. In a similar vein, the Toronto artist Cheryl Sourkes has been creating artworks using still images taken through Web cameras and posted on the Internet.[72] Similar video stills, and other surveillance devices, appear in the work of Jill Magid.[73]

Beyond the creative act, it is rare for artists to engage more directly within the advocacy community. Sometimes, however, art is used by individuals in specific contexts of resistance. Hasan Elahi is a conceptual artist with an Arab-sounding name who, post-9/11, has been subjected to constant FBI surveillance, including many interviews as well as polygraph tests. Although cleared of suspicion, he has also been obliged to report his whereabouts to the FBI to avoid detention. He then realized that if he had to tell the FBI, he might as well tell the world. So he hacked the signal of his cell phone to an ankle bracelet that can track his movements and report them on a map.[74] He also tries to document his life in a series of photos of his travel movements, his recreation, his eating habits, and even his banking records that give a record of his purchases. All of this record is placed on his Web site. He sees this self-surveillance as both an art form and his perpetual alibi for the next time the FBI questions him.

There are other examples of actors who do come to privacy advocacy through their art. The best illustration is a German group called FoeBuD.[75] Two full-time activists—Rena Tangens and padeluun—were originally inspired in the early 1980s by the music of the French composer Erik Satie, who coined the term *musique d'ameublement* (sometimes translated as "furnishing music"). This means music that is not there to fascinate people and make them passive consumers; it is meant to create a frame in which people feel comfortable and welcome—the audience becomes the leading character. In 1984, they organized a performance of Satie's work "Vexations" from his *Pages Mystiques*; the composer suggests that this two-minute piece could be repeated 840 times producing an atmosphere of calm and serenity. This music was performed by two pianists over fifteen hours. Rena Tangens and padeluun had arranged an all-white room with tables, flowers, and white food in such a way that people would actually like to stay for such a long time. It created a realization among that audience that they have time to self-actualize. But the space must create an arena within which people can be empowered, an important condition of which is that there is no surveillance, and thus no fear.

This philosophy also inspired their online activism. FoeBuD was one of the first groups in Germany to run a bulletin board in the 1980s. This was part of the independent BBS network called Z-Netz (Zerberus). Zamir Transnational Network, installed by FoeBuD member Eric Bachman in several cities in former Yugoslavia during the war, was the most important medium for peace groups, humanitarian aid, refugees, and ordinary citizens from 1992 to 1996, when the telephone lines between Croatia and Serbia were blocked. Along with the Chaos Computer Club, they engaged in some high-profile and early hacking campaigns. But they have since distinguished themselves from the CCC and have concentrated more on political issues, particularly raising awareness of the dangers and side effects of supermarket customer cards and RFID technology. Since 2000 they have organized the annual German Big Brother Awards. They are advocacy/activists, but at the same time they are always aware of their art background and see their advocacy work as part of creating a framework in which people can live. Thus, their house in Bielefeld, is both an artist's studio as well as a place within which other artists and activists can work.[76]

The public surveillance cameras in New York City motivated the creation of one of the most innovative "antisurveillance" groups in the world. Since 1996, the New York Surveillance Camera Players have been performing plays adapted by one "Art Toad" before public video-surveillance cameras. Examples include George Orwell's *1984* and *Animal Farm*, Edgar Allen Poe's *The Raven*, Samuel Beckett's *Waiting for Godot*, and Alfred Jarry's *Ubu Roi*, the subject of the very first performance in 1996 before a surveillance camera in Manhattan's Union Square subway station. They explained how this is done:

Surveillance cameras, though obviously designed to monitor and relay what they "see" are not allowed by law to monitor and relay what they "hear" . . . and so any performance by the Surveillance Camera players has to be a silent one. By rendering—reducing might be a better word—all of the dialogue of Ubu the King to a few expressions that would be clearly visible if printed on hand-held cards designed to look like speech bubbles in comic strips, M. Toad succeeded in creating a script that could be used by the SCPers.[77]

Part of this avant-garde style is dictated by federal law that restricts sound recording through surveillance video cameras. Thus, the group adapts many silent plays and employs signboards so as not to confuse observers about what they are doing.

Before long, the group achieved certain notoriety and attracted media attention, which occasionally attracted a police presence. Thus the complexity of surveillance mechanisms is exposed as one group of "watchers" (police) watch another group (the media) who had trained their cameras on the players as they were performing before the anonymous men and women tasked with having to monitor these technologies 24/7. The group has also made and published maps of camera locations and has offered guided tours based on those maps.[78] The project started in New York, but has inspired the formation of similar groups in other cities, and indeed countries.

The Players, therefore, try to render the surveillance transparent, to subvert its purposes by turning it into an entertainment medium, but also to complicate and disrupt the relationship between the watcher and the watched. The founder, Bill Brown, summarizes the group's approach through the concept of *détournement* borrowed from the tactics of the Situationalist International. They try to derail, satirize, and turn the cameras against their original purpose. Further, they are "not a professional theatre troupe, nor are they producers or actors in television shows; they are just a bunch of average Joes and Josephines who appreciate how boring it must be for law enforcement officers to watch video images constantly being displayed on the closed-circuit television surveillance systems that perpetually monitor our behavior and appearance all over the city" (New York Surveillance Camera Players, 22). Nothing they do, or advocate, is illegal. They have nevertheless used one artistic medium, the theatrical performance, to express their activism and to educate citizens about the threats to privacy of public surveillance systems.

Concluding Observations

Privacy advocacy can be expressed through traditional activism, through scholarly research and teaching, through consultancy, through hardware and software development, through journalism and through various forms of artistic expression. There are few pure stereotypical cases within the privacy advocacy community. Most self-identified privacy advocates wear a number of hats and juggle several responsibilities. Nevertheless, the analysis does suggest that we are not observing one community or coalition here. Roles are self assigned, but they are also imposed in multiple and conflicting ways by others.

It is also obvious that that there are no easy generalizations about what makes a privacy advocate. They are men and women, black and white, gay and straight, young and old, rich and poor, and so on. Some have religious beliefs and are active churchgoers; most are not. Most have higher levels of education, though their educational backgrounds are extremely diverse—humanities, sciences, medicine, business, social sciences, law, librarianship, computer science, and others. Some have personal experience of intrusions; others do not. There is no "constituency" from which they are drawn.

All, however, are animated by a fundamental belief that privacy is not only an important issue but one of the defining questions of modern times. All would share a profound sense that new technologies should be shaped to human ends, rather than vice versa. All have deep-seated worries about abuses of power by modern organizations using the latest technological tools. Since the 1990s, all would be animated by the excitement of being in at the first stages of the development of the Internet.

We have analyzed the types of groups that have arisen, as well as the various individuals. It is now time to explore in more detail what privacy advocates actually do. There are structures and identities. There is also behavior. What strategies are adopted to promote the cause? What works, and what doesn't?

4 The Strategies

Our strategy has always been to raise hell without breaking the law.
—Alan Borovoy, Canadian Civil Liberties Association

Four "Es": Establishing Rights, Exercising Rights, Exposing Violations, Encouraging Privacy Friendly Practices
—Pippa Lawson on the roles of CIPPIC

What, therefore, do privacy advocates do? What strategies and tactics do they pursue, and why should anyone pay attention to them? With few exceptions they do not speak for large constituencies mobilized through a mass membership. They generally have meager financial resources. According to most theories of group politics, they could safely be ignored. And yet they are not. What forms of politics do they engage in to ensure that they are not ignored?

There are many conventional ways to approach this question that focus on the targets of group pressure and resistance. Traditionally, pressure or interest groups have been conceived in relation to the institutions of the state. They obtain and mobilize resources (money, membership, expertise, information, and so on) and thereby compete to influence policymakers to support their agendas. Success is therefore dependent upon resources, broadly construed. In this "resource mobilization approach," a core group of sophisticated strategists works to harness the disaffected energies of a particular constituency (Zald and McCarthy 1979). They try to attract money and supporters. They capture media attention, and they thereby ensure that they cannot be ignored by those in power. There are several variants of this theory, dependent upon whether one approaches the problem from an economic, sociological, or political perspective. Traditionally, each has tended to assume that the major focus of resource mobilization is the state, and groups are conceived of, and legitimated, in terms of their relations with executive, legislative, and judicial institutions.

In contemporary conditions, this perspective falls short. Globalization has brought with it transnational activism, and with it a broader conception of what it means to engage in collective action. In their study of advocacy politics in international politics, Keck and Sikkink (1998, 16) offer a fourfold typology of tactics that international networks use in their efforts at persuasion, socialization, and pressure. Information politics relies on the ability to generate politically relevant information and to move it by the most effective means to the place where it will have the most impact, at the most critical time. Symbolic politics relies on the ability to call up symbols, actions, and stories that can interpret a situation in ways that makes sense for a particular audience within a particular culture. Accountability politics is an attempt to hold powerful agents accountable to previously stated policies or commitments. Leverage politics is directed toward those who have power in public or private organizations and who can effect change, by imposing a sanction or threat of some manner. This typology is developed in the context of human rights and environmental advocacy networks. It offers some interesting insights into privacy advocacy as well.

Information Politics: Promoting Change by Reporting Facts

There is a long tradition within social movement politics of inducing those in power to do something that they would not otherwise do through the constant reporting of facts and testimony about abuses of power and the resulting harms. This "human rights methodology" can be very effective in sensitizing public and elite opinion to the need for reform (Keck and Sinkink 1998, 45). The careful assembling, as well as the relentless repetition, of facts about, for example, slavery, racial discrimination, torture, child labor, prostitution, land mine mutilation, and so on have forced those issues onto institutional agendas and promoted change. This is not a power politics through which change can be effected through threats, through coercion, or by making life unpleasant for a target group—that is, the "leverage politics" discussed later. This is about the politics of persuasion, about speaking truth to power (Kennedy Cuomo 2005). There is a wrong that can be documented. Appeals are then made to the collective conscience of a society and of its political and business elites.

In the context of globalization, students of international economy stress that the extent to which regulatory protections might flow around the world (i.e., whether there is a "race to the top") relates in some measure to the work of transnational activists who can spotlight the behavior of firms and the lax standards of states. When firms go abroad, they take not only their capital investment but also their reputations, brand names, images, and so on. Activists in many countries are ready to use the media to shine the spotlight upon the socially irresponsible corporation and upon the weak regulations that facilitate such behavior. The "spotlight phenomenon" can expose questionable practices such as the use of child labor or the hiring of workers at below minimum wages (Spar 1998). Such pressures have led to global codes of conduct, standards, and seals to which companies have been forced to adhere.

What then are the equivalent "facts" for the privacy advocate? What are the "harms" that can be documented and relentlessly portrayed as incontrovertible evidence that reform is necessary? What is the equivalent of the testimony of human rights abuses? Several years ago, Robert Ellis Smith of *Privacy Journal* became tired of reading that privacy was an imprecise concept with only abstract relevance for the ordinary person. He published a book called *War Stories* (1993), a collection of anecdotes by ordinary Americans victimized by invasions of privacy. The stories came from many areas of American life, and they remain a powerful reminder of the direct harm (financial, reputational, psychological, and legal) that can occur through the inappropriate collection, processing, and disclosure of personal information. It is also a reminder that personal information need not be inherently sensitive for harms to result. Innocuous information in the wrong contexts can lead to severe consequences.

Nevertheless, this kind of specific documentation of direct harm to individuals is rare. There are three reasons. First, many privacy invasions often do not get seen as such. Their effects are more indirect, and only show up when other consequences arise: the denial of credit, the receipt of unsolicited telemarketing calls, an unwarranted tax audit, secondary screening at airport security, and so on. The root cause of these effects might be hidden from the subject, and therefore not identified as a privacy invasion as such. Second, and consequently, the privacy advocate has constantly to refute the argument that "if you have nothing to hide, you have nothing to fear." The vast majority of citizens go through their daily lives believing that surveillance processes are not directed at them, but at the miscreants and wrongdoers. For all the evidence that the monitoring of individual behavior has become routine and everyday, the dominant orientation is that mechanisms of surveillance are directed at others. Finally, there is nearly always a justifiable organizational purpose attached to surveillance mechanisms: internal or national security, the efficient provision of government services, lower insurance rates, better credit systems, and so on. Therefore, the harm is rarely regarded as unmitigated. It is normally viewed as a price worth paying for some public good.

For these reasons, the information politics of privacy advocacy has generally not been about adopting a "human rights methodology" and about documenting facts relentlessly about actual harms to real people. For the privacy advocate, the politics of information is more difficult. It relies upon argumentation about potential consequences. It often involves extrapolations from the experiences of similar surveillance systems in other times and places. Increasingly it involves considerable technical expertise, and sophisticated understandings of the operation of complex public and private organizations. It often requires a leap of faith, that many are unwilling or incapable of making, from a particular provision under discussion to larger arguments about the slow and incremental slide toward the "surveillance society."

An important part of the political struggle over information is whether or not an issue is defined in technical terms and therefore only subject to discussion by self-appointed experts, or whether it concerns a broader public constituency. Privacy advocates will try to frame the value context in these broader terms. By and large, privacy advocates will also try to enter the public debate about a particular practice earlier rather than later, and to generate relevant information about privacy implications in advance of the deployment of a product or service, or in anticipation of policy change. Advocates will talk about "getting ahead of the curve" and of the dangers of reacting to developments after human and financial resources have been devoted to a particular program or technology. And they need to perform this role with respect to proposals they support (such as a privacy protection bill) as well as those they might oppose.

At one level, privacy advocates engage in a constant fight to influence the discourse, the ways in which issues are framed, and the general understanding of privacy in relation to other values. In some contexts, this involves a process of going back to square one and of explaining in philosophical terms the nature of the problem. For instance, there has been a sustained attempt post-9/11 to insist that policy choices between privacy and security are a false dichotomy, and that there are many ways that security goals can be met without compromising privacy (Schneier 2004). They will, therefore, invoke a range of symbols and representations, discussed later, to attempt to connect this value to direct and common experience.

Privacy advocates also need to be informed about a number of technical and policy issues beyond that of privacy. Most advocates would contend that many surveillance processes are simply not going to achieve the social goals claimed, and should be blocked on the simple grounds of ineffectiveness. Barry Steinhardt of the ACLU has made this point repeatedly: "If a new program is not actually effective, the matter should end there. There is no need to engage in detailed balancing tests or evaluations of a program's effect on privacy if it is not going to increase security."[1] The information politics of video-surveillance cameras is a case in point. These schemes have raised the concerns of privacy advocates the world over. But it is also unclear whether indeed they do reduce or deter crime. The privacy advocate, therefore, has to immerse him- or herself in the criminological literature to draw some lessons about effectiveness. Increasingly, advocates have tried to engage the debate at that level in an attempt to appeal, for example, to the frames of reference of the resource-constrained city official who is accountable for crime rates and needs to do something about them.

Difficult choices also need to be made about the balance between more strategic or long-term research and the more short-term and immediate injection of argument into policy debate. Political scientists have written about, and analyzed, the "policy cycle" and have theorized about how these cycles vary over time and space (Howlett and Ramesh 2003). In a governmental context, where standards of democratic accountability normally impose some requirements for transparency, consultation, and open debate, advocates can inject relevant information at any stage of this cycle. They can attempt to shape which problems receive attention, which options are considered, which options are selected, and how the policy is implemented. Down the road, they can offer judgments about whether the policy has worked. Thus, in a context where there is open debate either about a pro-privacy measure (such as a data protection bill) or about a governmental scheme with implications for surveillance, the advocacy process is largely predetermined by the decision-making agendas of others.

Beyond the questions of timing, the advocacy community needs to make some fundamental decisions about whether to engage at all in the political process or to focus more on the general public. Some are suspicious of the political process, or are not conveniently located to engage with decision makers in the corridors or power. They will prefer to engage in public education. The PRC, for instance, provides helpful fact sheets on issues such as identity theft, employment background checks, credit reports, medical records, junk faxes, cellular telephones, and direct marketing. Others provide information for consumption within the broad network of privacy experts and advocates. The EPIC Alerts are a fine example, as is the EDRIGRAM. That information helps bind network members together and is essential for their effectiveness.

Others work well with reporters, are good at media interviews and have that ability to encapsulate the complex policy issue within the pithy one-liners that make good journalism. All, however, have to make judgments about the amount of time they can spend with reporters as well as the motives behind the story. All need to make decisions about which media outlets are worth talking to. But sympathetic journalists are also a source of information for privacy advocates, and can alert them to developments and events of which they may not have been aware. As with every other policy issue, media relations are a two-way street.

For those groups that do engage with the policy process, decisions need to be made about the appropriate institutional target, and those decisions are obviously influenced by the constitutional framework and balance of institutional powers in that particular country. Privacy advocates can, and do, spend enormous amounts of time injecting written and oral arguments into various stages of the policy cycle, and reacting to policy proposals developed by both executive and legislative agencies. In every country they spend a lot of time commenting on government reports, consultation documents, draft bills, and so on. They give written and oral testimony before legislative committees. They comment on reports and decisions from data protection authorities, where they exist. It is mainly in the United States, however, that they intervene in the judicial process, through the submission of amicus curiae (friends of the court) briefs.

The tactics of commentary vary from country to country, dependent on the political and administrative culture. For example, in the United States, as Chris Hoofnagle explains, the number of comments received by an agency is of critical importance:

In the United States it's the agency debates that are really important.... A lot of agencies count comments based on the number of commentators. For instance, the banking industry has around thirty different groups that it will use, and it will appear as thirty different comments on the agency records. And so privacy advocates have to counter that, and one way they do that is by doing big coalition comments. . . . Comments have to be read and considered under the Administrative Procedure Act. . . . Literally, you cut and paste the exact same comments and then have thirty different organizations file them and that counts as thirty against one.[2]

The provision of policy-relevant information also takes the form of letter writing. There are many examples where advocates have attempted to seize an initiative by writing a joint letter to an organization outlining privacy implications of certain proposals. Typically, these are never written without a number of organizations "signing on" and are made public from the outset. Thus, one organization will take the lead, consult, prepare a draft and then ask others for support. Most of the privacy campaigns against the big Internet companies, discussed in chapter 5, have employed this strategy.

Of course, advocates have to make tactical decisions about whether a particular proposal is worth the effort of commentary. In the United States, for instance, several bills might be introduced in different committees or subcommittees on the same subject at the same time, as House and Senate members wish to get their names associated with a particular issue and be able to tell their constituents that they are sympathetic to a problem and have tried to do something about it. Privacy advocates need to make judgments about which bills have any chance of being reported out. Another important dynamic in the United States is the delegation of quasi-legislative powers to regulatory agencies such as the Federal Trade Commission (FTC) or the Federal Communications Commission (FCC). The development of the American Do Not Call List, for example, was handled almost entirely by the FTC. Privacy protection cuts across many institutional competences. In the American separation of powers system, therefore, privacy-related proposals might emerge from one of literally hundreds of executive branch agencies, and from almost any House and Senate committee. The task of monitoring the policy process and of injecting relevant information at the key time is often daunting.

It is also of some interest how few privacy advocates admit to engaging in the old-fashioned art of "lobbying"—that is direct and face-to-face meetings with policymakers. The term does carry pejorative connotations and tends to be connected with private-sector interests. In some countries, the activity is frowned upon, especially at administrative levels. Most countries also have registration processes for lobbyists and this can create some constraints. Hoofnagle explains the subtle distinctions in the United States:

Under federal law, if you as the advocate initiate a conversation with the office of the member on some public issue, it is lobbying. So technically, I almost never lobbied. What we usually did was adopt a series of tactics to get staffers to call us. And tactic number one was to be quoted in the newspaper. So the staffer calls you up and says: "I saw you quoted on this issue, and I want to talk to you about it." Tactic number two is to get something on your Web site as soon as possible.... If they contact you, it is not lobbying. If they invite you in for a meeting or if they invite you to testify, it's technically not lobbying, it's education.[3]

These constraints often necessitate a kind of elaborate dance between outside advocacy groups and governmental actors. Groups will employ all kinds of tactics to draw attention to these issues without initiating contact, and thus violating their tax status. Of course, the ability to lobby or educate policymakers directly in large countries like the United States is directly dependent on geographical proximity. Thus, advocacy groups with offices in Washington, D.C., like EPIC, the ACLU, and CDT obviously have advantages over those that do not, such as EFF. Perhaps a good deal more lobbying goes on at the state levels. Rich Neumeister in Minnesota has no hesitation in saying that he engages in lobbying. He spends a lot of time in his state capitol. He marks up bills by hand. He directly approaches legislators and their staffers and continually and incrementally gets pro-privacy amendments to Minnesota law.

In parliamentary countries with traditions of executive dominance, the institutional landscape might be slightly simpler, but traditions of administrative secrecy often hamper the ability of advocates to unearth policy proposals and inject commentary at a relevant time. In Britain, for example, much of the effort of organizations like PI has been targeted against the Home Office, a notoriously secretive agency generally not open to consultation with privacy advocacy organizations. Parliament has, therefore, been the most important focus of attention, and not necessarily the House of Commons. Caspar Bowden of FIPR was closely involved with attempting to alter the provisions of the United Kingdom's Regulation of Investigatory Powers Act of 2000. As a neophyte to the political process, his reflections on lobbying in the United Kingdom are interesting:

There was a process of getting to know parliamentarians which was probably easier than I had imagined, but the other thing that became clear was that to have an impact on legislation it was virtually pointless to direct one's energy to the House of Commons, because of the large parliamentary majority.... It was much more fruitful, we found, than to develop relations in the House of Lords where there was no guaranteed government majority; and at that stage the Lords were being very feisty and minded to push to the limit their powers of opposition. The other thing that I think I have to say is that in the entire House of Commons

I counted there were only four people who had ever programmed a computer in their life.[4]

In other countries—Germany, for instance—there is little or no administrative tradition of consulting with civil society groups during the policy process. Groups such as Die Humanistische Union, therefore, have to appeal to individual members of the federal and Länder parliaments as well as to the political parties.[5]

There is also a general sense among privacy advocates in many countries that much of the "formal" consultation can be perfunctory. Sometimes it is undertaken because of legislative requirement. At other times, it is motivated by an administrative desire to go through the motions and give the appearance that a policy process has been open and broadly consultative. In most cases, advocates have to participate and provide comments for fear that their views will not be taken seriously at times when a process is genuinely consultative. Privacy advocates also have to be very careful about confidentiality, or nondisclosure, agreements. Sometimes, government executive agencies will agree to consult with outside groups, on for example a draft piece of legislation, on condition that they do not speak publicly. Some will agree to this compromise. Others will not. The choices can be vexing, because it may not serve anybody's interests to keep material confidential.

On a few occasions, an advocacy community will make a decision to boycott an entire process in protest against the underlying motives. In Australia in the late 1990s, there were several attempts by the government to introduce self-regulatory solutions for private-sector privacy protection. APF essentially boycotted the process in the belief that these efforts were devised to avoid legislation, rather than to pave the way for it. Such stands can only be taken when an organization is sufficiently cohesive, and when it has the credibility to make the wider case in the public arena. Similar dilemmas arose in Canada at the same time when privacy advocates were invited to take part in a process of negotiating a privacy standard through the Canadian Standards Association. In that case, advocates did participate. Their involvement did succeed in strengthening the resulting code of practice, to the extent that it could form the basis of federal legislation for the private sector (CSA 1996), but the decisions were agonizing.

Increasingly, and particularly with respect to government surveillance schemes with law enforcement dimensions, the politics can become shrouded. Schemes emerge in a variety of mysterious ways. They may be embedded or implicit in administrative regulation. Or they may be left vague and ambiguous, with the intention that later administrative decision will fill in the gaps. In recent years, privacy advocates have also had to cope with policy proposals migrating to international organizations when they might have failed at the domestic levels. Some international bodies have quite transparent mechanisms of consultation. Others are veiled in mystery. This has led to a phenomenon called "policy laundering" referring to the use of international forums as an indirect means of pushing policies that could never win direct approval through the regular domestic political process. A campaign coordinated by the ACLU, Privacy International, and Statewatch, contends that "in a rapidly globalizing world, this technique is becoming a central means by which the United States (and other nations) seek to overcome civil liberties objections to privacy-invading policies." A major illustration is the use of the International Civil Aviation Authority (ICAO) as a forum to advance global standards for travel documents, including the use of biometrics (Hosein 2004).[6]

It is commonly recognized that on the Internet "code is law" (Lessig 1999), which can have profound implications for rights and liberties. Technical design decisions can have intended, and unintended, effects upon values such as privacy. The impacts are genuine, but they are often complex and only felt in the long term. The key standards bodies, such as the Internet Engineering Task Force (IETF) or the World Wide Web consortium, generally operate outside the public eye, and have highly informal processes for outside consultation. There are a series of conceptual issues and capacity gaps that need to be overcome to improve public representation in standards-setting processes.[7] Many of the technical committees of the International Standardization Organization (ISO), working on technical and management standards with privacy implications, have been similarly impenetrable.[8]

We have been referring so far to advocacy in the context of policy changes by national governments or international agencies. In the vast majority of cases, there is a compelling public interest asserted on the other side of the argument. The information strategies with respect to private-sector practices tend to take on a different dynamic. With the private sector, intrusive practices often only come to light after a technology is deployed or marketed, when intended or unintended consequences for the capture of personal information come to light. Advocates will then be in a position of exposing those practices and their invasive nature. The current debate about RFIDs is an apt example. The work of CASPIAN, however, has involved exposing corporate plans to deploy this technology by researching and publicizing the various patent applications (Albrecht and McIntyre 2005).

For many privacy issues, of course, the distinction between the private and public sectors is impossible to draw. A contemporary example that exposes the strategies and dilemmas of privacy advocacy is provided by the first airport installation in the United States of a technology called "Backscatter X-Ray," a device designed to detect objects hidden under clothing that might be overlooked by the traditional metal detector. The device also generates a detailed image of the traveler as if he or she is undressed. The vendors addressed concerns that this was a kind of "digital strip search" by developing a display format that depicts the traveler as a "chalk line image" with sensitive body parts obscured. What is significant in this case is not the image viewed by the operator but whether or not the original would be stored for possible viewing later. EPIC asked these questions of both the Transportation Security Administration and the vendor, American Science and Engineering. The answers were less than forthcoming, and invited all kinds of questions and hypotheses about why such images would need to be remotely located and stored.[9]

This case is mentioned not because of the details but because if is fairly representative of the way that facts about privacy invasions arise and become documented. A technology is developed and introduced and justified in some public interest. It raises obvious privacy implications. Information, both speculative and factual, circulates rapidly around the various privacy-related lists and blogs. The company and the government respond with attempts at reassurance, which fuel further questions and confusion. The information flows tend to be rapid and horizontal. The facts elide with hypotheses and speculations. The reluctance, perhaps inability, of government and vendor to tell the whole truth contributes to a general atmosphere of suspicion.

Surveillance practices tend to develop out of the spotlight. Sometimes, the social and individual risks require expert analysis and explanation. Sometimes those risks might depend on the confluence of a complex set of institutional motivations and technological development. Thus, the information politics of privacy advocacy tends not to be about documenting facts of individual abuses, grievances and harms. It tends to be about an early and rapid response strategy that often does not leave time for research into technological capacities, institutional motivations, and public anxieties. Information about privacy invasiveness sometimes has to rely on hypothesis rather than fact. It must draw together certain assumptions about what could happen to personally identifiable information if certain worst-case scenarios materialized. Privacy invasions occur when technologies work as intended and when they fail. They occur when organizations have worthy motives, and when they do not (Bennett and Raab 2006, 25–26).

Symbolic Politics: Connecting with Culture

Politics is not only about the instrumental collection and dissemination of information. It is also about powerful symbols and how those in turn become catalysts for change. The imprecise and mostly disparaging use of the word "symbolic" in everyday parlance overlooks the fact that a politics based on facts alone, without a symbolic dimension, cannot exist. Symbolism has always been an unavoidable constituent of political reality. It represents a way for elites to present themselves, to prove their abilities, and to communicate their basic political preferences and standards (Edelman 1964).

According to some social science, the objective or material dimensions of politics are increasingly being overwhelmed by the symbolic. The presentation and packaging of politics tailored to the needs of a visual media culture is becoming increasingly important for the acquisition and retention of political power in democratic societies. Verbal and nonverbal symbols generate attention and reduce the complexity of political problems and communicate a certain vision of the world. While this production becomes political reality for a public with limited time to digest complex political issues, real political choices are made away from the media spotlight and remain shrouded in mystery. Central to the potency of a political symbol is that it is remote or set apart from the immediate issue or problem. Every symbol stands for something other than itself, and it also evokes a set of impressions beyond the immediate reference of the language used. The meaning of political acts, therefore, is not only about the objective consequences but also about the psychological and emotional needs of the respondents. Elites make assumptions about these needs and manipulate symbols accordingly (Graber 1976).

The politics of privacy and surveillance cannot be immune from these trends. Symbols are invoked quite relentlessly to justify surveillance measures. For example, the range of measures passed rapidly in the wake of 9/11 to combat terrorism were all wrapped up in the "Uniting and Strengthening America by Providing Appropriate Tools Required to Intercept and Obstruct Terrorism Act of 2001," producing the acronym

USA Patriot Act. The not so subtle implication is that any opponent of such measures must, therefore, be unpatriotic. Symbols to justify surveillance are also contained in audio-visual mechanisms. In 1993 in the United Kingdom, a gruesome killing of a three-year-old boy by the name of Jamie Bulger by two ten-year-olds, caused an immense outpouring of grief and anger. The CCTV tape of this little boy being led by the hand by his abductors through a shopping mall was shown continuously in the British media and did more to bolster public sympathies for video-surveillance technology than could any objective policy analysis. The British public, and its mass media, could see a direct causal link between the images captured and the ultimate apprehension of Jamie Bulger's murderers, even though they were caught by other means. A public myth was cultivated that CCTV led to the arrest. The Bolger case then became a potent symbol of the need for public systems of CCTV in the United Kingdom.[10]

How do privacy advocates find and use their own symbols to counter these powerful forces? Symbolic interpretation is part of a process by which they may create awareness, solidify their networks, and expand the constituency of believers. Over the years, this advocacy network has used the full range of written, audio, and visual techniques to advance the cause.

Not surprisingly, privacy advocates invoke the familiar specter of "Big Brother" and have attached that symbol to virtually any over-intrusive surveillance scheme—either governmental or corporate. Thus, CASPIAN heads its Web site, "RFID 1984."[11] They expose a company called UBI-SENSE whose products "combine the remote tracking power of Radio Frequency Identification with a modern-day version of the telescreen from George Orwell's novel *1984*."[12] Simon Davies has called different editions of his books "Big Brother." Commercial data brokerage firms, such as ChoicePoint, have been described as "Big Brother's Little Helpers."[13] In 2000, Intel was attacked for the personal serial numbers proposed for its Pentium III processor, and computers were festooned with "Big Brother Inside" stickers that distorted the company's logo.[14] No matter that Orwell's *1984* concerned the omniscient gaze of the state, rather than the private sector. No matter, that the form of monitoring through the telescreen was entirely visual. No matter that his novel was intended as a satire rather than a prediction. It is now a cliché, but the symbol of 1984 continues to be used to connote excessive surveillance.

Since 1998, several groups have organized "Big Brother Awards." This was originally the idea of Davies.[15] The first awards were given in the

United Kingdom in 1998. Since then there have been around seventy ceremonies held in around sixteen countries.[16] It is now affectionately called the "Orwells" and is typically staged as a spoof of the Oscars. A nomination process leads to a selection of the "Worst Public Servant," the "Most Invasive Company," the "Most Appalling Project," and the "Most Heinous Government Organization." Lately, they have also taken to presenting "Life Time Achievement Awards." The American award ceremony normally takes place at the annual Computers, Freedom and Privacy (CFP) conference, involves a variety of humorously clad performers engaged in various skits, and culminates in the award of the trophy of a boot stamping on a human face; according to Orwell in 1984, "if you want a picture of the future, imagine a boot stamping on a human face for ever." Advocates in other countries have invented other trophies to symbolize the repressive impact of surveillance: in Bulgaria a statue of a little cog within a big cog, in the Netherlands a statute of closing metal jaws, in Germany a statue of a human figure spliced by a sheet of numbers, and so on.

Some of these ceremonies are organized with greater care than others. In Germany, for instance, FoeBuD coordinates a very careful nomination process involving the analysis of a considerable amount of documentation by a jury of experts. In 2006, the ceremony was preceded by a street demonstration against the growth of surveillance in Germany entitled Freedom Instead of Fear (*Freiheit statt Angst*) and attended by about three hundred people. In this particular year, the prizes went to unsurprising recipients—the Association of German Insurers (for its "warnings and indications" databases), members of the legislature of the state of Mecklenburg-Western Pomerania (for legislation permitting eavesdropping in public places), the German Interior Ministers, and the Society for Worldwide Interbank Financial Communications (SWIFT). Phillips received the Technology Big Brother Award for the specification that CD burners write their serial numbers on the CD, thereby facilitating tracking of unlicensed bootlegging of music.[17]

This list is fairly typical of the recipients in other countries over the years, which have tended to be big state bureaucracies, large multinational companies, and prominent politicians. There are exceptions. In the United States in 2005, the Most Invasive Proposal award went to the Brittan Elementary School in Sutter, California, for its proposal to introduce RFID tagging for all students; the Big Brother Award was delivered personally to the principal by concerned parents. There have also been some surprising recipients. In Hungary in 2004, for instance, one award was given to the Hungarian Data Protection Commissioner, Attila Péter-falvi, for remarks he had made about the necessity of certain surveillance schemes. Acting like a good sport, Péterfalvi joined the ceremony and received the award, having earlier sent a letter to Privacy International threatening to withdraw support from the BBA process.[18] Other recipients have also shown up to receive their awards, sometimes suitably chastened and at other times regarding the entire ceremony as a bit of a joke. At the 1999 U.S. event, for instance, the representative from Microsoft proudly went to the stage to receive the award, adopting a "look what I've got" attitude.

In virtually all cases, the awards have gone to institutions or individuals that have already been in the media. In few, if any, cases has the award ceremony been used to "out" an organization. The news value is therefore variable. They did attract a lot of press attention at the outset in the United States and United Kingdom. They certainly have a larger impact in countries that have more recent histories of authoritarian rule; the symbolism of ridiculing state officials in Hungary, the Czech Republic, or Bulgaria is obviously a lot more potent than in more established democracies. The Big Brother Awards are now an institutionalized aspect of privacy advocacy and an enduring feature of the privacy advocacy network, even though it is a lot of work for advocates to pull them off effectively every year.

On the occasion of Orwell's one-hundredth birthday in 2003, EPIC collected a series of commentaries by privacy experts about his widespread influence on the privacy debate.[19] Gary Marx commented as follows: "George Orwell equated Big Brother with the harsh reality of a boot on a human face. The concept of the maximum security society is meant to characterize some softer social-control processes that have increased in importance and sophistication in recent decades, as the velvet glove continues to gain ascendancy over the iron fist." The reality is that contemporary personal information practices do not equate easily with crude symbols of repression. These images simply do not translate to the subtler, and more indirect, forms of surveillance. They run the risk of being viewed as "over the top."

So privacy advocates have attempted other symbolic strategies to communicate the incremental and hidden forms of contemporary information capture. One tactic is to emphasize the routine. On the ACLU Web site, for example, we see an interesting video about the ordering of a pizza. Caller ID allows the receptionist to identify the caller's name, social security number, address, and other information. The voice informs the caller,

Figure 4.1
"I Want Your Data for U.S. Army." (Distributed during EPIC's campaign against the Pentagon's recruiting database in 2005.) Reprinted with permission of the Electronic Privacy Information Center.

who wants the double meat version, that a scan of his medical records suggests high blood pressure and the necessity to pay a surcharge to cover the liability, in accordance with agreements with his health insurer. Further geo-positioning software indicates that the caller lives in an area where robberies have occurred, necessitating a surcharge to cover the extra risk for the driver. A scan of his credit card history also informs her that credit card limits have been reached and that cash would be necessary as payment for the tofu and sprouts pizza that he ends up having to order.[20] Each scenario contains that familiar grain of truth, which makes

Figure 4.2
"The Personal RFID Shield." (Distributed during EPIC's campaign against the installation of RFID technology in U.S. travel documents.) Reprinted with permission of the Electronic Privacy Information Center.

the entire story plausible, an effective symbol of the everyday, and creeping, nature of contemporary surveillance.

Other groups have tried to equate excessive surveillance with enduring national symbols. EPIC, for instance, employs the famous Uncle Sam image ("I Want Your Data for U.S. Army") to protest the construction of the Pentagon's recruitment database in 2005. On other parts of the EPIC Web site, photos of video surveillance cameras in Washington, D.C., are displayed against a backdrop of iconic American national

OBSERVING SURVEILLANCE

Figure 4.3
"Observing Surveillance." (The Observing Surveillance Project was undertaken by EPIC staff and documents the presence of video cameras placed in Washington, D.C., after September 11.) Reprinted with permission of the Electronic Privacy Information Center.

symbols.[21] The equation of surveillance technologies with historical symbols of repression are used in other ways. The NO2ID campaign in the United Kingdom has a photo on its Web site of protesters with barcodes stamped on their forearms. These symbols clearly convey analogies to the holocaust.[22] Similar images are invoked by the ACLU's pictures of chip implants on hands: "Don't Chip My Rights Away." These and other symbols are reproduced here (figures 4.1–4.8).

Humor is also seen as a necessary component of effective privacy advocacy. In its campaign against the RFID-enabled passport, EPIC produced "The Personal RFID Shield"—a piece of aluminum foil. Instructions for use: "1) Remove Aluminum foil from plastic bag; 2) Fold foil around RFID encoded document; 3) Drop document in your purse or wallet and go!" Stickers have also been popular: "For Reasons of Hygiene this Toilet is monitored by Video." Paralleling the Big Brother Awards, Privacy International has also organized "Stupid Security Awards"—an open competition to "discover the world's most pointless, intrusive, annoying and self-serving security measures."[23] At the height of the Monica Lewinsky scandal, CDT used the opportunity to post a "Privacy Quiz: The Lewinsky-Starr Edition," using the opportunity to

Figure 4.4
"Don't Chip My Rights Away." (Distributed during successive attempts to pass California legislation on the use of RFID.) Reprinted with permission of the American Civil Liberties Union of Northern California.

test people's knowledge about the kinds of intrusive behavior reported during this story and to make a point about the many shortcomings of American privacy law.[24] Question No. 1: "You are talking on the telephone with your friend, pouring your heart out about a love affair gone sour. Unbeknownst to you, your friend is tape recording the conversation. Afterward your friend plays the tape to people you don't even know and sends around a transcript of it. Did your friend break any laws?" The answer—it depends on which state you live in.

Symbols therefore get used in variety of ways to invoke the specter of authoritarian repression, to warn of the slippery slope, to link remote technological practices to everyday experience, to draw comparisons, and simply to lampoon. Symbolic politics only is effective when it connects to a broader set of cultural understandings. It operates at national levels, when current programs are equated with historical memories that

Figure 4.5
"Surveillance Society: Time Is Running Out." (ACLU's Surveillance Society Clock showing six minutes to midnight, reminiscent of the Doomsday Clock.) Reprinted with permission of the American Civil Liberties Union.

resonate within a particular country. It also has to operate at the international level. Symbolic politics can resonate; it can also seem pointless and overstated.

Accountability Politics: Living Up to the Rules

Organizations that process personal data must increasingly abide by the basic information privacy principles outlined in chapter 1. In most countries, these obligations are enshrined within data protection laws that cover both public and private sectors. Other rules are embodied within international agreements, to which organizations and countries might have subscribed. There is also a range of more self-regulatory measures: standards, codes of practice, privacy seals. Thus, even where legal rules do not exist, privacy advocates can still try to ensure that organizations do live up to their own public commitments. Once governments and corporations have publicly committed to privacy standards, advocates can use these positions to expose any discrepancies between rhetoric and practice.

In most countries, privacy advocates can and do use the rights enshrined within data protection, and other, legislation. In Canada, for instance, Pippa Lawson of CIPPIC has lodged a number of complaints under the Personal Information Protection and Electronic Documents

If you're watching everyone, you're watching no one

http://www.individual-i.com

Figure 4.6a
"If You're Watching Everyone, You're Watching No One."

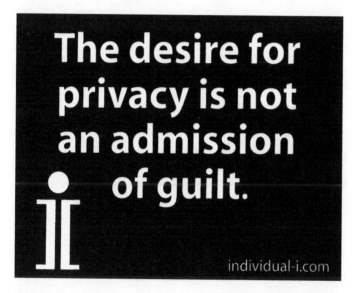

The desire for privacy is not an admission of guilt.

individual-i.com

Figure 4.6b
"The Desire for Privacy Is Not an Admission of Guilt." (Individual-I.Com Web site graphics in the public domain.)

Act (PIPEDA) with the privacy commissioner of Canada. For example, in 2004 she formed the view that Accusearch Inc., an American corporation based in Wyoming, was routinely collecting, using, and disclosing personal information about Canadians through its Web site for inappropriate purposes and without the knowledge and consent of the individuals in question.[25] She requested her own file from the company, was refused, and filed a complaint with the privacy commissioner of Canada. She

Figure 4.7
"For Reasons of Hygiene This Toilet Is Monitored by Video." (One of several stickers disseminated throughout Germany and other European countries by FoeBuD.) Reprinted with permission of FoeBuD (Germany).

Figure 4.8
"Lächeln ... Gleich Kommt das Vögelchen" (Translated as "Smile ... The little birds are coming soon" or perhaps "Watch the Birdie." A photo of early video-surveillance cameras in Helsinki.) Reprinted with permission of Julia Stoll and the Forum Informatikerinnen für Frieden and gesellshaftliche Verandtwortung (FIFF).

submitted that Accusearch Inc.'s activities were contrary to PIPEDA and called upon the commissioner to investigate. The commissioner refused, indicating that she did have not have jurisdiction to investigate a company residing in another country. Lawson appealed to the Federal Court, which determined that the commissioner did have jurisdiction and was therefore obliged to investigate the complaint. CIPPIC has also lodged complaints under PIPEDA against Winners, Sony, Ticketmaster, Info-Canada, and MBNA Mastercard.[26]

CIPPIC will file a complaint where it believes there is a key issue or that a part of the law requires clarification. In some cases, where jurisdiction is unclear, it will file complaints to both federal and provincial commissioners. In all cases, CIPPIC has publicized the complaint from the outset. The privacy commissioner of Canada, of course, is an ombudsman and under most circumstances is obliged to conduct a private investigation without revealing the identity of complainant or respondent. The summaries of any investigation finding even appear on the OPC Web site with names anonymized, a sometimes bizarre outcome when the informed reader knows exactly who is being written about. In other instances, CIPPIC engages with the company first to resolve any dispute. Often the potential of a public complaint against an organization is enough to effect a change in practices. The complaint process can be lengthy and difficult and may not yield the expected result.[27]

In some very high profile cases, advocacy groups have been able to lodge complaints to a number of different data protection authorities. The best example occurred in June 2006 when Privacy International decided to lodge simultaneous complaints to data protection authorities in 33 countries concerning revelations of secret disclosures of millions of financial records from the Society for Worldwide Interbank Financial Telecommunication (SWIFT) to U.S. Intelligence agencies. SWIFT is a worldwide financial messaging service that facilitates international money transfers. It stores all messages for a period of 124 days at two operation centers, one within the European Union and one in the United States—a form of data processing referred to as "mirroring." The messages contain personal data such as the names of the payer and payee. After the attacks of 9/11, the U.S. Department of the Treasury issued subpoenas requiring SWIFT to provide access to message information held in the United States. SWIFT complied with the subpoenas. The matter became public when the *New York Times* and the *Los Angeles Times* published details of these private arrangements.[28] The complaint alleged that the activity was undertaken without regard to the rights of citizens under data protection law, and that "the scale of the operation, involving millions of records, places this disclosure in the realm of a fishing exercise rather than a legally authorized investigation." They later filed further complaints to six other authorities, filed an FOI request to the Bank of England, and published an open letter to the CEO of the company. CIPPIC and PI also filed a separate complaint against Canadian banks to the OPC for failure to protect customer information from improper disclosures via the SWIFT network.

Thus a series of events was set in motion. Data protection authorities began investigating, individually and jointly. The U.S. government insisted that the programs were narrowly tailored. SWIFT hired an auditor to verify that the data transfers were legal; PI and the ACLU immediately exposed the close ties between the auditing firm and the U.S. government. The Belgian government issued a condemnation of the transfer. The Article 29 Working Group of European data protection authorities issued a finding that SWIFT was in breach of the EU Data Protection Directive and called for several remedial steps.

At this writing, the story continues, but the details of claim and counterclaim are not especially relevant. Whether or not these complaints succeed in forcing SWIFT to alter its practices is less important than the fact that a general and simultaneous complaint to so many data protection authorities generated news in each of these different countries, and began a process to render this from of surveillance transparent. Never before has an advocacy group issued so many complaints to so many different authorities; no doubt the global scale of the SWIFT operation permitted this rare opportunity. The action not only put SWIFT and the U.S. authorities on the spot but also demanded strong action from the data protection authorities, which have experienced a tense relationship with PI over the years.

The privacy advocacy community has generally not made extensive use of the complaints investigation and resolution process under data protection law. Advocacy groups are aware that data protection authorities are under-resourced, and that their legal powers are constrained by the various exemptions within the legislation. Some have less independence than others, dependent as they are on governments for funding. Some may be reluctant to take bold stances when they have the chance of being renewed in office. Some authorities, such as in Canada, are ombudsmen and do not have enforcement powers. Data protection authorities often have to adopt a more pragmatic approach and are therefore viewed with some impatience by the more radical privacy advocacy groups.

Complaints resolution also takes time, though there is some evidence that the investigative process can be expedited when the issue is attended by high levels of publicity. Some advocates tend to regard the process of complaint as more of a media moment, rather than a genuine opportunity to change practices.

American groups have had to rely on creative ways to use their patchwork of state and federal privacy legislation to hold organizations accountable, given that there is no federal privacy protection authority. Of course, the traditional American approach is one of litigation, an expensive and time-consuming option especially as damages from the abuse of personal information are difficult to prove. Within the U.S. advocacy network, EFF, and the ACLU pursue "impact litigation" and employ in-house attorneys to look for good cases to clarify and advance the privacy laws of the United States. And those laws are derived from the federal constitution (primarily the Fourth Amendment), state constitutions, federal statutes, state statutes, and regulation. Of course, both organizations litigate in many other areas of civil liberties and civil rights as well. Privacy protection has to compete for attention, and resources, within both.

Since its founding in the early 1990s, EFF has earned some notable victories within the courts. For instance, it successfully fought the government's attempts to track the location of mobile phone users without sufficient evidence. It won a settlement against Sony BMG on behalf of consumers who had purchased CDs and DVDs with flawed and intrusive software designed to limit the ability to make copies or transfer music onto unapproved portable media players. It has successfully challenged attempts to unmask the anonymity of users of bulletin boards, discussion groups, and blogs. EFF also supported Verizon in a successful challenge to a court ruling holding that the company must reveal the identity of one of it customers who had used the peer-to-peer file-sharing software Kazaa.[29]

One of the most visible challenges is the class action suit filed by EFF against AT&T in January 2006, accusing the company of violating the law and the privacy of its customers by collaborating with the National Security Agency (NSA) in its program to wiretap and data-mine Americans' communications. The lawsuit alleges that AT&T not only helped the NSA listen in on millions of ordinary Americans' Internet and telephone communications but also provided access to its databases containing records of most or all communications. In July 2006, a federal judge dismissed AT&T's motion to dismiss the case. In the meantime, the Bush administration urged Congress to legislate to halt these lawsuits. If passed, the proposed changes would forestall efforts to compel disclosure of the program's details.[30]

Litigation has also played an extremely important role within the politics of the ACLU. As the advocacy group with the most resources, and largest membership, it can afford to take on big cases to challenge U.S. surveillance programs. Although its most famous cases have not been related to privacy, at any one time litigation is being pursued nationally and at the state level on a variety of privacy issues. Most notably, the ACLU has led the fight in trying to defend the Fourth Amendment rights of Americans in the face of increasingly sophisticated electronic surveillance programs. At writing it is challenging in federal court the constitutionality and legality of the National Security Agency's electronic surveillance, arguing among other things that the Federal Investigation Surveillance Act (FISA) and Title III are the exclusive means by which the executive branch can lawfully engage in electronic surveillance.[31] In recent years, it has also engaged in less prominent litigation on Internet privacy and anonymity, on biometric technologies, and on educational privacy rights (such as strip searching in schools).

Other U.S. advocacy groups do not litigate, either because of lack of resources, or because they recognize that litigation is within the province and expertise of groups like the ACLU and EFF. Occasionally, a group, such as PRC, will act as a plaintiff in a suit or offer an amicus brief. Fundamentally, the economics of privacy litigation in the United States are such that unless you can create a class of injured parties where there is an opportunity to get significant damages, most American laws involve a lot of expense for the private litigant. Thus groups are looking for class action suits, under the limited range of statutes that allow damages to be claimed.

Privacy advocates, therefore, engage in accountability politics in other ways. One key strategy is the use of Freedom of Information Act (FOIA) requests. Most American groups have, at some stage, made FOI requests and regularly appealed to the courts if they have not been successful. In the United States, FOIA requests are quite easy. It costs the advocacy organization nothing. If the documents are obtained, there is a victory. If they are refused or heavily redacted, there is a story about government secrecy. Over time, organizations like EPIC in the United States and CIPPIC in Canada have developed the strategic skills necessary to target the requests on specific documents rather than broad information categories.

One prominent example is the attempt by EPIC to get to the bottom of evolving government programs for airline passenger profiling. These programs began as the Computer Assisted Passenger Profiling System (CAPPS), transformed into CAPPS II, then into "Secure Flight," and finally into the Automated Targeting System (ATS). At each stage, EPIC has made FOI requests, published the redacted documents on its Web site, and gleaned enough information in order to ask the further questions about these programs. EPIC and the ACLU were also able to get a handle on the CAPPS and Secure Flight systems by invoking the statutory obligations within the Privacy Act of 1974 to produce a notice in the Federal Register whenever a new "system of records" was being constructed. These notices are, to be sure, vague and insufficient. However, they do provide a starting point for further litigation and for FOIA requests.

Opportunities for American privacy advocates to hold the private sector to account have historically been quite limited. There is a lot of U.S. privacy protection law covering private-sector practices, each governing a slice of the U.S. marketplace and each with significant loopholes and limited opportunities to sue for damages.[32] U.S. private-sector privacy law has progressed incrementally and sectorally, leaving many areas of the U.S. economy with virtually unlimited abilities to collect, process, and disseminate personal information with impunity.

Recently, however, opportunities have arisen as a result of strong and multiple pressures for companies to be transparent about their personal information practices. Some of this pressure has originated from European advocates and regulators who have tried to enforce Articles 25 and 26 of the EU Data Protection Directive, which states that personal data should not flow out of the European Union unless the receiving jurisdiction can guarantee an "adequate level of protection." The main governmental response in the United States has been the negotiation of the "Safe Harbor Agreement," under which companies pledge publicly to abide by a set of privacy principles and thus to expose themselves to challenge to the U.S. Federal Trade Commission (FTC) for "unfair and deceptive trade practices," if it can be demonstrated that their behavior is different from their public statements. More generally, consumer concerns about Internet privacy have prompted most companies with a Web presence to develop and promulgate "privacy policies" and thus expose themselves to similar challenges. Some of these cases will be analyzed in greater depth in chapter 5.

In addition, the FTC is also responsible for the enforcement of the Fair Credit Reporting Act, the "Do Not Call" law, the antispam legislation, and the Children's Online Privacy Protection Act. There are clearly more opportunities to hold U.S. companies to account than in the past. Further, since January 2006, there have been an accumulation of fines levied on a number of U.S. companies for a variety of infractions. But opinions differ on the effectiveness of FTC enforcement. Bob Gellman, a Washington privacy consultant, asserts that "FTC fines are just the cost of doing business, and then only if you get caught. Since the odds are small, it is a legitimate business decision to ignore the FTC. If you get caught, you hire an ex-FTC staffer and negotiate a cheap fine." Marc Rotenberg of EPIC also contends that the "industry seems to know that if they can kick privacy complaints over to the FTC rather than worry about privacy rights of action, they're pretty much immune from liability. Further not a single U.S. company has been found to violate the safe harbor agreement."[33]

Privacy advocates have also been able to petition the Federal Communications Commission (FCC) under Section 222 of the Telecommunications Act. For instance, in 2005, EPIC and other groups petitioned for more stringent security standards for Consumer Proprietary Network Information (CMNI)—essentially the logs of calls—in response to concerns that telecommunications companies were selling such data to third parties for marketing purposes. The dispute revolved around whether implied consent (opt-out) arrangements were sufficient for such data, as the telecommunications and marketing industries had argued. The FCC decided in 2002 that opt-in or express consent is required for release of customer information to third parties, but permits opt-out consent for release of information to affiliated organizations.

These examples illustrate the difficulty of having to advocate for privacy protection when the legislative requirements are spread around a variety of provisions within different federal statutes, overseen by different regulatory agencies. Nevertheless, the U.S. advocacy groups have been far more likely to use the provisions within their relatively fragmented patchwork of laws, than have their European counterparts. It is indeed striking how few complaints have been lodged by European advocacy groups under their stronger and more comprehensive data protection laws. Complaints under European data protection law cost no money and very little time. There is a common view that data protection law, in Europe, Canada, and Australia, is so hedged around by exemptions that the data protection agencies are legally tied and cannot possibly effect real change.

Leverage Politics: "Naming and Shaming"

Leverage politics assumes that the group has some power and that it can get what it wants from those in authority by threatening some cost if there is no change from the status quo. Public choice theory would insist that the groups that can leverage the most power are those that have large and compulsory memberships—in other words, professional groups and labor unions (Olsen 1971). Compulsory membership produces a set of selective incentives for the members, and the benefits of group success are only enjoyed by members rather than by the wider population. The threat of the withdrawal of labor that is of vital interest to a national economy has historically been leveraged in order to obtain increased wages and benefits, better working conditions, and so on. In some countries, such groups can also deliver large numbers of votes for particular parties, and in the United States, enormous amounts of money to political campaigns through their political action committees.

Privacy, like other civil liberties and human rights, is a public good. If privacy advocates are successful in securing more effective privacy laws, then everyone in society potentially benefits regardless of whether or not they are a member of the organization. Few advocacy groups, as we have noted, have even bothered with a membership base. Moreover, privacy is rarely seen as an electoral issue. For the most part, politicians do not lose votes if they promote intrusive surveillance schemes, and they do not win them if they oppose such schemes. In the realm of electoral politics, the issue in every country tends to be overwhelmed by more materialistic concerns. Even if advocates had some financial clout and spoke for a large mass membership, there is no way that they could use that resource as leverage within the electoral process. So what can be threatened?

At the same time that the privacy advocacy network does not have resources in a traditional sense, they do have a powerful issue, and one that has continued to resonate with the mass public. Very few public or private organizations will say that they are against privacy and will probably not want to be regarded in public opinion as an opponent of the issue. Thus, the leverage politics of privacy advocacy is almost entirely about embarrassment, the loss of reputation, or what some commentators have called the "mobilization of shame" (Drinan 2001).

Privacy advocates have used subtle, and not so subtle, ways to name and shame organizations and individuals. We have already discussed the symbolic importance of the Big Brother Awards in several countries. We have also noted that these events are typically not used to "out" a particular company or governmental agency. They are organized retrospectively and the award winners are almost always organizations and actors who have already been publicly exposed. Other more prospective opportunities are, however, available.

The fact that a company is the potential subject of a complaint to a data protection authority, or regulatory agency, can be used by privacy advocates as leverage. If a questionable practice comes to light as a result of a consumer complaint, a whistleblower, or just through informal communications within the network, then in most cases the group will inform the organization and try to resolve without publicity. The threat of publicity, with or without a formal complaint, will always be in the background. Advocates need to make careful judgments about how to use this weapon, and these judgments will depend on a number of factors: whether the organization is a responsible player within the market; whether it has been in the news before; whether the practice is so egregious that it would definitely stir up public opinion; whether the facts are clear; and the commitments, resources, and styles of the advocates themselves. Some advocates are not naturally confrontational and will only use the threat of publicity as a last resort.

Some forms of naming and shaming are therefore quite easy. If there is an irresponsible company, a practice that few will defend (including many within the industry itself), and relatively clear facts, then a naming and shaming strategy poses few dilemmas. CDT's campaign against spyware is an example. In the context of an effort to work with industry in order to develop some definitions and best practices about online advertising, CDT convened the Anti-Spyware Coalition.[34] In so doing, it has therefore been able to identify the less responsible players. Beginning in 2004, CDT launched its first complaint to the FTC against Mailwiper, Inc., and Seismic Entertainment Media and their affiliates, alleging that they were engaged in deceptive and unfair marketing practices by changing computer users' Web homepages without their consent and then trying to convince these users that they needed the Mailwiper program called "Spy Wiper" software to protect their computers. In 2006, along with a group called StopBadware.org, they urged the FTC to shut down a site called FastMP3Search.com.ar, which self-executes the installation of Trojan horse applications, disables security software, sabotages valid Web addresses for legitimate security companies, changes homepage settings, and severely impairs computer speed and performance, all without user consent. More recently, other companies have been added to the complaints, and the FTC has sued some of these companies.

In each case, CDT warned the companies concerned. Jim Dempsey of CDT explains the process: "Almost always we tell the person beforehand and then offer them the opportunity to either tell us we are wrong or to change their practices. We've done this a lot in the anti-spyware arena. . . . We issue the press releases and we file a complaint with the FTC. We tell the company 'this is what we found. We are going to file this complaint with the FTC and we are going to issue a press release when we do it. Tell us that we are wrong, or not.'"[35] In such cases, a convergence of interests between consumers and the more responsible industry players has identified the free riders engaged in completely indefensible practices. This "outing" strategy was even given the blessing of the FTC. In February 2006, Commissioner Leibowitz stated that the FTC should publicly shame advertisers if the spyware problem does not decrease.[36] And "outing" is the correct language, because the publicity does involve the naming of companies that few people had hitherto heard of, and whose practices, to some extent, depend on their being able to operate in the shadows.

Other "outing" decisions are, however, far more difficult, especially where the effect of bad publicity could have competitive effects in the marketplace. Advocates therefore have to respond when asked why they have targeted one company rather than another, and consistency of principle is crucial. In their various campaigns for Internet privacy, for example, EPIC and other groups have targeted the companies whom they believed were the market leaders at the time. Generally, they have reacted to announcements that had already been made by the respective companies, as we will see in the cases concerning DoubleClick, Intel, and Microsoft, discussed in chapter 5.

In the case of DoubleClick, and its proposed merger of its online clickstream data with offline data on consumer purchasing habits owned by a company called Abacus Direct, advocates tried to leverage some pressure through an appeal to stockholders. In June 1999, the coalition addressed an open letter to the stockholders of Abacus Direct, calling on them to disapprove the merger, and alleging that they had been misled about the privacy risks inherent in the proposal. The same coalition later addressed a letter to the managers of socially responsible mutual funds. They called upon investors to divest their holdings in DoubleClick and Abacus as soon as possible, and add these companies to the screening lists of companies excluded from investment based on human rights criteria.[37]

CDT also organized an e-mail campaign not only to DoubleClick but also to sixty of its clients.

Probably the central strategy of CASPIAN has been to publicize the names of companies that, in its view, have been monitoring consumer behavior either through supermarket cards or, more recently, through RFIDs. Katherine Albrecht is not into legislative solutions, is distrustful of regulatory agencies and yet deeply committed to the marketplace and the principles of consumer choice. Its Web site is explicit: "CASPIAN operates under free market, Libertarian principles. We believe that a healthy free market depends on consumers having access to information that impacts them so they can work to ensure that their best interests are met in the marketplace. When consumers are not given pertinent facts, they get saddled with things like loyalty cards, CRM, retail surveillance, unbridled RFID usage, and the thousands of other offences to their dignity, privacy, and economic well-being that have sprung up in recent years."[38]

Thus, with its goal of consumer empowerment, CASPIAN has done its fair share of "naming and shaming" in the short time it has been in existence and has waged a number of campaigns against large retailers, including Benetton, Gillette, Levi-Strauss, Procter and Gamble, and Wal-Mart. CASPIAN also goes one step further than other American groups by calling for boycotts of certain products. Katherine Albrecht explains the value of this strategy:

I think a boycott works best if it's something that a company is rightly ashamed of—where you've actually got a situation where you've caught a company with its hand in the cookie jar or doing something that the vast majority of the public would consider unethical. At that point the boycott can serve a dual function: it gives people an opportunity to learn about the issue and a convenient place for you, as an activist, to direct people to the issue. Secondly, I think it puts other companies on notice. For many years if you typed in "Gillette" we were on the very first pages of search hits with our Boycott Gillette Web site ... that's terrible publicity for a company.[39]

The first boycott was against Benetton in 2003 after it was disclosed that the company had placed identification and tracking devices into its clothing products, including undergarments. CASPIAN called for a boycott of Benetton products and launched an "I'd Rather Go Naked Campaign."[40] There was considerable publicity, and Benetton was soon forced to cancel its plans to tag its products. CASPIAN followed this success with an attempted boycott of Gillette, after it was announced that this company was going to install RFID-enabled "smart shelves" that would sense when consumers picked up razor blade packets, trigger a camera shot of each customer, and relay those photos to store security. CASPIAN then began its "I'd Rather Grow a Beard" campaign and established a boycott Gillette Web site, which provided ways for consumers to express their dissent.[41] At this writing, both Web sites are still online.

The Benetton boycott was successful because of the novelty of the RFID debate at that time. Benetton had also been in the news for its advertising practices; many consumers were, therefore, already predisposed against the company. These boycotts were more important, however, because they served to rally activists to the cause, rather than because of any direct economic impact on the companies concerned. In more recent cases, companies have probably become more astute at how to respond to these tactics. Much of the subsequent debate has not centered on the rights and wrongs of RFID tagging, but on the specific commercial and technical conditions under which activated item-level tagging might be used beyond the point of sale. That debate can get complex and technical, and is of less interest to the mass media. Boycotts probably need to be used sparingly.

Another rare tactic is to target individual corporate executives. In its Boycott Gillette campaign, for instance, CASPIAN published the e-mail address of the Gillette executive allegedly behind the plan—thus not only outing the company but also the individuals within it. During the dispute over the Lotus Marketplace product, the e-mail address of Lotus's CEO was posted on newsgroups. He then received over thirty thousand messages opposing the product, and the proposed CD-ROM was never released (Gurak 1997). The Foundation for Taxpayer & Consumer Rights went one step further in October 2003. The group hired a "skywriter" to write part of the social security number of Citigroup's chief executive above its corporate headquarters in midtown Manhattan. The stunt was in protest to the bank's lobbying efforts in the Senate against certain financial privacy provisions.[42] The group also listed on its Web site the first four digits of the social security numbers of eight legislators who had opposed the bill. In April 2007, a Massachusetts advocate even threatened to publicly post the names of prominent individuals in Massachusetts whose personal information she was able to pull from public records from the secretary of state's Web site. The goal was to pressure the secretary of state to change the policy of making certain public records available to businesses that wish to check on existing loan encumbrances. The "Virginia Watchdog," one Betty Ostergren, has made it her goal to educate public officials about how easy it is to download personal information, such as mortgage papers, divorce decrees, tax liens, deeds, and power-of-attorney documents, from the Web sites of state and local agencies.[43]

At the 1999 CFP conference, Davies announced that "the time has come for us to get real about this struggle. We have to ratchet up the war for privacy just one more notch." He announced a campaign to "out" the people who use the World Wide Web to gather private data and redistribute it for profit. He proposed to identify the people who are collecting the data for money-making purposes, involving billboards with pictures of the privacy violators with their addresses, listing their assets, and supplying other sensitive personal information about them found on the Internet. The purpose was to get them to understand "how it feels to be violated this way. Hopefully they will understand the importance of the issue and how vulnerable people feel."[44] These tactics do raise sharp ethical dilemmas, and questions about whether advocates should be promoting the privacy cause by invading the privacy of others. The campaign never materialized.

In most cases, the circumstances that lead to the publicity of an organization's practices are complicated, often involving a number of groups beyond privacy advocates, including the media, members of the legislature, and the occasional whistleblower. Most privacy scandals are not a matter of one privacy advocacy group's discovering something wrong, and then taking a swing at an organization through a press release. The "outing" is often gradual and, to some extent, facilitated by an organization's own publicity. Typically there is no one "naming and shaming" moment against one organization, by one privacy advocacy group. The dynamics of privacy disputes, which we will examine more fully in chapter 5, do tend to be gradual, multifaceted, and complex.

Leverage politics does involve an expansion of the scope of conflict, however. It rests upon the principle that those with power normally have an interest in privatizing the fight and narrowing the terrain upon which conflicts are conducted. Those without power normally wish to expand and socialize the scope of the conflict, because they need allies (Schattschneider 1960). Politics is therefore not only about interests and issues but about the breadth of the political terrain on which they are fought. Leverage politics in the name of privacy protection tends to be constrained at every turn. There are ethical issues. There are questions about credibility and long-term effectiveness. There are always questions about being sure of one's facts. The mobilization of shame in the interest of expanding the scope of a privacy conflict is a sanction that needs to be used sparingly, and with careful considerations of the consequences.

Conclusion: Strategic Dilemmas

There are some forms of political activism that are notably absent from the analysis above. For example, the issue has rarely spilled onto the streets. To the extent that this street-level politics has been encountered, it is entirely associated with high-profile governmental schemes in countries outside North America. In Germany, for instance, there were several early protests in the 1970s and 1980s against the national census. In Australia in the late 1980s, there were street protests against the Australia Card. There were also occasional protests against the British ID card scheme. In Germany in 2006 and 2007, there have been marches against the proposals on telecommunications traffic data. When the Japanese government established its controversial "Juki Net" system, a national network of registration information on all Japanese residents, protestors shredded their identity cards on the steps of the Home Affairs Ministry.[45]

Resistance strategies are, however, more common at an individual level. A nice example is the retired city councilor from Kingston, Ontario, who paid his entire $230 Visa bill in 985 installments, often in pennies, to protest the outsourcing of credit-card processing to the United States.[46] As Gary Marx has argued, "humans are wonderfully inventive at finding ways to beat control systems and to avoid observation." He goes on to analyze eleven "generic techniques of neutralization" that are in fact aided by the logistical and economic limitations, contradictions, and gaps within surveillance systems. There are a range of moves that individuals both within, and outside, organizations can employ in order to subvert, distort, block, mask, or counter the surveillance system. Some of these tactics may be of questionable legality. However, they are rarely countenanced as part of any collective, or political, strategy (Marx 2003).

The privacy advocacy network is therefore confronted with a series of choices and dilemmas within the frameworks of information, symbolic, accountability, and leverage politics. In any complex case, each of these forms of politics will be observed in different measures. Each involves dilemmas, however. In conclusion, it will be useful to summarize these tensions.

The first is expressed by many advocates as an inside versus outside choice. Some groups will prefer to engage with governmental agencies and the private sector, to understand the other side's interests and arguments, to work out differences, to establish compromises, and to develop pragmatic solutions. They will recognize that compromise is not an ugly word. They will prefer to make some progress on an issue, even if it is not the ideal. In other language, the inside versus outside choice is expressed as the dilemma between the advocates and the "pragvocates." These tensions are faced by every advocacy organization.

There have been two cases in the history of U.S. privacy protection that have highlighted this tension more than any others. The 1994 conflicts within EFF over CALEA, and between EFF and other organizations, had widespread ramifications. John Perry Barlow was, on this occasion, an insider and defended the decision to try to improve a bad bill, rather than walk away on principle (quoted in Li 2003, 70): "Politics is simply the art of the possible. If you're a purist, you go down to defeat almost every time, and the things you care about ultimately suffer. Maybe your honor and dignity will remain intact, but the environment or civil liberties or whatever your cause is won't. Sometimes you have to do a bit of nasty dealing. We got right down to the floor of the sausage factory, getting ourselves smeared with blood and pig fat, and it wasn't all that pleasant. But we did what we felt we had to do, and I'm proud of that." Judgments about the "art of the possible" are of course premised on a guess about the future, that indeed a law was going to happen anyway.

A second and later conflict occurred over involvement in a project called the Platform for Privacy Preferences (P3P), a World Wide Web Consortium standard that allows Web site operators to make a machine-readable version of their privacy policy. Consumers then use their P3P enabled browsers to read the site's privacy policy and are notified whether the policy matches the user's privacy preferences. The P3P standard was incorporated into the major Internet browsers, including Windows XP. These efforts were, for a while, very controversial among privacy advocates. Some, such as Jason Catlett of Junkbusters contended that the program should be disbanded because "it has come to be used by some as an excuse to delay the progress of genuine enforceable privacy rights in the US.... Unjustly, it has been marketers and lobbyists, not the P3P researchers, who have portrayed P3P as the golden pot of consumer privacy just waiting at the end of the technology rainbow."[47] EPIC called the program "pretty poor privacy."[48] In response, proponents of P3P responded that this tool was never intended to be the panacea and should not be "trotted out as a reason to discourage regulatory or self-regulatory efforts to protect privacy" (CDT and Ontario IPC 2000). The conflict split the online privacy advocacy community, and once again exposed the difficult dilemmas when advocates work and negotiate for less than the ideal.

There is a general consensus that any network needs both insiders and outsiders. The work of those who work on the "inside" is assisted by the existence of advocates pursuing the outside strategy and continually making the more fundamental arguments for privacy within the media, and to the mass public. There is also a general assumption that a group like CDT tends to favor a more inside and pragmatic strategy, actively engaging with the companies and policymakers, whereas those like EPIC tend to be more confrontational. The media has occasionally reported on the different personal styles of Jerry Berman of CDT and Marc Rotenberg of EPIC.[49] However, these categories are misleading. They are tendencies, and very dependent on the case concerned. Some groups do prefer initially to engage with an organization rather than to go to the media. But sometimes "inside" strategy breaks down, and groups are forced to stop negotiating and start opposing. Sometimes, those groups that are more ready to state their opposition publicly decide that it would be beneficial to work initially on the "inside."

A second dilemma concerns the scope of concern, the broad versus narrow dilemma. In the United States at any rate, an interesting division of labor has gradually been witnessed as different advocacy groups have entered the scene and found a particular niche. Some groups, as we have seen, do try to cast their net widely and advocate for a broad range of privacy interests. Others choose focus, wishing to be known as the best and most informed on a particular subject. Again, the network benefits from having groups that can understand the breadth of the issue, as well as those that can dig relentlessly on a few significant topics.

A third dilemma arises with respect to timing, and is best addressed in terms of long-term research versus short-term advocacy. Privacy issues are complex and require research. Research takes time and money. Privacy advocates sometimes need to articulate concerns without having the benefits of accurate research. They have to be "in the game," and also maintain an academic's commitment to getting the facts straight. The two requirements are often at odds. Privacy advocates sometimes have to act, and speak quickly and publicly. And sometimes they get caught out. They must therefore develop techniques to express the privacy interest in ways that do not necessarily bring into question the motives and behavior of public officials and private corporations, if they are not in full possession of the facts of a particular situation.

A fourth dilemma concerns membership. Some advocacy groups have bothered to develop a membership; others have not. With a membership, the group leaders can make claims about the number and range of people for whom they speak. Without a membership, the group can speak and act more quickly, expeditiously, and surgically. It is also very difficult to obtain a membership without the use of mailing lists. Some advocates will, therefore, not go to the trouble of developing a membership and collecting membership dues, out of principle. Others refuse because they are no good at organizational management and do not want the hassle of collecting subscriptions, reminding people when money is due, and maintaining the necessary records.

Finally, and inevitably, strategic choices do depend on finance. Most groups are designated as nonprofit groups and are registered as such under the relevant national tax legislation. In the United States, for instance, most of the advocacy groups are designated as tax-exempt charitable groups under 501(c)(3) of the Internal Revenue Code, meaning that none of their earnings can accrue to any individual or shareholder. However, the sources from which advocates might receive funding are very limited, if they make decisions not to accept money from government or the private sector. That leaves membership dues, foundation grants, as well as the cy pres awards that stem from successful class action suits and that are distributed to public interest groups, on application. Advocacy groups find themselves competing for similar and limited pots of money, from similar sources. Constant dilemmas arise, therefore, about whether to take money from government or the private sector—for the attendance at conferences, for giving speeches, for producing reports, for commenting on proposals, and so on.

As in any public interest advocacy network, these tensions create personal rivalries and jealousies, some of which have endured. They produce some entrenched attitudes about what does and does not work. They sometimes accrue into a politics of blame and blame avoidance. They can produce some embittered views of who is true to the cause, and who has "sold out." But the ultimate, and only relevant, question is "what works"? That question can only be addressed with reference to some key cases in North America and elsewhere, where the privacy advocacy network has indeed made a difference. Those cases form the subject matter of chapter 5.

5 Cases and Conflicts

I'm sorry that a community this young should have to face a fight this savage, for such terribly high stakes, so soon. But what the heck; you're always bragging about how clever you are; here's your chance to prove to your fellow citizens that you're more than a crowd of Net-nattering Mensa dilettantes.
—Bruce Sterling

Largest anti-surveillance street protest in Germany for 20 years—On Saturday, 22 September 2007, more than 15,000 took to the streets of Berlin under the slogan "Liberty instead of Fear—stop the Surveillance Mania!"
—EDRI gram, September 26, 2007

The privacy advocacy network that we see today has been shaped by the issues it has addressed, and the battles it has fought. We have referred to a number of these controversies along the way. It is now time to examine them in more detail. Under what circumstances do privacy issues escalate into conflicts? What roles have privacy advocates played over the years? What lessons have been learned? How have these conflicts shaped the views and behavior of today's privacy advocates?

There is probably a "normal politics" associated with privacy. The day-to-day, and quite routine, collection and management of personal information leads to a string of issues concerning consent, access, security, retention, and so on. New technologies are deployed. Questions are raised by advocates about privacy implications. Sometimes the issues fade quickly. At other times, they drag on and become mired in technical and legal detail. The normal politics of privacy involves the quite relentless and painstaking attempt to understand the policies and proposals of government and business and to inject privacy argumentation and reasoning.

Sometimes, however, this normal politics is punctuated by cases that reach higher levels of public and political consciousness and that affect the very structure of conflict and the nature of the discourse. These are

paradigmatic cases with high stakes and far-reaching implications, beyond the boundaries of the particular issue at stake and the domestic circumstances of individual jurisdictions. These cases have come to define
which privacy problems have been regarded as the most significant during
different decades. They have shaped the experiences of privacy advocates
and produced enduring understandings about privacy, and how to advocate for it in the face of relentless pressures.

I have chosen to present these cases historically, as they exemplify the
dominant privacy concerns of different decades. For many years, it was
conventional wisdom that there have been only two occasions when privacy protection was really elevated to the level of a major conflict producing political crisis: the disputes over the census in Germany in 1983 and
1987, and the conflict over the proposed national identification system in
Australia in 1988 (the Australia Card). As concern over the consolidation
of personal databanks migrated from government to the private sector,
concerns arose about marketing practices, the paradigmatic case being
that of the Lotus Marketplace product. The nature of the Internet, and
its capacity to capture personally identifiable information, became the
major question of the mid-late 1990s, with major conflicts over the Clipper Chip, the MS Passport applications, DoubleClick, and the Intel Pentium III processor. In recent years, the dominant stories have focused on
the many instances of identity theft and data breaches.

Much has been written about each of these conflicts. The focus of this
analysis is from the perspective of the privacy advocacy networks. What
role have they played in these events? What lessons have they learned?
How have these cases shaped the perceptions and behaviors of the key
actors?

Census Protests

The national census provides a regularized, obvious, and concentrated
moment when personal data is collected by the state on every citizen.
The census therefore tends to focus the attention on privacy issues like
no other process. It concentrates the minds of ordinary citizens, who
may not otherwise be privacy aware, on the reasons for collection, the
scope, the rules about access and retention, and the protocols for security.
As David Flaherty reminds us, "The census provides a recurrent opportunity in every country for people to oppose the collection of personal
information by government agencies. The census, as one of the very few
universal and compulsory data collection activities, generates some basic

hostilities." He contends that early census disputes "helped to spark the original data protection movement" (Flaherty 1989, 80).

One of the earliest examples of significant protest against a census occurred in the Netherlands in 1971, the last year that a comprehensive census was held in this country. Public concerns about privacy, and a lack of trust in the Dutch Bureau of Statistics, caused a high nonresponse rate even though nonparticipation was an offense. Long memories of World War II and how the Nazis had terrorized the Dutch people with access to local records, as well as fears of the linkage of statistical with administrative records, were cited as the cause of this resistance. Later in the decade, the Dutch government decided to conduct a pretest of the planned 1981 census. The nonresponse rates were so high that the census was cancelled. These incidents also inspired the creation of the major Dutch organization, Privacy Alert (Stichting Waakzaamheid Persoonregistratiie), and motivated the early activism of individuals like Jan Holvast.

The disputes over the censuses in Germany in 1983 and 1987 took place at a time when few countries had data protection legislation, and even fewer had data protection commissioners. These cases were, therefore, a quite early test of whether this issue could resonate with the general public, and in this case a public with bitter and relatively recent memories of the effects of centralized authoritarian rule. The German story begins in March 1982, when the Bundestag passed enabling legislation for a census of the population in 1983. At the time, there were few voices of protest. The legislation regulated the content of the questions, the method of execution and the various requirements for confidentiality and access to the results (Schwartz 1989, 687–689). The Federal Data Protection Commissioner at the time, Hans Peter Bull, had been consulted and had recommended certain changes.

Nobody was prepared for the storm of protest that erupted. The issue appears to have reached public consciousness as a result of a large peace rally in late 1982. Organizers advised people that if the government could not tell the public where the proposed U.S. missiles were to be based, then the people should not reveal information about themselves to the government. The resurgent Green Party, which had won a substantial number of seats in the Bundestag, then took up the issue, using the census as a vehicle to attack the government, and to criticize the increasing appetite of state bureaucracies for information on German citizens. They also alleged that certain questions in particular could be used to identify illegal aliens, draft dodgers, tax evaders, welfare cheats, and antiwar protestors. The census became a major issue during the federal election of March 1983, at which the Christian Democratic Union (CDU) of Helmut Kohl took power (Butz 1985).

In a few weeks, many other groups, including trades unions, called for a boycott. Influential newspapers called for the census to be stopped, as did many members of the Bundestag who had previously supported it. Opinion polls indicated that 52 percent of the population did not trust the questions, and 25 percent were prepared to risk prosecution by not completing the form (Flaherty 1989, 79). Influential public figures, such as Günter Grass, joined the voices of dissent. Banners appeared on buildings encouraging nonparticipation. Government reassurances about the data protection safeguards did little to quell the anxieties. Even Commissioner Hans Peter Bull's statements that fears about the census were unfounded fell on deaf ears. The *Volkszählung* had become a symbol of an overintrusive German state (Appel and Hummel 1987).

Two lawyers challenged the constitutionality of the census law on the grounds that it constituted an invasion of privacy. In April 1983, the court decided to postpone the census until its constitutionality could be clarified. In a decision in December 1983, it indeed found that some of the planned uses were unconstitutional. More important, the decision placed German data protection law on a firm constitutional grounding. It articulated a broad right of "informational self-determination" and established that the constitution gives the individual the right to decide the circumstances under which personal data may be processed: "the individual is placed at the center of the data collection process to insure his awareness of the fate of his information and to encourage his participation in the discussion and debate regarding the use of personal data" (Schwartz 1989, 691). The decision had broad ramifications throughout Germany and the rest of Europe.

The 1987 census was, therefore, conducted within this new legal framework. There were fewer questions and clearer rules about anonymization. Despite the fact that the Federal Statistical Office spent an enormous fraction of its budget on public relations, this census still provoked much controversy and resistance. The Green Party again led the opposition. Fears about record linkage, about the absence of a strict separation between statistical and administrative uses of the data, and about the associated proposals for a machine-readable identity card again dominated the debate. The census went ahead, but there was significant nonparticipation. It was the last time a comprehensive population census was conducted in Germany. Statistical surveys of a sample of the population are now the norm.

Subsequent conflicts over census operations in different countries have not inspired anything like the level of opposition seen in Germany. To some extent, statistical agencies have learned some hard lessons about the limitations of their abilities to reassure a skeptical public with assurances about legal and technical safeguards. Flaherty concludes that the 1983 German census controversy was "in no way a highly rational activity, nor one that was devoid of partisan politics" (1989, 82). These early census battles did, however, teach the early privacy advocates of how easy it can be to promote resistance, when there is a sympathetic political culture and a set of political interests that coincide with those of privacy protection. It also produced a deep-seated skepticism about the technocratic and compromising instincts of official data protection authorities. The German protests were extraordinary, and they have been remembered. Twenty years later, contemporary resistance to schemes for the retention of telecommunications traffic data, as expressed in the epigraph at the top of this chapter, reflect these heady days of an antisurveillance politics in Germany.

Card Games

One reason why national census schemes inspire such resistance is that they represent one defined moment of interaction with the state. The census possesses symbolic importance, notwithstanding the fact that census disputes are often mired in highly technical and legalistic questions about data protection. Proposals for national identity cards produce similar reactions. All modern societies have developed systems to establish that their citizens "are who they say they are." Those systems have evolved over time as new forms of biometric technology and the demands of a complex, mobile, and globalizing world have provided more efficient and reliable forms of authentication. The pocket-sized card remains, however, an enduring symbol of the process of self-identification in our interactions with different state and private agencies (Bennett and Lyon 2008). Most countries have obliged their citizens to obtain and carry some form of identification card for a long time. The notable conflicts have arisen in societies that have attempted to propose quite comprehensive identity card systems, marking a radical departure from historical practices.

The story of the Australian government's attempt to impose an Australia Card on its citizens has been told a number of times, and has reached almost mythic status in Australian history (Clarke 1987; Greenleaf 1987). The idea for the card was raised at the national Tax Summit in 1985, convened by the then Labor government. The initial reasoning behind the scheme was to combat tax evasion, welfare fraud, and illegal immigration. The plan consisted of a central register containing information about every member of the population, a unique personal identification number, an obligatory and multipurpose ID card, and statutory obligations to produce the card on request by specified government agents. The government introduced legislation in parliament in 1986 that was blocked by the opposition parties in the Senate. The failure of this legislation was a trigger for the double dissolution of Parliament and the calling of the 1987 election. The government was returned, and decided to press on with the idea. The bill was reintroduced, together with promises of a subsequent bill dealing with data security issues. As a result of a technical flaw in the bill, however, (the fact that the date for implementation was not part of the legislation) it was obvious to the government that the opposition would defeat the bill by disallowing the accompanying regulations. The government announced a few days later that it was withdrawing the bill.

Social opposition to the scheme, however, was very slow to mount. The Australia Card was the trigger for the election but it was not an election issue. The few privacy advocates in Australia at the time had great difficulty getting any attention. Indeed, the return of the Hawke government and its immediate announcement that it would reintroduce the legislation signaled to a lot of people that the fight was lost.[1] A last-ditch effort coordinated largely by Simon Davies produced an extraordinary increase in opposition in a short time and motivated the creation of the Australian Privacy Foundation. The launch in the ballroom of a major Sydney hotel was professional and very well attended. It had a broad membership, both ideologically and professionally, and embraced an important blend of people with media experience, academic credentials, and name recognition in other fields.

Opposition from the public mounted through letter writing, public meetings, and rallies. Roger Clarke concludes: "The issue gave every impression of developing into the most divisive social issue at least since the Vietnam War and possibly since the Second World War, but with the additional aspect that demonstrations were not confined to the capital cities" (1987). Davies calls it a "massive movement" and a "tidal wave." He notes that the "the passion of those weeks approached the point of open civil disobedience; public demonstrations against the ID card began to turn nasty." The rhetoric in favor of the card was also ratcheted up, as proponents of the card sought to discredit the motives and intelligence of the resistors (Davies 1992, 37).

Like the German census conflict, the Australia Card question was tied up in both the minutiae of parliamentary procedures as well as the high stakes of electoral politics. It also had much to do with underlying surveillance concerns, beyond the issue of the Australia Card. The resistance arose quite quickly and unexpectedly, reversing initial public support in dramatic ways. The opposition was framed squarely in terms of "privacy" and the various opposition groups and personnel were embraced by the umbrella organization of APF, giving the organization a real boost. It inspired the key actors and cemented some close and enduring ties and friendships. No other national privacy organization has begun with such publicity and success. APF then earned a reputation as a force in Australian politics far in excess of its membership or resources.

The issue of an Australian national identity card resurfaced in the post-9/11 climate of antiterrorism measures. Dubbed "Australia Card II," the proposal was initially floated in the summer of 2005, ostensibly as a method to control illegal immigration and to prevent terrorists from entering the country. Opposition again mounted from the opposition parties, from backbenchers in the governing (Liberal) party, from business leaders, and from the media, and APF again played an important leadership coordination role. The government, however, decided to adapt its proposal rather than withdraw it. In April 2006, it announced a new Access Card, a single card to replace the Medicare card and various benefit cards issued by Australian social services and veterans' affairs agencies. The overall purpose seems to have shifted from one of the control of illegal immigration to that of streamlining access to government services.

The card was supposed to be voluntary, though "voluntary" cards can easily become de facto mandatory cards. It comprised a national identification number, a national identification database, a biometric photo, and was to all intents and purposes compulsory for anybody wishing to access medical, social security, or veterans benefits. The battle has also focused on the cost estimates, the secrecy of various consulting reports (including a Privacy Impact Assessment) and the inadequacy of consultation with privacy advocates. Nevertheless a bill was introduced in December 2006, and rammed through the House of Representatives. As in the 1980s, however, it ran into serious opposition in the Senate, with government members joining the opposition to recommend withdrawal and resubmission. The minister withdrew the bill in March 2007.[2] The new government of Kevin Rudd, elected in November 2007, have scrapped the plans completely.

In this case, APF was one of several groups in opposition, and the resistance did not reach anything like the level of that in the 1980s. The torch has also passed to a younger generation of privacy advocates, such as Anna Johnston, even though some of the original campaigners from the 1980s, such as Roger Clarke and Graham Greenleaf, are still very active. Clarke explains: "A nucleus gained self belief, and that nucleus grew. We are now 20 years on, but that self belief has been projected through the "grey beards" that emanated from 1987 and that has carried through into the contemporary scene. So the younger members carry that kind of confidence (almost swagger) when they walk into the Minister's office."[3]

The early Australia Card conflict also shaped the views and experiences of Davies, who provided much of the media savvy during the Australia Card dispute. After he had established Privacy International, he moved to Great Britain and helped lead the resistance to the British Identity Card scheme introduced by the Blair government in 2005. A NO2ID campaign was also launched signing up group and individual members.[4] The British Identity Card Bill finally passed, but support declined over the course of the legislative passage. Significant parliamentary opposition, led by the House of Lords, also damaged its credibility. Again it reached the level of high politics, with denouncements of Davies and his colleagues by Home Secretary Charles Clarke, as well as by Prime Minister Tony Blair, in the media and in Parliament. Relatively high levels of public support waned as a public and media became more skeptical. It is not clear whether it will be implemented with the same vigor by the government led by Gordon Brown.

Resistance to ID card schemes has also surfaced in countries with more long-standing traditions of centralized citizen identification schemes. The French national identification system, for example, has its roots in the system of "bertillonnage" at the end of the last century, a method of identification on the basis of multiple biometric identifiers. It has administered a national identity card system since the 1920s, with significant amendments during the Vichy regime, and in the 1950s and 1980s (Piazza 2004). A recent proposal for a biometric card called INES (Secure Electronic National Identity) involves charging citizens for a biometric card that would become compulsory within five years of initial issuing. For the first time, the card was to be connected to various national registers, including births, deaths and marriages, fingerprints, digitized photographs, and passports. The biometric data were to be included in a chip, and capable of remote access through an RFID.

The project was suspended by then Interior Minister Nicolas Sarkozy in 2005, and at the time of this writing it is not clear whether now President Sarkozy is inclined to support its reintroduction. But INES has attracted widespread and unprecedented opposition and resistance. A coalition was set up in the spring of 2005.[5] In May 2005 this group launched a petition against INES, mocking it as "Inepte, Nocif, Effrayant, Scélérat" (Inept, Harmful, Scary, Nefarious). Then there is a more radical group called Pièces et Main d'Oeuvre[6] that arranged a hoax in June 2005, wherein a fake four-page leaflet bearing the logo of the Isère General Council was delivered to thousands of mailboxes in Grenoble. An official-looking leaflet extolled an imaginary new biometric "life card" and urged Isère dwellers to request one at once. Opposition also came from the communist and socialist deputies in the National Assembly. The Commission Nationale de l'Informatique et Libertés (CNIL), the official data protection authority in France, also voiced skepticism (Lanial and Piazza 2008).

Another country in which the politics of national identification systems has reached the highest levels of political and public attention has been Japan. The Japanese have always had a system of residential registration. Thus new residents in a neighborhood are required to attend the local government office, where they dutifully report their presence and give details of their family. On moving residence, they must again notify local authorities and get a report to take to the office of the next place in which they will be living. This official tracking has been accepted by most Japanese for decades (Ogasawara 2008).

In 2002 the central government introduced a national integrated system to place these data on a computer network (Juki Net) and to assign an eleven-digit identification number to everyone. The reaction and resistance astounded both the government and outside observers. Protesters, decorated as bar codes, took to the streets. Public opinion polls showed huge opposition to the system, and a campaign was organized by the influential journalist, Yoshiko Sakurai, to try to get it abolished. It was also opposed by some local municipalities, a few of whom defied the government and refused to be a part of the computer network.[7] Court challenges commenced, demanding either a scrapping of the system or the recognition of an individual's right to opt out. In the first ruling on the system in 2005, the Kanazawa District Court endorsed a new right for the Japanese, analogous to the decision of the German constitutional court to informational self-determination. The ruling said the right to privacy is guaranteed under Article 13 of the Japanese Constitution and that the names, addresses, dates of birth, and gender listed in the basic resident registries, as well as code numbers assigned by municipalities to residents, are private information that each resident has the "right to control." The ruling said that refusing residents' requests for removal of their data from the system was a violation of this right and unconstitutional. Other court challenges followed, and other courts reached different judgments (EPIC 2007, 603). What began as an attempt to integrate national and local registration systems, and to bring them into the era of "e-government," is still mired in litigation and mistrust about security breaches.

Japan is typically regarded as a more deferential and centralized political culture and unlikely to produce such levels of resistance. But the same could also be said of Australia and the United Kingdom. On the other hand, countries such as France with long histories of popular protest have possessed national identification cards for many years. The common thread appears to be the perceived reach of these systems, with the attendant financial and administrative costs, that create a widespread reaction across generations, ethnic groups, and people of different political affiliations. Davies has suggested that campaigns against national ID cards go through some predictable phases:

During the first stage of the debate, a popular view is usually expressed that identification, per se, is not an issue related to individual rights. When an identity card is proposed, the public discussion is initially focused on the possession and use of the card itself.... The second stage of public debate is marked by a growing awareness of the hidden threats of an identity card: function creep, the potential for abuse by authorities, problems arising from losing your card. Technical and organizational questions often arise at this level of discussion.... The final level of discussion involves more complex questions about rights and responsibilities. At this stage, the significance of the computer back-up and the numbering system enter the picture.[8]

Where established privacy advocates have the experience to ask the right questions and produce credible analysis, and have the media savvy to couch the opposition in terms that will appeal to a popular audience, then experience suggests that national identification policies can run into trouble. And governments have learned these hard lessons, with the result that more contemporary national identification policies tend to be introduced more gradually, and with symbols that are perhaps more palatable. Thus the new Australian policy is termed an Access Card.[9] The Canadian government now talks of a national Identity Management policy. And the United States has embarked on a steady process of standardizing the drivers' license systems of the fifty states, with biometric identifiers.

American privacy advocates have denounced Real ID as a sneaky method to introduce a de facto national ID card "through the back door" of state vehicle and licensing authorities. Under these circumstances, and within the context of post-9/11 fears of terrorism, the opposition is far more difficult to muster than in earlier years, even though several states have decided not to participate in the scheme. Echoing themes from previous ID card disputes, the ACLU has declared Real ID a "real nightmare"—"Real Invasive, Real Red Tape, Real Expensive, Real Pointless."[10] Some states have already resolved not to cooperate, primarily for financial reasons.

Marketing Schemes

The attention of the privacy community shifted in the late 1980s and early 1990s to the activities of the private sector, and in particular its collection, use, analysis, and dissemination of personal data for marketing purposes. At the same time, scholarly analysis of surveillance began to stress the everyday or routine nature of the phenomenon. The capture of personal information did not need to be associated with grandiose and bureaucratic schemes. It was beginning to occur in the "mundane, ordinary, taken-for-granted world of getting money from a bank machine, making a phone call, applying for sickness benefits, driving a car, using a credit card, receiving junk mail, picking up books from the library, or crossing a border on trips abroad" (Lyon 1994, 4). Surveillance became, therefore, a process of sorting and classification, as well as one of observation and investigation. It began to be denounced for its discriminatory, as well as its intrusive, effects (Gandy 1993).

The very routine nature of information about personal transactions also provided a dilemma for privacy advocates who had to make the case that the accumulation of vast quantities of mundane information could be just as dangerous and intrusive as the targeted collection of more sensitive data. They also had to counter the perception that the dangers were trivial when the only effect is annoyance at a telemarketing call, a mail promotion, or an unsolicited e-mail. On the other hand, the proliferation of telemarketing literally brought home the effects and extensiveness of the personal information economy. Privacy advocates could therefore fight, throughout the 1990s, for more stringent regulations on the collection, processing and dissemination of marketing data, and struggled with the marketing industry over the proper standards for individual consent, secondary uses and the rules for "Do Not Call" lists. This has been the "normal politics" of privacy with respect to direct marketing. One major conflict, however, rose above the normal politics—the Lotus Marketplace dispute in the early 1990s.

This was a database program developed jointly by Lotus Development Corporation and Equifax, the former producing the software, and the latter providing the personal information from its Consumer Marketing Database. The product was announced in April 1990, and was to be released on eleven CD-ROMs in two editions. The Business edition of this program contained information about seven million businesses in the United States that could be easily searched. This edition was not so controversial and was released in October 1990.

It was the Households edition of this program that caused the anger. The product contained the following data on each household: name, address, age range, gender, marital status, household income, dwelling type, telephone numbers, and past purchasing behavior, on about 120 million people and 80 million households in the United States. The software allowed for quick and flexible searching by various parameters. Thus, a small business owner could enter a set of parameters of people in a particular area with certain characteristics, and then buy the full list by contacting Lotus and paying for the code to access the encrypted data on the disk. The corporations pointed out that this product was only providing small businesses with the same information that had been available to large corporations for a long time, through centralized data brokerage firms such as Polk, Acxiom, TRW, and others. The difference, however, was the distribution of this application as a desktop application. The end user owned the database and controlled its use, without the same restrictions on the proprietary databases of the centralized data brokerage firms. Furthermore, disks allowed only read-only memory (ROM), meaning that errors could not be easily corrected without writing to Equifax and hoping that changes would be made on the next edition of the disks. There was also no easy provision for opting-out.

Lotus and Equifax had considered consumer privacy issues before the release of these products. They had conducted focus groups, and had consulted with privacy experts, including Alan Westin. They insisted that there was a screening process to ensure that the product would only be used by legitimate businesses, and distributed a privacy protection pamphlet. They pressed home the point that the encrypted data could only be downloaded after the access code was received from Lotus. Indeed, the initial publicity in the mainstream press, as well as in trade journals for the direct marketing and software industries, was praiseworthy (Gurak 1997, 23).

The privacy concerns surfaced quite quickly, however. Marc Rotenberg, then of CPSR, Evan Hendricks of Privacy Times, and Janlori Goldman, then of the ACLU, were critical in both media and congressional testimony. Mary Culnan, a professor at Georgetown University, produced some of the early analytical work (Culnan 1991). The companies corresponded with these advocates and even organized a demonstration of the product at CPSR offices.

It wasn't until criticism was posted on the online newsgroups that the protest exploded. These online networks were new, but they were also read by some of the most sophisticated computer professionals who could circulate informed technical information about the product. Of particular importance were the RISKS Digest, and the famous Whole Earth Electronic Network (WELL). The speed and efficiency with which messages circulated throughout this community in late 1990 and early 1991 were a novelty and became part of the story. In addition to debates about this product, individuals posted information about how one should remove one's name from the database, together with the address, telephone number and e-mail address of the CEO of Lotus. Some also posted form letters to be sent to Lotus. The posting and reposting of critical commentary triggered subsequent waves of protest, and over thirty thousand people contacted the company to request that their names be removed from the database.

The companies had little idea how to respond; traditional press releases were found to be useless against information and misinformation that was popping up all over these new networks. Even when Lotus did try to post to some newsgroups, their more traditional and "business-like" tone only served to anger protesters further. In January 1991, Lotus announced that it would cancel its Household product citing "public concerns and misunderstandings of the product, and the substantial, unexpected additional costs required to fully address consumer privacy issues" (Gurak 1997, 123).

This episode is invariably cited as a substantial victory for privacy and for the potential for online activism. It did produce one of the first online communities that rapidly, organically, and informally prevented a privacy invasive product from being marketed. There is no doubt that companies drew important lessons from this episode. As the Internet matured, so it has been easier and more efficient to mobilize protest. On the other hand, organizations are also savvier about how to respond. Further, as the Internet matured, the privacy issues tended to revolve around the very nature of the medium, and whether or not it was going to be possible to communicate and browse with anonymity. The Lotus Marketplace dispute demonstrated the potential for online activism but it was just about one product. It was, therefore, a forerunner for a string of more fundamental issues that consumed the attention of the privacy advocacy network in the mid-1990s and beyond.

Crypto Wars

The most prominent question for privacy advocates in the mid-1990s concerned the availability of strong encryption for online communications, in the face of a series of attempts by governments to enforce the same measures and standards for surveillance as exist for offline communications. We have already discussed the attempts to restrict the distribution of the PGP e-mail encryption program in chapter 3. But the dispute that clearly came to symbolize the competing tensions between privacy advocates and law enforcement was that of the "Clipper Chip"—a code name for the encryption system proposed by the Clinton administration in 1993. This was a high profile and high-stakes debate about the future of the new communications media. The history is long and technically complex. It shaped the attitudes and perceptions of American privacy advocates like no other conflict before or since.

The story really begins with the Computer Security Act of 1987, which required the National Institute for Standards and Technology (NIST) to develop a new standard for computer encryption. The growth and complexity of online communications required a more complex algorithm than that known as DES, which only required one key, was developed in the 1970s for the stand-alone mainframe generation of computers, and had been compromised many times. The U.S. government was deeply concerned that new technologies were outpacing the ability of law enforcement to perform the same legal surveillance of e-mail communications as they had enjoyed with respect to telephones. They feared that authorized wiretaps would be rendered meaningless if communications could be encoded with an unbreakable encryption technique. In collaboration with the National Security Agency (NSA), NIST developed an escrowed encryption standard (EES), which could be encoded within a tamper-resistant integrated circuit (the Clipper Chip), using a far stronger encryption algorithm (known as Skipjack), which could then be inserted into various communications devices. This new federal standard was announced in April 1993.

The central feature of this new standard was "key escrow." The new standard required the use of two encryption keys, one to encrypt and the other to decrypt the message. Each key was to be held by two different government agencies, to ensure that both could only be obtained with proper court authorization. In theory, therefore, messages would be more difficult to intercept, because decryption could only take place when both keys were used together. But the Clipper proposal embodied a "back door" that would have allowed the government to decrypt the traffic for law enforcement and national security purposes through a "Law Enforcement Access Field." The effect was likened to a little keyhole in the back of the combination locks used on the lockers of school children. The children open the locks with the combinations, which are supposed to keep the other children out, but the teachers can always look in the lockers by using the key.[11] Others used the analogy of leaving one's front door key at the police station (Levy 2001, 251).

The Clinton administration was adamant that cryptography needed to be controlled in order to prevent criminals and terrorists from using it to hide their activities. They believed it a balanced proposal. Further it was initially proposed as a voluntary standard. It only affirmed that the federal government itself would buy the clipper devices from the manufacturer (AT&T) for installation in its own communication devices. Further, it was argued that the key-escrow feature would only be triggered under the same conditions for wiretapping that had been developed under the standards of the Fourth Amendment. It was billed as an attempt to bring U.S. encryption policy into the digital age (Levy 2001, 248–249).

There were many different arguments advanced against Clipper (Froomkin 1995). There were technical concerns raised about the vulnerability of the Skipjack algorithm. There were questions about human vulnerability in the key-escrow system; if one could bribe officials within the two government agencies, then one could also tap into any link for which they hold the keys. Further, the system was constructed in such a way that once the keys were revealed, then they would be known for ever. The fact that the system was designed in secret also raised suspicions that the various vulnerabilities had not been adequately subjected to the critical evaluation of the scientific community.

At a policy level, critics pointed out that his radical change in policy was being proposed without a statute and a proper process of public comment. The 1987 Computer Security Act actually bars the NSA from working on systems designed for public use. Opponents were also not persuaded by assurances that encryption keys could only be accessed by law enforcement under a court-ordered warrant, when such warrants are rarely refused. Clipper also compromised privacy in advance of due process. The American system, it was argued, prevents anticipatory interference in free speech unless there is a demonstrable evidence of wrong doing. At root, there was a logical problem. If Clipper remained a voluntary standard, then the key-escrow feature relied on the theory that the people worth catching would be smart enough to use cryptography but stupid enough to use a government-designed system with backdoor access for law enforcement. This led to suspicions that Clipper was being designed as a de facto mandatory standard, and that the purchasing power of government would ultimately force all computer and telecommunications manufacturers to install Clipper-enabled devices. The implications of this proposal were also not lost on foreign governments, whose secret diplomatic communications might also be compromised.[12]

In retrospect it is quite remarkable that the Clipper proposal produced the storm of protest that it did. These are complex technical and policy questions. The opposition was hardly coordinated, but it was fierce and broad-based. It stemmed from the civil liberties community, including the newly formed EFF and EPIC as well as the ACLU. It also came from an organization called the Digital Privacy and Security Working Group (DPSWG), a coalition of over fifty communications and computer companies and associations, and consumer and privacy advocates. It came from major software corporations such as Microsoft and Lotus, who calculated that a key-escrow encryption standard would hinder their ability to export to foreign markets. The opposition even came from anti-Clinton commentators such as Rush Limbaugh (Grossman 1997, 56).

The Clipper proposal was initially staunchly defended by the administration. It was then relaxed in 1996 to allow users a choice of escrow agencies, and inevitably dubbed "Clipper II." Clipper III soon followed, allowing companies to export un-escrowed cryptographic products, in exchange for building escrow into future products. To all intents and purposes, the Clipper Chip idea was dead, although interpretations have differed as to what killed it.

In some accounts, this was a victory for a new grassroots form of Net activism. Like the Lotus Marketplace case, but a couple of years on and with the assistance of quicker and more extensive Usenet newsgroups as well as file transfer protocol (FTP) sites for the posting of relevant documents, a network of young, technologically informed, and largely male activists coalesced and mobilized. The most visible and novel manifestation of this opposition was the petition drive organized by CPSR. To participate, individuals had to send a message to clipper.petition@cpsr.org with the message "I oppose Clipper." They received a return message confirming their vote, and were encouraged to distribute the announcement to others. CPSR collected over fifty thousand signatures and passed the petition along to the White House. This strategy was effective because it was innovative. The grassroots activism also extended to a boycott: "Don't buy anything with a Clipper Chip in it. Don't buy any product from a company that manufactures devices with Big Brother inside. It is likely that the government will ask you to use Clipper for communications with the IRS or when doing business with federal agencies. They cannot, as yet, require you to do so. Just say no."[13]

The importance of these activities should not be exaggerated, because there was also a good deal of more traditional lobbying. Congressional hearings served to reinforce opposition from some key legislators, and especially Senator Leahy and Congresswoman Cantwell. Particular efforts were directed toward lifting the embargo on cryptography exports, which for the administration was an essential mechanism to manipulate the marketplace to favor clipper enabled products. The strong support for Cantwell's bill (H.R. 3627) forced the administration eventually to compromise on the key-escrow provisions of Clipper (Levy 2001, 267–268). Advocates also pressed the issue of legal authority. Clipper, as proposed, represented a significant policy change without congressional legislation or financial authorization.

Other accounts have stressed the importance of lining up business opposition. In this respect the work of the Digital Privacy and Security Working Group (DPSWG) deserves mention. It was described as a "diverse forum of over 50 computer, communications, and public interest organizations working to develop and implement policies that protect personal privacy and network security on the expanding and rapidly changing global information infrastructure."[14] This coalition was originally founded in 1986 at the time of the passage of the Electronic Communications Privacy Act (ECPA). It since played a critical role in the 1994 debates over the Communications Assistance for Law Enforcement Act (CALEA), and was therefore well positioned to coordinate a response to Clipper. There were several important reasons why the high-tech industry was opposed to Clipper. There were severe implications for American competitiveness in this rapidly developing market. There were implications for the secrecy of companies' negotiations with government agencies. There were also concerns about the potential for industrial espionage, and so on. For these reasons, the Clipper Chip was never likely to become an industry standard when opposed by some of the biggest computer and telecommunications companies. Thus, when the OECD issued its cryptography guidelines in 1997, despite heavy American pressure in favor of key escrow, it advised that the "development and provision of cryptographic methods should be determined by the market in an open and competitive environment" (OECD 1997).

Perhaps the final nail in the coffin was the research conducted my Matt Blaze of the AT&T's Bell Labs research facility. Through a series of unlikely events, Blaze was hired as an outside evaluator of the Clipper technology. In a relatively short period, he discovered a way to hack into a section of the Law Enforcement Access Field (LEAF). To his surprise, he encountered no objections to publishing his results from either the NSA or AT&T. Further to his surprise, the story was considered worthy of the front page of the *New York Times*.[15] The flaw, discovered by Blaze, was not insurmountable, but it did serve to undermine the trust in Clipper and in the engineers and consultants of the NSA. According to Wendy Grossman, "the plan pretty much died there" (Grossman 1997, 60).

The story of public-key cryptography then proceeds along a complicated series of parallel and overlapping tracks. As the Internet progressed into an essentially decentralized and privatized medium, so it became increasingly difficult for governments to impose centralized cryptography policies. Public-key infrastructures (PKI) using trusted third parties (TTPs) emerged as the standard method for governments and corporations to guarantee levels of security and authentication in the rapidly evolving era of e-government and e-commerce. The Clipper controversy is also important for the impact that it had on privacy advocacy. It energized a fledgling Internet community, and it taught privacy advocates the importance of forging coalitions with elements within the corporate sector, and indeed with companies that turned out to be on the opposite side of later controversies.

Web Conflicts

The Clipper controversy was about the privacy of communication. As the Internet was transformed into a medium for electronic commerce in the mid to late 1990s, so the attention shifted to the circumstances under which corporations and governments could discover an individual's browsing behavior. One normally has the freedom to walk anonymously along a high street or through a shopping mall. Should not the same standards apply on the World Wide Web? Why should the provision of online commerce or electronic government also bring with it an expectation that the vendors or service providers might now the identity of those people visiting their Web sites? Again the very character of this new medium was as stake. Three major disputes deserve discussion, relating to chip processor identification (Intel), online advertising (DoubleClick), and identification management (Microsoft).

Chip Identification: The Intel Processor Serial Number

The first dispute concerned Intel. In February 1999, the company announced that its new processor (the Pentium III) would contain a unique identifier called the Processor Serial Number (PSN) to facilitate inventory control especially in large organizations where the same machines may be used by several people. A PSN could also be of considerable value in tracking stolen processor chips and hence preventing chip theft. It would also allow owners the benefit of an extra layer of authentication to protect them from fraud. In any electronic transaction, users would also be able to specify, in addition to name and password, that access would only be authorized on a PC with their own PSN. Further, Intel proposed that access to the PSN on Pentium III-based PCs should be controlled in one of two alternative ways: by a software control utility that was loaded and run when the Windows operating system is started, or through the PC's BIOS setting.[16] If the latter, then Intel recommended that the default setting should enable PSN access.

At one level, the debate centered on highly technical analysis about the real effectiveness of these controls, and whether or not the Windows operating system, or indeed any installed software could access the PSN regardless of the owner's wishes. It was soon clear that the potential for the surveillance of identifiable individuals was dependent on a complex set of conditions relating to the relationship among the PSN, the other hardware configurations of different manufacturers, the settings on the Windows operating system, and so on. Security experts weighed in, pointing out the vulnerabilities of the PSN to hackers, virus and worm writers, and unethical software suppliers. As with Clipper, the larger issue about the potential for access by law enforcement and intelligence agencies was also raised.[17] The technical analysis swiftly was swamped by fears that the PSN would create a kind of de facto comprehensive identification system for the Internet. The reactions were swift, widespread, and directed to a number of different audiences.

Four days after Intel announced the PSN feature, EPIC and Junk-busters called for a consumer boycott of the company. Various actions were recommended: writing to PC makers like Compaq, Dell, Gateway, Hewlett-Packard (HP), and IBM refusing to buy a product with "Big Brother Inside"; adding a line to the bottom of e-mails and usenet postings—Protect privacy, boycott Intel: http://www.bigbrotherinside .org; adding similar banner ads to Web sites; and distributing a "No Way Out" flyer.[18] Advocates also targeted other companies. On February 16, CDT wrote to the CEOs of nine major equipment manufacturers asking them to specify their corporate policies on the Pentium III chips.[19] A similar letter followed on February 22 from EPIC, Junkbusters, and PI to the CEOs of Dell, Gateway, HP, IBM, and Compaq. They followed this up with a stronger call for these companies to suspend all company products that incorporated the chip in the light of a report that the serial number could be read through software, regardless of whether it had been turned off. On February 28, they also called upon the managers of socially responsible mutual funds "to bring economic pressure to bear on Intel to permanently disable this dangerous feature."[20]

At the governmental level, the advocacy groups made a complaint to the FTC arguing: "(a) The PSN will become a de facto standard Global User Identifier (GUID); (b) The GUID will be used by companies in information practices that are unfair; (c) Such practices will become known to consumers, some of whom will avoid participation in e-commerce because they apprehend that their privacy is at risk by doing so." They also charged that Intel had engaged in false claims and deceptive trade practices contrary to Section 5 of the Federal Trade Commission Act. In response to the initial publicity, Intel stated that they would change the chip's identifier from "normally on" to "normally off." The advocates contended, however, that they had not changed the chip at all, merely their recommendations to PC manufacturers on how the chip is configured by software. In addition, EPIC filed FOIA requests to fifteen federal agencies, including the NSA and the FBI, to determine their level of involvement in the creation of the PSN. Such involvement would not have been unprecedented given the collaboration between the government and AT&T over the Clipper Chip. No agency ever acknowledged any involvement. The FTC never pronounced on the complaint.

Intel responded by releasing a software program to disable the number, and then a BIOS modification. Most PC manufacturers chose also to turn off the feature. That is essentially where the issue stood for over a year. In

April 2000, Intel quietly let it be known that it would not be including the PSN in its next generation Willamette Chip. "The gains that it could give us for the proposed line of security features were not sufficient to over-come the bad rep it would give us," an anonymous source was quoted.[21] None of the subsequent generation of Intel processors has been produced with any similar feature.

Coming on the heels of the abandonment of the Clipper Chip, this about turn in policy by the world's leading chip manufacturer was seen as a significant success for the privacy advocacy network (Leizerov 2000). The company was clearly caught off-guard by the speed and breadth of the opposition, though the privacy advocacy coalition was not as large as that assembled to fight later battles. There also seemed to be two somewhat separate centers of gravity, CDT on the one hand and Junkbusters/EPIC on the other, with scant mutual referencing on the re-spective Web sites, and little overlap in terms of supporting signatures on letters. For instance, there were two separate complaints to the FTC in February 1999. One was authored by CDT and supported by Consumer Action, Privacy Rights Clearinghouse, and Private Citizen, Inc. The oth-er, coordinated by Junkbusters, was supported by EPIC, PI, the Center for Media Education, Private Citizen, Inc., Privacy Rights Clearinghouse, and Privacy Times. CDT pointedly did not join the boycott, contending that it would be ineffective against a company with Intel's market posi-tion. These divisions have persisted in subsequent campaigns.

Online Advertising and DoubleClick

The first, and still probably most important, dispute over online advertis-ing involved the practices of DoubleClick, in 1999 the Internet's leading advertising company. It delivered banner ads to over fifteen hundred client Web sites and had technology that tracked Internet users as they moved from one client's site to another. DoubleClick watched the sites that people visited, the terms they typed into search boxes, and the ads they clicked. All of this was achieved through cookies, the small text files that are logged in the cache of the user's computer. Some cookies are designed to expire once the browser is closed. Others are persistent, and may be used to identify a user when he or she returns to that site. Double-Click observes these cookies to make inferences about individual inter-ests, and to deliver specially targeted banner ads through a proprietary technology known as Dynamic Advertising Reporting and Targeting (DART). However, there was no real reason for privacy advocates and regulators to be concerned about these practices, so long as there was no chance that DoubleClick could identify individual users. Both Double-Click, and its clients, had posted privacy policies indicating that this "clickstream data" was indeed anonymized.

That changed when DoubleClick acquired a little-known company, Abacus Direct, in June 1999. Abacus Direct compiled offline data on consumer purchasing habits, primarily through agreements with catalog retailers and other direct marketing companies. Abacus Direct's repository reportedly held data on over eighty-eight million U.S. households. The combination of the Abacus database with DoubleClick's profiles of clickstream data provided the companies with the ability to identify positively someone browsing the Web with personal information and to deliver targeted online advertisements. As the press release boasted, these combined resources would provide their clients with "comprehensive, full service marketing and advertising solutions." Chairman and CEO Kevin O'Connor claimed that this merger "further enhances our ability to deliver the right advertising message, to the right consumer, at the right time."[22]

Despite company promises that consumers would always be able to opt out from the databases, the proposal was immediately attacked by a coalition of privacy advocates, including Junkbusters, EPIC, Privacy International, the U.S. Public Interest Research Group, and the Privacy Rights Clearinghouse. The media campaign was initially triggered by an open letter sent on June 21, 1999, to O'Connor and copied to key members of Congress. In this letter they announced that the campaign would include: an appeal to shareholders of both companies, a call to the FTC to disapprove the merger, a request for socially responsible mutual funds to divest holdings in these companies, a public education campaign, and a call for congressional oversight.[23]

Particularly innovative was the appeal to stockholders. In June 1999, the coalition addressed an open letter to the stockholders of Abacus Direct, calling upon them to disapprove the merger, and alleging that they had been misled about the privacy risks inherent in the proposal. The same coalition later addressed a letter to the managers of socially responsible mutual funds. They called upon the socially responsible investors to divest their holdings in DoubleClick and Abacus as soon as possible, and add these companies to the screening lists of companies excluded from investment based on human rights criteria. CDT also organized an e-mail campaign not only to DoubleClick but also to sixty of its advertising clients.

The approach to the Federal Trade Commission initially contended that the merger was itself illegal under a piece of legislation called the Hart Scott Rodino Act, a 1976 law mandating a thirty-day waiting period during which regulatory agencies might assess whether the proposed transaction violates antitrust laws. The coalition also relied on the fact that DoubleClick had registered its compliance with the Safe Harbor program, the agreement with the European Union under which U.S. companies declare their commitment to basic privacy principles to facilitate international data transfers from the European Union. Any breach of those principles renders the company open to challenge for "unfair and deceptive" practices under the Federal Trade legislation. The proposed merger, and the intended uses of personal information, appeared directly to contradict DoubleClick's privacy policy.

By March 2000, although shareholders had approved the merger with Abacus, DoubleClick's stock price had dropped 20 percent, largely on concerns related to privacy issues. The FTC opened a formal Double-Click investigation. States attorneys general were also becoming involved through its National Association of Attorneys General. In addition, there were a mounting number of lawsuits on the basis of a number of state and federal privacy statutes, as well as on common law grounds. The response of other Internet advertising companies, clearly threatened by DoubleClick's dominance, was to negotiate a Network Advertising Initiative (NAI) that subscribed to the fair information practices developed by another industry group, the Online Privacy Alliance.

DoubleClick was soon isolated and, despite initial periods of denial and resistance, backed down. O'Connor was quoted in a *New York Times* article in the spring of 2000: "I made a big mistake. It was wrong to try to match that information in the absence of government or industry standards, so until there is an agreement on it, we will not." He continued, "It became clear that the overwhelming point of contention was under what circumstances a name could be associated with anonymous Web activity. Now we're just happy to get this behind us and move on."[24] The FTC dropped its investigation in January 2001. DoubleClick settled federal and state class action lawsuits addressing online privacy for $1.8 million in April 2002. In August 2002, in a settlement reached with ten states, DoubleClick agreed to pay a further $450,000 for consumer education. The company also agreed to be more transparent about tracking of Web users' online activities, to develop more explicit data retention policies for offline data, and to offer Web users access to their own marketing profiles. It also undertook to provide users with the ability to opt in to an e-mail notification system that will alert the user to any changes within DoubleClick's privacy statement, and to not share user data collected on behalf of one of its clients with any person other than that client or as directed by that client. DoubleClick was also to retain an independent firm to review compliance of the terms of the settlement. It also appointed a new chief privacy officer and established a consumer privacy board to oversee its activities.

The DoubleClick campaign was a success for the international privacy advocacy network, in part because of the initial intransigence of the company, but also because the proposed merger was relatively easy for the average citizen and investor to grasp. Advocates were able to provide the relevant information to the public and to regulators, to appeal to relevant symbols, to force the company to be accountable, and, in particular, to exert some leverage through the shareholders and investors.

The economic value of being able to identify who is browsing where and when was simply too enormous for other companies to ignore. Advocates therefore needed to be extremely vigilant of other efforts to link clickstream data with personal identifiers. At the time of writing, Double-Click is again in the news as a result of the proposed takeover of the company by Google. On April 20, 2007, EPIC, CDD, and US PIRG filed a complaint with the FTC, requesting the commission to investigate the proposed acquisition; in December 2007 the FTC approved the proposed merger. Similar complaints have been made in Europe and in Canada. Advocates are deeply concerned about the enhanced ability of Google to record, analyze, track, and profile the activities of Internet users. Companies including Microsoft and AT&T have also complained that the merger would limit competition in the online advertising market.

Online Identity Management: Microsoft Passport

Web advertising companies, like DoubleClick, try to collect information on people behind the scenes through hidden cookie technology so that they can send targeted ads. But this approach for sharing information only works for advertisements. Microsoft, however, developed a different strategy by providing a proprietary online identification and authentication service known as Passport. This was an online service that made it possible for users to sign in to any Passport-participating Web site or service, using a single e-mail address and a password. Once customers signed into Microsoft services, they became a part of the Microsoft Passport Network, which meant that the same credentials could be used to access many different Microsoft sites and services, as well as services provided by their affiliates. For those who are privacy conscious, a 64–bit encrypted unique ID number could be assigned to one's credentials, and sent to the different sites or services. Passport was to store user data in a central database. The supposed benefit to consumers was that it would allow them to use one login and password to access all the Passport web sites, and thus avoid password fatigue. The benefit to the Web sites was much greater, because of the potential to pool and share that information.

In March 2001, this system was revamped into a product called Hailstorm. Microsoft planned to create services that included MyAddress, MyProfile, MyContacts, MyNotifications, MyInbox, MyCalendar, MyDocuments, MyApplicationSettings, MyWallet, MyUsage, and MyLocation. A wide range of consumer information would have been collected and subsequently disclosed by means of HailStorm, including a person's telephone and fax number, home/business address, location; a person's name, nickname, birth date, anniversary, other special dates, and personal photograph; a complete list of all names/contact data of all contacts contained in an electronic date book. Microsoft revised its privacy policy, and declared its intention to join the Safe Harbor regime.[25]

For the company, Passport, Hailstorm, and the other related services were entirely consensual. Others were not so sure given the dominant place of the Microsoft Internet browser and the consequent likelihood that the standard for Internet authentication was being developed. Questions were raised about the automatic registration with Passport when one opens a Hotmail account, the fact that failure to enroll in Passport could result in exclusion from certain Web sites, the difficulty of deleting a Passport account, the vulnerability to hacking, the fact that individuals using public computer terminals may inadvertently pass on their information to the next user, and the question of law enforcement access to personal information within the Passport system. It was clear to outsiders that Microsoft was attempting to build a massive database on online consumer behavior. Indeed, the company admitted as much. The business plan used in the unrelated antitrust suit revealed that the company's goal of the Passport online identification and authentication system was to "create the largest and most leveragable database of profiles on the planet" and a "subscription relationship with every user on the Internet."[26]

In July 2001, the campaign against Microsoft began in earnest. EPIC and a coalition of consumer advocacy groups filed complaints with the FTC detailing the privacy risks associated with Passport, especially when used through the new XP operating system. The complaint was premised upon the claim that Microsoft was engaging in unfair and deceptive trade practices intended to profile, track, and monitor millions of Internet users. The coalition ordered the commission to investigate these practices and to instruct Microsoft not to violate Section 5 of the Federal Trade Commission Act. Later that year, the same coalition further called on the FTC to investigate the information collection practices of Microsoft through Passport and to order them to revise the XP registration procedures, block the sharing of personal information among Microsoft areas, incorporate techniques for anonymity and pseudo-anonymity that would allow users to gain access to Microsoft Web sites without disclosing their identity, and incorporate techniques that would enable users to integrate services provided by other online companies. They also requested that the commission conduct an investigation to determine whether Passport complied with the requirements of the Children's Online Privacy Protection Act.[27] When the FTC showed reluctance to act, the coalition began pressing key congressional committees as well as the state attorneys general.[28]

The Europeans also got involved. Early in 2002, Dutch European Commission member Erik Meijer submitted a series of questions about the legality of Passport under European data protection law to the European Commission. Frits Bolkestein, then commissioner for the internal market, assured Meijer that the commission "is looking to this as a matter of priority, in connection with national data protection authorities, as regards the system's compatibility (or not) with EU data protection law." Bolkestein summarized the requirements for building a database of personal information consistent with EU data protection law. These included a requirement that Microsoft have a specific, legitimate purpose for collection of the data; a right of access to the information collected; the requirement that consent be freely given when required; and notice to national data protection authorities.[29] In July of that year, the EU Internet Task Force began an investigation of Microsoft's Passport system to see if it complied with European data protection laws. At issue was whether Passport users were aware that their data was transferred to a party other than Microsoft.

In August 2002, Microsoft agreed to settle FTC charges regarding the privacy and security of personal information collected from consumers through its Passport web services. As part of the settlement, Microsoft agreed to implement a comprehensive information security program to protect the privacy and confidentiality of consumers' personal information collected through its Passport and Passport Wallet services, including credit card numbers and billing information stored in Passport Wallet; to provide consumers with identical security at those sites regardless of whether they used Passport Wallet to complete their transactions; and provided parents control over what information participating Web sites could collect from their children.[30] In September 2002, EPIC wrote a letter to the FTC, urging the commission to closely monitor and resolve Microsoft's future security breaches.[31] In February 2003, the European Commission (EC) announced that Microsoft Corporation was going to "substantially modify" its Passport service to conform to EU privacy laws.[32]

The central position of Microsoft, however, has meant and will mean that it will continue to be scrutinized very closely. It has, for example, made great strides in developing more privacy-friendly identity management systems. In the fall of 2006, it launched a new global identity management system based on seven Laws of Identity, and won praise from some privacy advocates, as a more reasonable effort to base the technology on some central privacy laws.[33] In November 2005, the company called upon Congress to enact a federal privacy protection law citing: "the increasingly complex patchwork of state, federal, and even international laws related to data privacy and security; the potential for consumer fears about identity theft and other online dangers to dampen online commerce; and the increasing consumer desire for more control over the collection and use of online and offline personal information."[34] The move won praise from many privacy advocates.[35]

Data Spills

In each of the previous cases, powerful interests on the other side of the debate have sought to defend the particular scheme or program for personal data processing. Various public interests were, and are, articulated in favor of census surveys, national identification programs, and key-escrow cryptography. In the private-sector cases, a variety of arguments for letting the "market decide" were advanced: if consumers did not like these products, they could opt out or choose others. Regardless of the cogency of these various arguments, the point is that organizations felt able to defend their intentions and their practices. There was a debate about rights and wrongs.

The final, and most recent, category of conflicts concerns practices that are essentially indefensible. The privacy news of the first years of the twenty-first century has been dominated by cases of data breaches. The stakes are high for consumers, because one tape missing, one laptop stolen, or one unshredded pile of forms in a garbage dump can compromise the privacy rights of millions of individuals. The cost to the reputations of companies, in terms of lower consumer trust, is also high. Since 2005, the Privacy Rights Clearinghouse has been documenting the extent and frequency of data breaches, and has estimated that, as of January 2008, around 218 million records of American citizens have been compromised by a staggering variety of state, federal, and local agencies, and private corporations.[36] Similar stories have arisen in every advanced industrial state, to the extent that larger questions about legal obligations for organizations to notify consumers about data breaches have become one of the most difficult, and hotly debated, topics among privacy experts (Schwartz and Janger 2007). Data breaches can occur through willful attempts at identify theft, or through sheer sloppiness. One highly publicized example of each will highlight the role that advocates have played.

There is no doubt that the contemporary attention to data breaches is partially attributable to the most high-profile case of its kind, involving ChoicePoint. Few had heard of this giant commercial data brokerage firm before the scandal erupted in 2004, although it did receive a Big Brother Award in 2001. EPIC and others had been pursuing the practices of the company through FOIA requests, and on the basis of the information contained therein, wrote to the FTC in December 2004. Among other things, EPIC argued that some of ChoicePoint's data constituted "consumer reports," thus subjecting both the information seller and the buyer to regulation under the Fair Credit Reporting Act. Later in December 2004, ChoicePoint answered the EPIC letter, disputed the allegations and called for a national debate on their practices.

That debate occurred both in the online and offline media, and revealed that the company had sold personal information on at least 145,000 Americans to a criminal ring engaged in identity theft.[37] Criminals essentially tricked the company by posing as legitimate businesses and thus gained access to various ChoicePoint databases. They obtained names, addresses, social security numbers, credit reports, and other information. As a result, a number of suspicious accounts were opened in the name of nonexistent debt collectors, insurance agencies and other companies. At that time, California was the only state that required disclosure of data breaches, and so the firm sent around 3,500 letters to California residents telling them their personal data may have been stolen by criminals who set up fake companies and downloaded information from

ChoicePoint. The company initially suggested the theft of information might be limited to that state. On meeting with law enforcement officials, they decided to mail an additional 110,000 letters to the other victims.

This revelation led to an FTC investigation, to legislative hearings, and to a final settlement. The FTC charged that ChoicePoint violated the Fair Credit Reporting Act (FCRA) by furnishing credit histories to subscribers who did not have a permissible purpose to obtain them, and by failing to maintain reasonable procedures to verify both their identities and how they intended to use the information. The agency also charged that the company violated the FTC Act by making false and misleading statements about its privacy policies. The settlement obliged ChoicePoint to pay $10 million in civil penalties and $5 million in consumer redress to settle these charges. It was also obliged to implement new procedures to ensure that it provides consumer reports only to legitimate businesses for lawful purposes, to establish and maintain a comprehensive information security program, and to obtain audits by an independent third-party security professional every other year until 2026. ChoicePoint's name became synonymous with identity theft. The Web site Consumerist.com named it the second worst company in America. It received a "Lifetime Menace Award" from Privacy International. The company was "named and shamed."

The ChoicePoint case really was not a "breach" or a "spill" at all because it was the company's corporate policy to sell these data. The second illustration stemmed from sheer corporate sloppiness. In the spring of 2000, Eli Lilly and Company launched Medi-messenger, an e-mail service associated with the company's Prozac Web site. Interested subscribers enrolled in the program at Prozac.com, and thus signed up for their own personalized e-mail reminder to take their medication. At the time of enrollment, subscribers were invited to view the Prozac.com privacy statement, which said that the privacy and confidentiality of the personal information subscribers provided would be protected. In 2001, the company decided to discontinue the Medi-messenger program. An Eli Lilly employee created an e-mail message using the Medi-messenger enrollment information and sent a single message addressed to all 669 subscribers, stating that the service was being terminated. The problem was that all e-mail addresses were apparent.

The ACLU then complained to the FTC, arguing that the company had been negligent, and that its privacy notice was misleading in claiming that appropriate security measures were taken. The FTC agreed. By making visible the e-mail addresses of all its Medi-messenger subscribers in a single message, Eli Lilly's claims of protecting subscribers' privacy constituted unfair or deceptive acts or practices because inadequate measures were implemented to train employees and to protect Medi-messenger users' private information. Although Eli Lilly unintentionally disclosed private information, it did not admit to violating any laws, and no fines were imposed; yet it agreed to provide more internal security measures to protect end user privacy, and to publish yearly written reviews by qualified persons of its security measures.[38] The FTC has since conducted several enforcement actions against companies in which no compromise of security has occurred. In those cases, the FTC reviewed the business' security practices and found that they did not fulfill assurances about security made in the companies' privacy policies.

In countries with comprehensive privacy protection statutes, such breaches are typically investigated by the respective data protection authorities. In Canada, for example, there have been several such investigations, the most notable being the inquiry into the Canadian Imperial Bank of Commerce (CIBC) in 2004. In this case, faxes containing the personal information of CIBC customers were misdirected by various branches of the bank to a company in the United States and another in Dorval, Quebec. The only action taken by the bank was to request that the faxes be shredded. The bank took no further action, and did not notify the customers concerned. The commissioner concluded that "the bank's privacy practices were seriously tested by these incidents, and they failed. These incidents are a wake-up call not only to CIBC but to every organization in Canada that collects, uses, or discloses personal information in the course of its commercial activities."[39]

The frequency and variety of data breaches have brought the importance of appropriate privacy and security measures to the attention of the general public in a remarkable way. The various problems are typically framed and conflated in the media as "identity theft" even though most data breaches do not necessarily result in severe and fraudulent activity.[40] Public interest organizations have grown up specifically to educate consumers, help victims, and lobby for better laws.[41] Ordinary individuals are affected not only by media reports but more especially by the process of direct notification that they might be a victim and by the considerable inconvenience when credit cards have to be changed, with implications for online banking and for automatic bill payments. Furthermore the apparent risks can be invoked to some effect when broader identification schemes are being debated. At the same time, they are indefensible.

For the most part, they do not require systematic campaigns to sensitize individuals and organizations of the harm. The public conversation can focus on the remedies rather than the inherent rights and wrongs.

Conditions for Success

Each of the cases described in this chapter reached high levels of public and political attention. Each involved the collection and processing of personal data on millions of people. For the most part, we have been talking about grand schemes with huge implications. Each resulted in abandonment or substantial changes in the schemes initially proposed. The early census protests meant that no further national censuses occurred in Germany and the Netherlands. The Australia Card proposal was defeated, with the result that the public regarded the contemporary scheme for an Access Card with greater skepticism. Lotus Marketplace never happened. Centralized key-escrow encryption schemes are a thing of the past. Intel never implemented its Processor Serial Number. Double-Click did not get to merge clickstream data with offline databases. Microsoft was chastened by its initial scheme for online authentication. And public and private organizations cannot adopt a cavalier attitude toward information security given the loss of reputation and consumer trust that can arise from data breaches.

To be sure, these "success stories" might have been temporary and they may be exceptional. Moreover, we can never determine whether it was the appeal to privacy that stopped or altered these schemes, or whether they would have collapsed anyway, as a result of other and more powerful forces. But in a rhetorical climate that contends that societies are drifting inexorably toward a surveillance society, it is relevant to pose the question: why, in these cases, were the interests of powerful governmental and corporate players thwarted? What conditions prevailed in these cases? The answer can be stated forthrightly in terms of a wider theory of political action. In each case, privacy advocates employed an appropriate blend of information, symbolic, accountability and leverage politics.

In each there was a relatively coordinated information strategy targeted at both the general public and political and business elites. Further, in each there was serious research, sophisticated analysis, and technical and legal expertise marshaled and presented. In each the privacy advocacy network had to be taken seriously because it made a credible effort to get its facts straight. They were then providing a valuable resource for public and political debate. These cases are all characterized by the fact that the network was contributing value-added to the debate, by advancing facts—and not just speculation and hypothesis. On the Australia Card campaign, Roger Clarke emphasizes the importance of a "combination of a highly accurate understanding of technological, legal, and social systems coupled with media savvy."[42]

The costs of getting the facts wrong should not be underestimated, especially where advocates have little access to the industry and have to rely, to some extent, on questionable media reporting. As Chris Hoofnagle, formerly of EPIC, explains: "Sometimes that leads to error. And the problem with making errors is that the denial industry begins. If you make an error, they will crucify you on it. They will harp on about it. It does not matter what they have done."[43] Yet in most of these cases, the preponderance of suspicion about who was shielding, eliding, or even misrepresenting the facts in the end tends to rest with the other side. Davies recognizes that "the most powerful booster in the promotion of privacy is the word 'deception.' You usually find that a privacy violation in combination with secrecy or deception ends up creating quite a stir … People are prepared to say the government or the company has the benefit of the doubt as long as they are open. But when they find out there's secrecy and deception people say the deal is off. It's very powerful to be able to say that this has happened behind your back. That's the most powerful imagery or message you could couple with the privacy issue."[44]

At important moments in each of these disputes, the public agency or business lost the confidence of the public because of disingenuous statements, or strategic errors of communication. Privacy advocates rarely catch an organization in an obvious lie. But overtime they can question the consistency between public statements and the empirical realities of a technology, service, or program. The "how can X and Y both be true" questions persisted in these debates and over time reduced the credibility of the organization. For example, how can the Clipper chip be promoted as a voluntary standard, when the last people who would use such technology are those whom law enforcement hopes to catch? How can the new Access Card in Australia not be an identity card, when its features closely parallel those of the old Australia card? How can it be true that the German census information would only be used for statistical, rather than administrative, purposes? And so on.

In each of these cases, the debate about the facts was also accompanied by skilful uses of symbols that appealed to the wider populace. Davies reflects on the lessons learned from ID card conflicts: "Most public opposition to administration strategies such as numbering systems, identity cards or the census are structured around an organized campaign of negative imagery (Big Brother) and a more systematic process of public education. In the Netherlands and German anticensus movements, and in the campaign against the Australia Card, hostile imagery sat comfortably alongside a strong intellectual foundation of opposition."[45]

But Big Brother has become a cliché, so the task is to spice up the more objective and analytical information in original ways that appeal to the media. Roger Clarke's favored spice is "pepper": "When the time is right there's got to be pepper. But the pepper has got to be measured. We do have to say things that are reasonably peppery otherwise the media won't cover it but also because it won't get noticed even if the media does cover it. It must sting the organizations that are behaving inappropriately. But it must not be such that everybody can just brush aside the advocates because they are obviously just a bunch of rag-bags, saying 'look how they talk?'"[46] In each of the cases discussed here, there was plenty of potential to add the right amount of pepper to the media commentary. The opportunities were partly provided by the extraordinary scale and ambition of the surveillance programs being resisted. Each in their own way involved the potential for the building of massive databases of personal information, which were easy to caste in the over-reaching, omniscient, intrusive symbolism of Big Brother. Clearly some commentators went too far and became discredited. Others obviously used the right amount of "pepper."

As I argued in chapter 4, symbols have to resonate within a culture, especially when there is an existing level of mistrust with the organizations concerned. This is a striking feature of the cases described here. They either involved programs introduced by governments whose standing in public opinion was at the time relatively low. Or they related to organizations (e.g., Microsoft and Intel) whose market dominance had provoked mistrust for other reasons. Or they concerned companies (such as DoubleClick and ChoicePoint) about whom the majority of people had never heard. Privacy advocates were able to employ their symbols against large organizations whose standing in public opinion was already fragile. Their arguments against surveillance resonated, and reinforced images of remote and uncaring organizations.

In each of these cases, the privacy advocacy network engaged in efforts of what we have termed accountability politics. In the German census dispute, complaints were lodged with the federal and state data protection commissioners. In the Australia Card case, there were complaints to the federal privacy commissioner. In JukiNet, there were a series of cases brought before local courts. The Clipper chip proposals and the Intel PSN were subjected to a series of FOIA requests. DoubleClick, Microsoft, Intel, and ChoicePoint were the subjects of FTC complaints. Microsoft was investigated by European data protection commissioners. Over time, it appears that the privacy advocacy network has become more expert in seeking opportunities to use different official avenues of redress. The network should also remember that any commitment to privacy protection by a government agency or a business provides an opportunity to demand accountability, however weak and qualified that commitment might be.

In few of these cases, however, did a resulting judgment precipitate the downfall of the proposal in question. Official complaints might provide an initial "media moment," but the investigative processes always take time. Any impact is often felt after the fact. Official complaints can also be a two-edged sword. They may result in a clarification of law that was not consistent with the expectations of advocates. They do serve, however, as mechanisms to get at the facts, and on occasion to force the organization to reach a settlement. As we have noted, the threat of complaint can also be used as leverage. No private corporation wants it known that it is the subject of a complaint to a regulatory body, nor do its shareholders and customers. In each of these cases, there were attempts to leverage results through the power of negative publicity.

Any contemporary privacy campaign ideally needs, therefore, a combination of information, accountability, leverage, and symbolic politics: clear presentation of facts and analysis, ideally backed up by research; a media strategy that presents those facts with symbols that resonate with the wider culture; the use of official avenues of redress, both domestically and internationally; and the judicious use of opportunities to name and shame that affect reputation and image.

It is probable, therefore, that this combination of strategies cannot be effectively pursued without a coalition. This is one further trend. In the early years, privacy advocacy groups did tend to go it alone. Now, there are explicit attempts to make common cause and to use the expertise in other advocacy groups to bring the full range of political resources to bear. In each of these cases, campaigns were waged by a number of groups, brought together on an ad hoc basis to fight the case in question. In some of these cases—Clipper, for example—the coalition building went beyond the privacy advocacy network to embrace sympathetic corporations. There is therefore a growing recognition of the importance of finding a consonance between privacy and other political agendas. How have these efforts affected the privacy advocacy network? What other groups and interests have been marshaled to the cause? What is the "glue" that binds them, and how does the Internet provide this "glue"? These questions will be addressed in chapter 6.

6 The Networks

More than one of my respondents for this project referred to the above passage from Monty Python's *Life of Brian* in depicting the privacy advocacy scene today. There is disagreement over strategic direction as well as perennial competitions for funding. There is a good deal of suspicion by those on the "outside" of the deals made by those on the "inside." Some actors have been around for a long time. Historical legacies can create personality conflicts that endure and can be detrimental. Here is Gus Hosein of PI: "There's this trend in the NGO community to call it "civil society." This is an oxymoron, because we are not civil and we are not a society. We fight over funding. We fight over issues. We fight over attention. A lot of us don't even like each other."[1]

Yet internal competition and conflict within a network are not peculiar to privacy protection. Every social movement exhibits internal struggles, which sometime spill over into personal tensions. More important than the personalities is the nature and strength of the network itself. This chapter concerns the connections within the privacy advocacy network, and between that network and other organizations. I have used the concept of the privacy advocacy network to describe the very loose set of organizations and individuals in civil society who have engaged with the privacy issue over the years. In chapter 2, I concluded that there were privacy-centric, privacy-explicit, and privacy-marginal groups. Beyond that there is an almost limitless universe of potential groups who might in the future have to engage with the issue. In chapter 3, I depicted the network at the individual level, concluding that there is a loose collection of privacy/activists, privacy/researchers, privacy/consultants, privacy/ technologists, privacy/journalists, and privacy/artists—all of whom have to negotiate different and overlapping roles and obligations in their work. But to what extent and in what ways do these individuals and groups "network"?

Network analysis can be conducted at different levels of abstraction. According to Manual Castells, "networks are open structures, able to expand without limits, integrating new nodes as long as they are able to communicate within the network, namely as long as they share the same communication codes. . . . A network-based social structure is a highly dynamic, open system, susceptible to innovating without threatening its balance" (1996, 470). While social networks have existed at other times, new information technology provides the basis for their pervasive expansion throughout the entire social structure. Castells contends that networks constitute the new logic of modern societies, and are substantially altering all social, political, economic, and cultural processes. The power of networks and the flows of information they facilitate are thus more important than specific interests: "the power of flows takes precedence over the flows of power" (Ibid.). The "network society" is exactly the kind of social organization within which new social movements can be expected to challenge hierarchies and existing discourses. It is exactly the kind of decentralized and open form of social structure that would allow resistance to the centralized concentration and accumulation of personal information. According to Castells, it should permit an antisurveillance politics of the kind documented in previous chapters. We will return to these larger themes in the concluding chapter.

For Castells, the notion of the network has become a way to label contemporary advanced industrial "information" societies. It is then elevated to the status of an all-encompassing general theory with its own set of norms and discourses (Barney 2004, 179). At a less lofty level of analysis, there is a new science of network analysis that has gained increasing popularity among academics of different disciplines concerned with trying to understand the complexity of social organizations in the context of globalization and advances in information technology. There is, of course, nothing new about loose, leaderless, and amorphous networks; the student movements of the 1960s are a prominent example. The Internet, however, has provided a kind of laboratory of human behavior through which political and social organization can be studied and compared with equivalent processes in the offline world.

At this level, networks mean something very particular with some clear empirical referents: nodes, ties and flows. A node is a distinct point in the network (e.g., an individual, a firm, a computer, an NGO). Ties connect one node to another (e.g., mail, e-mail, contracts). Flows (e.g., speech, data, money) pass along these ties between the nodes. As Darin Barney explains: "Attached to each of these three elements is a number of variables which, taken together, condition the character of any given network. Nodes can be powerful or powerless, active or dormant, stationary or mobile, permanent or temporary, net sources or net recipients of various kinds of flows. Ties ... can be strong or weak, private or public, singular or multiple, unique or redundant, sparse or dense, parallel or intersecting. Flows ... can be copious or minimal, constant or intermittent, one-way or reciprocal, uni-or multidirectional, balanced or imbalanced, meaningful or meaningless" (2004, 26). The various permutations of these variables thus determine the degree of centralization, hierarchy, openness, accessibility, inclusiveness, intensity and interactivity of the network.

The ultimate purpose of this chapter is to advance our understanding of the characteristics of the privacy advocacy network. We know something of the "nodes" from chapters 3 and 4. But what are the "ties" that connect the actors and organizations together, and that determine the "flows" of information. Four are important to discuss at some length—conferences, campaigns, coalitions, and more generally the impact of "net activism."

Privacy Conferences

The policy community associated with privacy attends, and has always attended, an enormous number of conferences, workshops, symposia, forums, and other events. These more traditional forms of networking have historically been the principal means by which privacy advocates have connected and shared information. There is no evidence that the scope and frequency of conferencing has decreased as online methods of networking have proliferated. Conferences may be organized by governmental agencies, by the private sector, by academic institutions, or by a combination. Privacy advocacy groups have played significant roles in all.

Robert Ellis Smith has an interesting take on privacy conferences: "I think also the interdisciplinary aspect of this issue has something to do with it. You don't find that in any of the other movements. Here I think it is quite unique where you get academics, activists and business people all in the same room. No privacy conference can function with only one of those segments."[2] Not only is this view a reflection of the overlapping nature of the privacy issue, embracing government, the private sector, and civil society. It also reveals an interesting dynamic about these different communities. It suggests that there are few occasions when advocates or activists can convene in order set priorities and plot strategy. Indeed, one of the only conferences of privacy advocates/activists in the last decade was organized by *Privacy Journal* itself, discussed in chapter 3. Even then, this conference of "privacy activists" still involved participants with governmental and business affiliations.

Civil society advocates do not have much money. They depend on governmental, academic, or private-sector sponsorship to get together. This produces interesting dynamics and occasional conflicts. It is quite commonplace for speeches and presentations to be given critical of the very organizations that are paying for the hall rental, the microphones, and the refreshments. Many of the more vocal privacy advocates see no conflict, but there must be limits. However much advocates wish to see the issue in terms of "us" and "them," the practicalities of privacy conferences mean that the civil society groups are not necessarily seen as distinct from governmental, academic, and industry participants. They are an essential part of one larger network, certainly playing different roles, but also in constant engagement on formal and informal levels with representatives from organizations who may be responsible for the very surveillance they are challenging.

Indeed, there has probably only been one regularly scheduled conference that has had the reputation of providing a forum for privacy advocates to speak their minds, regardless of who was in the audience, or who was paying for the coffee. The annual Computers, Freedom and Privacy (CFP) conference has been mentioned before. It began in 1991 primarily in an effort to bring together the law enforcement and hacker communities in the United States to improve mutual understanding. Its original raison d'être was to provide a forum where those in government and business could start to understand the Internet and its subculture at a time when tensions were running high. The first few years saw a fascinating interaction between different communities with different assumptions about how this new communication space should evolve, with different discourses, and different modes of behavior. As Wendy Grossman put it: "In this period, the raw meat thrown to the conference lions tended to be hapless government officials who had no idea anyone cared—until they had to face a room full of 500 heavy-metal crypto heads quivering with passion and outrage."[3] Hotels with vulnerable security systems were sometimes victims of some high-tech pranks by the assembled hacking community. In 1994, one of the visiting FBI agents actually arrested a conference bystander under the impression that he was the hacker, Kevin Mitnick.

More important, the CFP conference became institutionalized and developed its own culture. Discussions extended well into the night in "Birds of a Feather" (BOF) sessions. It gained a reputation as *the* conference to attend if you wanted to keep up with the many social and political implications of evolving technologies. In the words of Roger Clarke, "The program and delegates' list is such a 'who's who' that you keep an eye on the name-badges around you, in case you get the chance to finally meet the meat behind a long-known cyberspace persona. And that you do. Everyone's accessible, and interested in sampling the views of anyone who's interested enough to turn up."[4] The participants, the discussions, and the culture mirrored the fascinating evolution of the global networks and the World Wide Web. Over the last ten years, CFP has not had the same flavor. Despite efforts by successive conference chairs to return the conference to its more controversial roots, it is less confrontational, and therefore less well attended. By 1996, as Lorrie Faith Cranor noted, the "old cyberspace as electronic frontier—occupied by early settlers, the techno-elite—was giving way to the new cyberspace as electronic suburbia."[5]

Beginning in the mid-1990s, the annual meeting of the international privacy and data commissioners began to involve outsiders to a greater extent. Civil society groups were invited, initially as observers, and subsequently as participants on relevant panels. This conference is now a major international event, with significant sponsorship. It is typically used by the host to gain media and political attention to the issue within his or her respective country. In 2006, for instance, Richard Thomas, the U.K. information commissioner, used the opportunity to launch a major international study on the surveillance society (Surveillance Studies Network 2006). Individual privacy advocates can play important supporting roles at this conference. Some civil society groups also use the opportunity to organize their own one-day workshop in advance of the main event, such as that organized by the International Civil Liberties Monitoring Group in advance of the Montreal Commissioners' conference in 2007. But the international privacy and data commissioners conference is primarily designed for the data protection authorities themselves. It allows them to draw lessons from their counterparts overseas, and occasionally to declare common statements on issues of common interest.[6]

A further conference we should note is the World Summit on the Information Society, which occurred in Geneva in 2003 and Tunis in 2005. These were high-level events, endorsed by the UN General Assembly and involving thousands of participants from most countries of the world. Each summit also required much preparatory work through an elaborate Working Group structure. The final declarations from the Geneva and Tunis summits refer to the importance of privacy. The former, for instance, declares that "within this global culture of cyber-security, it is important to enhance security and to ensure the protection of data and privacy, while enhancing access and trade."[7] The Tunis Declaration called upon all stakeholders to "ensure respect for privacy and the protection of personal information and data, whether via adoption of legislation, the implementation of collaborative frameworks, best practices and self-regulatory and technological measures by business and users."[8]

However, both references are buried in these respective documents, indicating that privacy was never going to be a prominent issue for the large numbers of developing societies concerned about economic infrastructure questions, and the more authoritarian regimes fixated on national security issues. Ralf Bendrath, one of the co-coordinators of the Privacy and Security Working Group of WSIS has documented the difficulty of injecting privacy and civil liberties language into these documents in the face of strong security agendas. He and his colleagues lobbied tirelessly to improve the language from a privacy perspective, and thereby inject the issue into the broader debate about the information society. But the results were disappointing, and civil society groups eventually disassociated themselves from the official summit documents, and distributed their own set of commitments. More important than the results of WSIS were the networking opportunities. Bendrath's conclusions are instructive:

As the WSIS example has shown, privacy advocacy groups are much more successful if they work toward roughly the same goals as the private sector, even if coming from different angles. This has repeatedly been the case in the past, e.g., in the U.S. "crypto wars" against the Clinton administration's plan to install a backdoor in encryption systems ... However, as those past privacy lobbying efforts which were lost have also shown, the notion of privacy still has to struggle with the "security" agenda. Privacy also has still some way to go before it becomes a value that is supported and taken serious by a broad majority of players.

To the majority of WSIS governmental delegates, or even civil society groups, privacy remained a marginal issue, abstract in content, and much harder to grasp and advocate than, for instance, freedom of expression.[9]

Privacy Campaigns

For much of the 1990s, and beyond, the privacy advocacy network has engaged in campaigns against specific measures or programs. There is, of course, no common understanding about what does, and does not, constitute a "campaign." It is probably the case that most advocates would regard campaigns as relatively broad based and involving a number of different actors. Campaigns generally also imply some duration, or at least more than an ephemeral interest in a topic. Beyond that, there is considerable variation across four dimensions—the nature of the launch, the breadth, the duration, and whether they are uni- or multi-centered. We can analyze these variations with reference to some of the cases discussed in chapter 5.

With some campaigns, and particularly those that predated the Internet, there is an official "launch." The Australia Card campaign, for instance, was formerly initiated on August 31, 1987, at the Sebel Town House in Kings Cross, Sydney. The media attended in large numbers, and the campaign led the evening news across Australia. APF was inaugurated at the same time and the campaign gained momentum from that time on. Another example is the Global Internet Liberty Campaign (GILC), unveiled by EPIC and the ACLU at the 1996 meeting of the Internet Society, and funded by the Open Society Institute's Internet Program. This campaign brought together a diverse group of new, and established, human rights and civil liberties organizations from five continents. However, it lacked institutional and policy focus and its activities waned by the end of the decade.[10]

Typically, however, it has not been common to launch a campaign with a public event at one defined moment. The campaign against Lotus Marketplace emerged spontaneously, initially within the mainstream media, and then through electronic bulletin boards. There was little orchestration of these online protests. The campaign against Clipper also emerged quickly and spontaneously within a number of newsgroups, although there was more orchestration by the EFF and CPSR. The former convened the Digital Privacy and Security Working Group (DPSWG). The latter coordinated the electronic petition that had its origins in a letter sent to President Clinton by CPSR, and signed by a number of famous cryptographers. Marc Rotenberg explains: "Soon the letter became a petition. And then researchers, students, and company CEOs put their names to the statement. In all, more than forty-seven thousand people on the Internet said "I oppose Clipper" and supported our effort to send a clear message to the White House that it was not for the government to prevent citizens from using good tools for privacy protection. The Clipper campaign was probably the most successful petition drive ever organized on the Internet."[11] However, it is very difficult to pinpoint a specific date at which a "campaign" against Clipper was officially launched.

This pattern of spontaneous and unpredictable action from a multitude of "netizens," combined with a certain prompting and orchestration from those within the privacy advocacy network, characterizes the other major privacy campaigns of the 1990s. The campaigns against DoubleClick, against Intel, against MS Passport, and later against Google's Gmail product were all a blend of spontaneous protest and more centralized orchestration. These campaigns were not "launched." They didn't need to be. They evolved organically through a steady accumulation of dispersed actions, which occasionally came together in a concerted manner, and more often did not.

The breadth of campaign support is also an important variable to consider. The typical pattern by which campaign support is mustered is for one group to take the lead, perhaps draft a letter or a complaint, and then circulate for support. Other groups then sign on. The strategy is a common one within social movement politics. It is, as Lee Tien of the EFF remarks, not difficult to get people to sign on, provided someone else is doing the work:

The strategy of coalition building and the strategy of getting other people to do work tend to converge. It helps that we are [the] EFF because we have a pretty high profile and people will pay attention to us. If I suggest to a number of people that a certain issue is important and we ought to do something on it, we then get the usual suspects to sign on. We do the initial heavy-lifting and then they will come in. That often will work.... A lot of time we'll just do it and see if anybody picks up on it. It depends on how much time we have, and how well we know this issue.[12]

There is also an assumption that the longer and more diverse the list of groups endorsing a particular campaign, the greater the chance of success. When we examine the history, both in the United States and elsewhere, the connection between the size and diversity of campaign support and the ultimate success is far from clear. There have been some very widely coordinated campaigns that have achieved next to nothing. For example, in the wake of the publication of the Patriot Act after 9/11, a broad-based coalition was formed in opposition called the "In Defense of Freedom Coalition." It involved around 150 organizations, 300 law professors, and 40 computer scientists, from different countries, all of whom subscribed to a ten-point statement about the attacks of 9/11. But the coalition was not established to support or oppose specific legislation, and has had very little impact on, for example, the Patriot Act, or on its later reauthorization under the sunset provisions. The coalition has been dormant since 2004.[13]

It is also worth examining the successive campaigns against Google, which since its startup in 1998 has been gradually and systematically trying to "organize the world's information and make it universally accessible and useful." Its foundation is, of course, the search engine, which depends on a Web crawler that accesses indexes and caches web content. It also applies a precedence algorithm that sorts the pages that match any given search-string into a sequence that is designed to be helpful for the particular user. Google now provides many services that are increasingly interlinked and interleveraged. Some have been developed internally. Others have been acquired through takeover.

Privacy concerns first arose in a major way in April 1, 2004, when Google launched its free e-mail program, Gmail. The program automatically stores, processes, and maintains e-mails, contact lists, and other data, to relieve the user of having to manage or delete e-mail messages. Gmail is supported by advertisers who buy keywords, and uses "content extraction" on all incoming and outgoing e-mail in order to target the advertising to the user. For example, if the user is having an e-mail conversation about arranging a game of golf, Gmail might present the user with ads about golf vacations, golf products, alternative courses, and so on.

The privacy advocacy network soon sprung into action, and the campaign was broad and transnational. On April 6, thirty-one privacy and civil liberties groups signed an open letter, coauthored by the World Privacy Forum and the Privacy Rights Clearinghouse, asking the cofounders of Google Inc., Sergey Brin and Larry Page, to suspend scanning of e-mail text for ad placement, set clear data retention and deletion dates, and establish detailed written privacy policies about data sharing among its business partners. Of particular concern was the privacy rights of nonsubscribers who had not consented, and indeed may not even be aware that their communications were being analyzed or that profiles were being compiled. On April 9, the EFF announced that it was engaging in talks with Google about this service. On April 19, 2004, PI filed a

complaint asking the privacy and data protection commissioners of many
of the EU countries to investigate the privacy implications of Google's
Gmail service. On April 23, APF wrote a letter to the Australian Federal
Privacy Commissioner expressing concerns regarding Google's violation
of the Privacy Act of 1988.[14]

Particular attention focused on legislative developments in California.
In February 2004, State Senator Liz Fitgueroa had introduced Bill SB
1822 in an attempt to address privacy concerns with regards to the sale
of social security numbers. In April, the bill was amended heavily to pro-
hibit a provider of an electronic mail or instant messaging service from
knowingly divulging or deriving personally identifiable information, user
characteristics, or content of an electronic mail or instant message while
the electronic mail or instant message is being electronically stored by
the provider. With this legislation, scanning was only allowed with the
consent of all parties. In May, EPIC, the World Privacy Forum, and the
Privacy Rights Clearinghouse also sent a letter to California Attorney
General Bill Lockyer calling for an investigation of the Gmail service for
possible violations of state eavesdropping and wiretapping laws. The
letter pointed out that California law requires the consent of all of the
parties involved. If Google were found to be in violation of California's
Penal Code 631, Gmail users could face possible civil and criminal penal-
ties.[15] A separate letter was also sent out on this day to Google cofounders Sergey Brin and Larry Page, notifying them of Google and Gmail
users' possible liability.

Google's response was to defend itself strenuously. They lobbied
against the California bill and secured the removal of the major consent
provisions; the Online Privacy Protection Act went into effect in June
2004. Even though Google changed its main privacy policy as a result of
this legislation, nothing in the law prevented the Gmail service from being
implemented as planned. Google also convinced the California attorney
general that there was no potential exposure of Gmail users to the provisions of California's penal code. European data protection authorities
were also powerless, because there was no way to prove that Google
were in any way dishonest about their intentions, nor planning to profile
personally identifiable information.

Google also quickly and effectively waged its own media campaign,
especially in the computer trade press. A series of sympathetic articles
appeared. For a while, also free Gmail accounts were only available on
a very limited basis to Google employees and friends. They skillfully
manipulated the anticipation of this new service by sending out free

e-mail packages to many journalists. For a few weeks, invitations to open a free Gmail account were actually being sold on eBay. Google also skillfully used the power and centrality of its Web page to convey a very strong message that there had been a lot of misinformation circulated about Gmail, that e-mail content was not going to be shared with third parties, that Gmail did not violate the privacy of nonsubscribers, and that the provision of information by Gmail subscribers was entirely consensual.[16]

Thus the Google campaign had a rather different outcome from those against DoubleClick, Intel, and Microsoft. There was immediate pressure exerted on a number of fronts, but the Gmail service was introduced, and to this day operates basically as planned. The privacy advocacy network was left with a lot of questions about the extent to which consumer profiling actually takes place within Google, about the relevance of several important patents registered in Google's name, and with a series of admonitions to the privacy-conscious Internet user to subscribe to other e-mail services. Google was also clearly prepared for the protest, and responded with a brilliantly coordinated media strategy of its own. It had learned from previous privacy campaigns.

At time of writing, Google is also under scrutiny from the network for the privacy implications of its StreetView application, as well as for its proposed takeover of DoubleClick. Unlike some of the other campaigns, therefore, this is ongoing, and perhaps open-ended. Many of the others, such as those against Intel, DoubleClick, Microsoft, or ChoicePoint, were defined by a relatively precise endpoint when the company backed down, or settled a complaint, and a "victory" of sorts could be declared. Because of the breadth and power of Google, however, the campaigns against its various applications seem more multifaceted, complex, and inextricably tied to far larger considerations about market control.

Other campaigns have also been quite open-ended. On the face of it, the NO2ID campaign in Britain initially lost in its attempt to derail the U.K. identity card scheme. However, it is still very active and in so being has continued to critique the implementation of the card scheme, the costs, and the technical requirements. The campaign thus claims that the credibility of the entire scheme has been seriously undermined, and the government of Gordon Brown is reported to be far less enthusiastic than that of Tony Blair.

Finally, with some campaigns it is possible to locate a central group that is responsible for the coordination, and the bulk of the work. The typical dynamic when an issue arises involves a fairly frantic set of conversations within the network, possible conference calls, and checking with experts. Then somebody undertakes to do the "heavy lifting" and requests others to sign on. Occasionally one group takes the lead. Sometimes, more than one centre of gravity evolves, and two or more nodes in the network are visible. In the Clipper campaign, for instance, there was a clear coalition clustered around CDT and its DPSWG, and another centered on the work of CPSR. Two sets of complaints, again emanating from both CDT and EPIC, were lodged against the Intel PSN. The particular network configurations within individual campaigns sometimes have to do with disagreements over strategy. More often they are the result of serendipity, and of who happens to have the time to drop other things and perform the necessary work at the critical time according to a short deadline.

The coordination of privacy campaigns takes time and effort. Some groups do not bother. They will, like PI, simply do their own thing and invite others to join if they so wish. They will eschew attempts at coordination and compromise in favor of rapid action. Despite some considerable successes, the pragmatic and decentralized evolution of these privacy campaigns convinced some in the network that more durable coalitions needed to be forged. The period since 9/11 marks a new, and distinctive, phase in the history of the privacy advocacy network.

Privacy Coalitions

There has been quite a long history of attempts to bring the privacy advocacy network together in the form of more durable and institutionalized coalitions. At the first CFP conference in 1991, for example, the U.S. Privacy Council was established. The purpose was to "build a consensus on privacy needs, means, and ends, and will push to educate the industry, legislatures, and citizens about privacy issues."[17] It formed a newsgroup (alt.privacy), but little else was achieved. It expired in the early 1990s. Similar efforts have been attempted in Canada to link together the disparate groups and individuals within a Canadian Privacy Council.

The need for coordination in the United States is perhaps greater than elsewhere because of the absence of an institutionalized data protection authority. A group called the Privacy Coalition has been meeting in Washington, D.C., since 1995. It is described as a "non-partisan coalition of consumer, civil liberties, educational, family, library, labor and technology organizations" all of whom have agreed in writing to a "Privacy Pledge":

Recognizing the need to protect this essential freedom, I, (insert Member's name), pledge to my constituents in (State and District) and to the American people that I will support a privacy framework to safeguard the rights of Americans in this information age.

This framework includes

1. the Fair Information Practices: the right to notice, consent, security, access, correction, use limitations, and redress when information is improperly used,

2. independent enforcement and oversight,

3. promotion of genuine Privacy Enhancing Technologies that limit the collection of personal information and legal restrictions on surveillance technologies such as those used for locational tracking, video surveillance, electronic profiling, and workplace monitoring, and

4. a solid foundation of federal privacy safeguards that permit the private sector and states to implement supplementary protections as needed.

The coalition formalized its organization in February 2001, and holds monthly meetings coordinated by EPIC and an annual summit in January of each year.[18]

The breadth of this coalition is interesting. In addition to the "usual suspects" it now includes a good number of more conservative groups, such as the American Association of Christian Schools, the Eagle Forum, the American Conservative Union, the Free Congress Foundation, the Liberty Coalition, and the National Rifle Association. This membership serves really as the core for a larger network of potential groups that might come together for individual campaigns. Three major campaigns have so far been launched. In October 2005, coalition members signed on to a letter urging the Secretary of Defense to end the "Joint Advertising and Market Research Studies" Recruiting Database, which was to include name, date of birth, gender, address, telephone, e-mail address, social security number, ethnicity, high school, education level, college, and intended field of study for more than thirty million Americans who are sixteen to twenty-five years old. In 2006, the Privacy Coalition also coordinated a campaign against the proposed exemption of several systems of records by the Department of Homeland Security.[19]

The most extensive campaign was the 2007 opposition to the REAL ID initiative, the proposal requiring states to issue harmonized drivers' licenses by May 2008. Among other strategies, the campaign encouraged individuals to submit comments on the draft regulations for this scheme through the federal government's public submission portal.[20] In the sixty-day comment period, the DHS reported receiving around twelve thousand comments. In just around ten days, a coalition of fifty groups was formed, as well as around eighty separate blogs. The coalition against Real ID also includes some "strange bedfellows," ranging from the National Center for Transgender Equality to OpenCarry.org, a group advocating the ability openly to carry firearms.

The model cannot, and does not, discriminate. Anybody willing to sign the privacy pledge is welcome. The fact that much of this coalition building occurs in cyberspace, thus obviating the need for face-to-face meetings, obviously assists the process. Further, whereas some groups can sign on without serious internal consultation with members or boards, others (such as Common Cause) have quite lengthy and bureaucratic processes before public commitments to a particular campaign can be made. The organizers of the privacy coalition clearly envisage that this model provides a more efficient way to marshal support for a particular cause, than does the more pragmatic and decentralized campaigns of the past. However, they do exhaust a lot of time and effort, possibly drawing resources away from other initiatives.

Another group that defines itself as a "coalition" is the Coalition for Patient Privacy, centered in Austin, Texas: "We are parents, patients, doctors, lawyers, nurses, advocates, industry insiders, social workers, caregivers and caretakers. We are people who use health care services and citizens who want to restore our fundamental constitutional right— the right to medical privacy."[21] The coalition was formed in the wake of the passage of the privacy regulations made pursuant to the 1996 Health Insurance Portability and Accountability Act of 1996, and especially as a result of the belief that these rules had been interpreted too loosely to permit the sharing of patient medical information. The coalition runs an electronic petition, and has been pressing Congress to strengthen patient consent provisions in the wake of a weakening of these rules in 2003, and wider measures to establish interoperability standards for electronic health records. This coalition is also broad-based, and includes conservative groups such as the Christian Coalition of America, the Free Congress Foundation, the Republican Liberty Caucus, the American Conservative Union, and Right March.com.

The quite recent phenomenon of embracing the privacy interests of those from all sides of the political spectrum is also evident within other coalitions in other countries. A Canadian coalition, the International Civil Liberties Monitoring Group (ICLMG), was formed in 2002 to monitor the implementation of Canadian antiterrorism legislation. It brings together over thirty NGOs representing the labor movement, environmental organizations, refugee and immigration advocates, humanitarian and international development advocates, faith-based organizations, as well as civil liberties and human rights representatives. Their concerns are the broad human rights implications of counterterrorism measures, including racism, refugee protection, and political dissent. The coalition also includes faith-based groups, and notably the Canadian Friends Service Committee (CFSC) of the Religious Society of Friends (the Quakers). Deeply concerned about the implications for world peace as a result of overreactions to the 9/11 attacks, the Quakers have been very active in the ICLMG. As the CFSC explained to its members: "Before December 2001, this issue was not on the agenda as an active concern in any CFSC committee. Well, after the attacks of September 11th, our usually quiet meetings for worship became quite noisy. Expressions of grief and sorrow were followed by searching for nonviolent responses and by a renewed commitment toward working for peace."[22]

In April 2005, the Quakers, through their Friends' Committee on National Legislation, joined the ACLU, the ICLMG, Statewatch, and Focus on the Global South to launch an International Campaign Against Mass Surveillance. A report entitled "The Emergence of a Global Infrastructure for Mass Registration and Surveillance" was published with the launch of the campaign. The report begins: "Governments have begun to construct, through numerous initiatives, what amounts to a global registration and surveillance infrastructure. This infrastructure would ensure that populations around the world are registered, that travel is tracked globally, that electronic communications and transactions can be easily monitored, and that all the information that is collected in public and private databases about individuals is stored, linked, data-mined, and made available to state security agents."[23] As of December 2006, an impressive 180 groups from all over the world had endorsed the campaign. On the other hand, endorsement can require no more than the submission of a very brief endorsement form with name of organization, country, contact person, and e-mail address.

Efforts at coalition building have also been seen recently in Europe. The European Digital Rights Initiative (EDRI) was discussed in chapter 2. Begun in 2002, its initial rationale was to coordinate the work of European civil liberties groups at the European level, as well as to counter the U.S. dominance within the privacy advocacy network. It currently embraces twenty-five privacy and civil rights organizations from sixteen different countries. It has been particularly active on issues relating to data retention requirements, spam, telecommunications interception, copyright and fair use restrictions, the cyber-crime treaty, rating, filtering, and blocking of Internet content and notice-and-takedown procedures of Web sites. It ceases to have a permanent office in Brussels, and so its main visibility is gained through the weekly publication of the EDRI gram, a biweekly newsletter about digital rights in Europe.

The issue of data retention in particular has provoked widespread opposition. A Data Retention Directive, requiring ISPs and phone companies to track and stockpile every user's call, e-mail destination, and Web access for later access by law enforcement, was passed by the European Parliament in 2005. All member countries were supposed to pass enabling legislation by September 2007, but few have. A campaign has been mounting, especially in Germany, to prevent such legislation. In addition to court challenges and legislative strategies, the issue has also sparked street protests. The Working Group on Data Retention (Arbeitskreis Vorratsdatenspeicherung) has been coordinating a coalition of around fifty local and national groups.[24] Three protests have so far been organized in Frankfurt, Bielefeld, and Berlin. The latter attracted around fifteen thousand people on September 22, 2007. The campaign slogan "Freedom Instead of Fear" (*Freiheit statt Angst*) also indicated that the coalition had adopted a more general aim to challenge the rise of the surveillance state.

There is, of course, no common understanding about when a campaign becomes a coalition, and vice versa. Campaigns tend to be more temporary, and perhaps more focused. In the language of network theory, a coalition implies one or more relatively permanent and active nodes, with relatively strong, multiple, dense, and intersecting ties. The flows of information within coalitions should be constant and multi-directional. It is also probable that coalitions should embrace groups with a genuine and specific interest in a cause, rather than a general and undifferentiated grievance against the government of the day. Sometimes, coalitions against the surveillance issue of the moment can provide an easy vehicle for groups to express more general political opposition. Coalitions can appear, from the outside, to be broad but superficial if the only demand for membership is the delivery of a pledge by e-mail. Nevertheless, the period since 9/11 has been characterized by a notable effort to broaden the range of interests within the privacy advocacy network, and to establish, through groups such as the Privacy Coalition, a more permanent and institutionalized network that perhaps can respond to surveillance schemes with a greater efficiency than occurred in the 1990s. Perhaps the implications of the REAL ID proposals, for example, are sufficiently broad that it can genuinely embrace a range of very diverse groups. It might, as Deborah Pierce of Privacy Activism believes, be a "harbinger of things to come." It might reflect the fact at last that privacy groups have realized the need to pull together.[25]

Privacy coalitions are always, however, likely to shift as issues rise and fall from political agendas. As Smith observes: "You get a bunch of people who come into the movement because they care deeply about medical records, and tomorrow we're talking about wiretapping, and they say 'what am I doing here?'"[26] This heterogeneity raises larger questions about the potential for the development of a larger social movement that will be discussed in chapter 7.

Privacy and Net Activism

The modern privacy advocacy network has been fundamentally shaped by the Internet. We have seen that many groups have arisen principally out of profound concern about the character of this new medium. The conflicts with Intel, Microsoft, DoubleClick, Google, and so on, have shaped advocates' perceptions of their roles, their strengths and their limitations. Privacy advocates were some of the first to see the potential of this new medium to mobilize support in the challenge to surveillance practices. The use of the Internet is not without its conundrums for privacy advocates. The near dependency of Internet users on the Microsofts, Googles, and Intels creates dilemmas when that very technology is being used to denounce the practices of its manufacturers. The Internet has been both an instrument of surveillance, and a tool through which that surveillance can be denounced.

Many privacy advocates are technologically very astute and have been some of the first to develop online petitions, e-mail campaigns, Web sites, and electronic newsletters and to use the potential of social networking sites and blogs. We can therefore observe an interesting ten-year history of interaction between this network and the various technologies of the day. The case will permit us, in conclusion, to interrogate some of the prevailing hypotheses about the effectiveness of Net activism. Is this potentially a major example of new forms of democratic participation that can reinforce counterhegemonic tendencies? Or is Net activism just another ephemeral expression of "electronic panics" with little lasting impact on social movement cohesion, or public policy?

We have already mentioned several ways in which the Internet has been used to support various expressions of information, symbolic, leverage and accountability politics. As new methods of online communication became available they were used—rapidly. The early online communities, such as the Whole Earth 'Lectronic Link (WELL), were arenas for the discussion of privacy on the Net as early as the mid-1980s. The privacy movement was one of the first to mobilize mass e-mail petitions. It was one of the first to understand the potential for the professionally designed Web site and the electronic newsletter. As the more cumbersome electronic bulletin boards and LISTSERVS gave way to social networking and the "blogosphere," so privacy advocates also embraced these new practices.

For many participants in the network, this embracing of online activism was a conscious choice. It demonstrated a rejection of Luddism. Nobody could accuse an organization like EPIC of being against the progress of technological development if, at the same time, it was using advanced technology to communicate its message. Further, in these early campaigns, there was a need to demonstrate that civil society groups were as adept at using the Internet as were powerful governmental and corporate agencies. Campaigns such as those against Lotus and Clipper were significant because of their boldness, taking both corporate interests and governmental bureaucracy by surprise, and serving as an example to other activists. These campaigns exerted leverage because they were early. They would not have anything like the same impact today.

The Internet has also supported the many efforts at accountability politics, especially through the immediate publication of a documentary record about the various conflicts. Letters to companies and to government agencies were immediately placed on the relevant Web sites. Responses were also posted. A fine example is the campaign against the Intel PSN. Deidre Mulligan was then at CDT:

With the Intel Pentium Serial Chip case, I wrote to all the OEMs [original equipment manufacturers] and said 'look I understand that you are going to use these chips, what are you going to do to protect privacy? Is it going to be on or off in the BIOS? What are you going to do here?' And I said 'I'm going to put the results to these questions up in ten days, so get back to me.' The OEMs had leverage over what Intel did in the future. I didn't necessarily think that the customers as end-users had leverage but I thought that the OEMs did, and they didn't want to be left holding the bag.[27]

This entire correspondence was, and is, available on CDT's Web site.[28] Most privacy advocates have proceeded with a presumption of publicity, when disputes like this arise. As a publicity tool, the Internet provides an effective and immediate instrument for accountability.

It is perhaps with respect to the more routine provision of information about privacy that the Internet has been the most benefit. Groups like EPIC, for example, gain a reputation through their regular provision of useful information. The Web site is updated everyday. The EPIC News Alert goes out to online subscribers once a week. The international survey of *Privacy and Human Rights*, the 2007 edition of which runs to eleven hundred pages, is published annually (EPIC 2007). In Europe, the EDRI gram is published bi-weekly. These, and other sources, provide information not just for the devotees, but for any individual or group interested in privacy questions. They support academic research, and provide resources for governmental agencies, including the many data protection authorities. The politics of privacy is as much a battle over information as over other resources.

Web sites are not just catalogues informing users about information and events, but also instruments to mobilize support and pressure. The contemporary privacy advocacy Web site will combine the provision of information resources in multimedia format with instruments to mobilize and connect. The recent German demonstrations against data retention were supported by a very popular wiki.[29] On CDT's Web site, you can "Adopt your Legislator" and be alerted when your own members of Congress are about to vote on policy issues affecting online civil liberties. Other strategies for encouraging communications with those in power include: the provision of form letters of protest; the publication of e-mail addresses of relevant government departments and corporate CEOs; and the circulation of online petitions. EFF's Web site incorporates easy-to-use e-mail and fax options for communicating with federal and state legislators about relevant bills of the day, and for posting comments on controversial proposals, such as those about Real ID. Privacy Activism is the group within the network that has made the most effective use of social networking sites like Tribe.net, MySpace, Free Association, and Yahoo! Each has active and expanding group discussions on privacy issues. Occasionally, the online networking spills over into face-to-face meetings in the coffee shops about privacy.[30]

Opinions differ, however, about whether this volume of online activity is effective. The campaign against the Communications Decency Act in the United States in the late 1990s illustrated a sharp contrast between the old-fashioned lobbying techniques of the Christian Right and the strategies of online activists. It elicited a biting critique from Simon

Davies: "While the politicos have been raping the Constitution, netizens have been preaching to the choir.... Congress and the White House have come to believe that the Net is useless as a political weapon—and that its users are incapable of organized political resistance. If netizens want to stem the hemorrhage of remaining freedoms, this passive stance must change—and fast. Yet all that impassioned ASCII amounted to little more than a digital wank-off session, as netizens wasted time preaching to the converted."[31]

Whereas in the 1990s, online strategies were often seen as novelty, and something to be reported in its own right, they are now commonplace. There is now a clear recognition that the online presence should be a component of a sound and integrated media strategy for any advocacy group. Online strategies should complement dealings with the traditional media. But how has this relatively long history of online activity affected the network itself? Do the e-mail campaigns, online petitions, blog discussions, electronic newsletters, and sophisticated Web sites serve to coalesce the privacy advocacy network? Does this activity deepen the sense of shared commitment as well as broaden the range of individuals and groups involved? These questions go to the heart of contemporary debates about the nature and importance of "cyber-activism."

The Privacy Advocacy Network and Cyber-activism

There is now a significant theoretical and empirical literature on the effects of the Internet on social and political activism. For many social activists and advocates, the Internet has transformed their work. It enables them to breach barriers of geographical distance, cost, time, and, to some extent, censorship. The Internet clearly has the potential to radically disrupt traditional assumptions about how groups do, and should operate, and how other actors should respond to them. Some certainly see Internet activism though grassroots networks as an exciting form of democratic participation with significant counterhegemonic implications. Research has demonstrated that the Internet does not make collective action impossible just because individuals are socially and geographically isolated one from another (Brunsting and Postmes 2002).

Others are more skeptical, pointing to the inherently isolating properties of the medium that weakens social connections, and thereby undermines the normative ties that bind communities together. The skeptics point to the extreme, disruptive, and confrontational actions that tend to be reported in the popular media. They also suggest that Internet advocacy is ephemeral and thin. It gives rise to "electronic panics" rather than sustained campaigns. As Ron Diebert explains, "the fear is that rather than a world of democracy, the future holds an increasing logistical nightmare of thousands upon thousands of niche interest groups buzzing around every conceivable international forum where nothing is achieved but endless gridlock" (2000, 256).

The truth is obviously somewhere in between. The Internet provides advantages and also carries risks. The task in the conclusion of this chapter is to examine the literature on cyber-activism with a view to understanding the conditions under which the Internet is more likely to establish effective online networks. There is no question that this form of political participation is different. But does the difference make a difference, both to the cohesion of the privacy advocacy network, and to its effectiveness in the political arena? There are clearly a number of aspects of Internet activism, noted in the general literature, which are also exhibited with respect to the privacy advocacy network.

Cyber-activism, as many have noted, grows from an environment characterized by a multiplicity of senders and receivers. It is a plural and flexible network, easy to join and capable of rapid restructuring as organizations arise, leave, adapt, and redefine themselves. Pressure is no longer the result of hierarchical attempts at interest aggregation, but of a multiplicity of agents using the Internet as a medium to establish relationships across diverse structures and locations. Not only is the Internet a faster communications medium, it has ushered in a qualitatively different set of political dynamics. For example, organizations that are older, larger, and resource rich have tended to rely on Internet communications to amplify their preexisting communication strategies and routines. New, resource-poor organizations, on the other hand, that challenge existing state and corporate hierarchies are defined in important ways by their Internet presence. They are more likely to embrace the new medium and use it in innovative ways (L. Bennett 2004, 125).

This network structure is also arguably more resilient. Large and flexible coalitions exhibit what Gerlach has termed "the strength of thin ties" (Gerlach 2001).[32] Attacks by opponents might succeed in lopping off one or two arms of the multiheaded hydra, but they cannot fundamentally destroy the network. When the costs of entry and exit are relatively low, and there seems to be a danger of hijack, participants may leave and return with different roles and affiliations. Movements dominated by large hierarchical structures, on the other hand, are more vulnerable to crisis from within, and opposition from without.

The Internet does not cause contemporary activists to organize in non-hierarchical, distributed, and flexible ways. But it does reinforce the existing biases of many contemporary activists, who want to get things done, rather than worry about rules and organization. Here's Roger Clarke on APF: "Organizations like ours.... do not sit there with mission statements, and nice long lists and tick things off and allocate resources. Organizations like ours get out and do things. Movers do things. Certainly from time to time, we need to put out a call 'can anybody handle this one?' And more often than not, somebody manages to put their hand up."[33] If privacy advocates can reach their objectives without the prerequisites of group organization and aggregation, then that is the overwhelming preference. The Internet clearly facilitates that preference.

A further advantage of cyber-activism is its ability to cast the spotlight on bad corporate behavior from afar. It can promote the phenomenon of "witnessing at a distance" (Ribeiro 1998), thus facilitating the rapid and widespread sharing of information and opinions about practices anywhere in the world. Research in other policy areas has demonstrated that transnational activists can and do spotlight the behavior of firms and the lax standards of states that facilitate that behavior. When firms participate in a global economy, not only do they export their capital investment; they also take their reputations, brand names, and images. The "spotlight phenomenon" can expose questionable practices such as the use of child labor, the hiring of workers at below minimum wages, environmental degradation, or the effects of landmines. Under pressure, multinational firms are reluctantly forced to accept responsibility for the abuses perpetrated by foreign contractors and subsidiaries. Such pressures have led to global codes of conduct to which companies have been forced to adhere (Spar 1998).

The privacy advocacy network, without explicitly recognizing it, has developed a particularly important tradition of spotlighting. Whether the respective campaigns were successful or not, the network has been able rapidly to expose the worse effects of third-party cookies, of key-escrow encryption, of the construction of online databases through search engine data, and so on. These practices might not have the immediate and visceral impact of campaigns against other forms of corporate abuse, but they have altered the debate, placed these issues on political agendas, and served serious warnings to irresponsible corporate actors. The "spotlight phenomenon" has also contributed to the raising of international privacy standards (Bennett and Raab 2006, 274).

Cyber-activism serves the privacy advocacy network well because the issue itself is more amenable to the capacities of the Internet, than are some others. Privacy is an inescapably global question. Populations everywhere are affected by the corporate policies and behaviors of the Microsofts, Googles, and Intels. Unlike some environmental questions, where the impacts are felt disproportionately depending on location, with privacy there are universally felt impacts. Cyber-activism in support of some environmental causes, for instance, will have a variable impact on the cohesion of the network depending on whether that activism is about clearcut forests, polluted oceans, toxic waste dumps, or whatever. Here, the ubiquity of the resource to be protected (personal data) can inspire a more universal set of concerns. The Internet has provided the tools through which a technologically sophisticated, possibly "geeky," privacy advocates network can convey those concerns to government and business, and build a far larger network than was possible before.

At the same time, the risks and weaknesses of Net activism, documented in other studies, are observed here as well. Most computer-mediated communication is asynchronous. Synchronous tools (like the telephone, audio and web conferencing, instant messaging) enable real-time communication and collaboration at a single point in time. Asynchronous tools (e-mail, blogs, discussion boards) enable communication and collaboration through a "different time-different place" mode, allowing people to connect according to each individual's convenience and schedule. Asynchronous tools are useful for sustaining dialogue and collaboration over a period of time and for providing people, perhaps within different time zones, with resources and information that are instantly and continuously accessible. They are also helpful in capturing the history of the interactions of a group, and in allowing for a collective memory to be more easily formed. They permit users to manage their time more efficiently, to prioritize, to avoid disruption of creative processes, and to separate work from social life. But these advantages also reduce the emotional and human qualities of direct communication. Asynchronous communication is disembodied and unconnected. It does not permit senders or receivers accurately to judge the motivations, emotions, and attitudes of one another. It demands no instant feedback. In a political context, it changes the dynamics and nature of collective action, and perhaps militates against the building of social trust (Franklin 1999, 150–155).

Asynchronous communication can, therefore, make it difficult to achieve common idea framings. It does not permit the deeper generation of ideological arguments of justification. The openness of the networks invites diverse activists from diverse groups to join campaigns, but also contributes to ideological and identity "thinning" (L. Bennett 2004, 134).

Indeed, in some instances, groups might join networks and campaigns in the expectation that there will not be the penetrating analysis of different political perspectives. For instance, there is an unwritten rule within the Privacy Coalition that everyone sticks strictly to the issue at hand—privacy. Any deeper penetration of the ideological reasons why groups from both the right and left would find the issue interesting might easily expose contradictions and conflicts, and weaken the coalition. So some contentious issues, like abortion or gun control, just don't get discussed, either online or offline. A condition for the formation and persistence of the coalition is, therefore, the very absence of discussion about the deeper ideological reasons why the group might be interested in the privacy issue. This obviously contrasts in stark ways with the intense squabbling over the "true" meaning of doctrine that has characterized and splintered many groups on the Left and the Right.

Thus networks such as the Privacy Coalition can demonstrate a breadth of concern and can allow groups to give voice to their various interests, but they do not produce the collective action "frames" that are normally associated with the growth of social movements over the long term. They do not produce any kind of permanent sense of an "us" and a "them." It is not only that the public interest advocates can come and go, depending on their commitment to and interest in individual issues; it is also the case that some interests that might very well be defined as a "them" for one dispute can become an "us" for another. We have already documented the perceived value among the privacy advocacy network of forging allies in the private sector. Yet some companies can be enemies at one moment, and allies the next. Some individual actors can be within civil society at one moment, and move through the "revolving door" to work for the corporate sector or the government the next.

The degree of ideological discourse and identity-framing seems to be inversely related to the number and diversity of groups in the network. This very openness permits diverse groups to expand the universe of issues and diversify organizational agendas. The logic of the open network makes connections between disparate issues and groups possible, but it also produces intellectual dilemmas. For groups like EPIC, the hub and orchestrator of the privacy coalition, the philosophy that any civil society actor can be a privacy advocate, and anybody can join these campaigns, clearly broadens the potential for political effectiveness. But that breadth also incorporates a danger that the universe of privacy issues can expand and proliferate, complicating the problem of issue framing for a protean concept that is notoriously difficult to frame in the first place.

There is also the risk that an ideologically thin network is more amenable to temporary campaigns rather than long-term strategic partnerships. "Strange bedfellows" have been a feature of coalition politics for a long time. Experience has suggested, however, that such coalitions dissolve quickly as soon as a particular battle is over. The relative speed and ease of coalition formation on the Internet is ideally suited to the kinds of transitory campaigns waged in the name of privacy. However, it is by no means clear that this succession of campaigns is building anything more permanent. Neither is it clear that any one group within the privacy advocacy network has the sufficient credibility, resources, and inclination to do anything more. There have been some tentative efforts to cement linkages across campaigns. However, it is too early to tell whether these initiatives represent a more permanent presence that can develop the true sense of solidarity and belonging characteristic of more established social movements.

Research has also demonstrated that the openness of online networks can serve to diminish group identity, and change organizational structures and processes. The Internet is not simply subordinated to the agendas, routines, and structures of existing hierarchical organizations. It shapes the organizations and the relations between them. Lance Bennett identifies a number of organizational dynamics from his case-studies of online activism. Organizations may be transformed because of the demands of network actors. They may move on to other networks to protect their roles and identities as hub organizations. They may split away and produce successor networks (L. Bennett 2004, 136–140). Bennett's arguments suggest that for groups like EPIC, for instance, the hub and orchestrator of the Privacy Coalition network, there is a danger that its agenda can be altered by the myriad interests of the groups it is trying to coordinate. The groups at the "hub" can sometimes be overwhelmed by the procedural demands of coalition-building, rather than the substantive value and the policy goals. The Internet is not just a communication medium, it is an organizational principle.

The transitory nature of Internet campaigns risk also being interpreted as "electronic panics." The analysis of earlier campaigns, such as those conducted in the name of the antiglobalization movement, has suggested that the medium itself has the tendency to spread contentious politics (Ayres 1999). The medium encourages the rapid dissemination of "facts" that may not be accurate. It exaggerates the level of opposition and polarizes the debate. It can, in some interpretations, reinforce a contemporary tendency in modern politics to engage in "moral panic." This term typically refers to the phenomenon by societies occasionally to obsess about practices deemed deeply unsettling to established cultural norms. Reason and perspective give way to hyperbole and hysteria. In their more extreme forms, certain groups are held up as scapegoats, and scorned by a majority as the cause of any manner of social problems (Cohen 1972). More generally it is a term applied to any irrational and exaggerated attempt to construct problems in social and political terms and to demand any kind of collective response.

Moral panics are often at the heart of the more intrusive surveillance systems, as individual cases of crime or deviance become constructed as representative of a larger problem demanding a general response in terms of video surveillance, drug testing, national identity cards, genetic databanks, RFID tagging, or whatever. But moral panics can also be fomented on the other side of the debate. Much of the early battle over cryptography, for example, had such a flavor, with the proponents arguing for surveillance capabilities like key escrow to ensure that the Net was not taken over by terrorists and child pornographers, and the opponents warning against the slide into the Orwellian state. Particularly in the early campaigns, the novelty of online activism motivated overenthusiastic netizens to communicate their outrage at particular practices, without checking facts, and without the discipline imposed by organizational membership. Folklore quickly developed, sometimes at odds with the seriousness of the particular intrusion.

Laura Gurak has carefully documented the various instances of misinformation that circulated within online discussion groups about the Lotus Marketplace product and the Clipper Chip. The speed and power of online communications produced in each case an "online ethos" and a misplaced trust in the self-regulating power of the Internet to weed out false and misleading postings. Instead, there was an exigency to respond that produced inaccurate or exaggerated information (Gurak 1997, chap. 6).

Another illustration is the dispute in September 1996 about the Lexis-Nexis "P-TRAK" personal information database. This product compiled a variety of personal information from public sources for resale to the legal community for use by general legal practitioners, litigators and public attorneys, as well as law enforcement agencies and police departments. The way that misinformation circulated about this product was likened to the age-old game of "telephone," where one person whispers a message to another in a chain to the point at the end where it bears absolutely no relationship to the original (Chick 1996). The amount of misinformation that circulated about P-Trak, and especially about the extent to which the social security number was collected and shared (in possible contravention of federal law), prompted a stiff response from the company on the major privacy newsgroups of the day. In the case of Privacy Forum, the moderator even intervened by calling the company lawyer to try to establish some facts. However, disputes such as these are often more about the protest than about the facts. They are characterized by a pattern of claim and counterclaim, rather than the search for the truth. Like other electronic panics, the result was the "cyber-diffusion of contention" supporting Jeffrey Ayres' point that the "Internet holds the power to turn unreliable and unverifiable information into a global electronic riot" (Ayres 1999, 132).

Conclusions: Usual Suspects and Strange Bedfellows

The privacy advocacy network is a very modern example of transnational activism. Yet in many ways, its structure is not unlike that of other social movements. According to Gerlach, the most common types of social movement organization are characterized by three features. They are segmentary: "composed of many diverse groups which grow and die, divide and fuse, proliferate and contract." They are polycentric: "having multiple, often temporary, and sometimes competing leaders or centers of influence." And they are networked: "forming a loose, reticulate, integrated network with multiple linkages through travelers, overlapping membership, joint activities, common reading matter, and shared ideals and opponents" (Gerlach 2001). This analysis was based mainly on the observation of the environmental movement, but it is a relatively accurate depiction of the network described in this chapter. The privacy advocacy network is composed of multiple groups and individuals with varying commitments to the central value of privacy. It is nonhierarchical in the sense that no one group is considered more important than any other. There is no one person who can claim to speak for the network as a whole, any more than there is one group that is representative of the entire movement. It is an open network. It has no defined limit. It expands and contracts depending on the issue and the opponent.

What then are the ties? What makes it a network, distinguishable from the mass of organizational and individual actors within civil society? We have discussed the importance of conferences, campaigns, and Net activism. There is no question that the privacy advocacy network is now broader, larger, and more diverse than it was twenty, or even ten, years ago. It is also clear that the Internet is largely responsible for this transformation not only because of its facilities as a communication and networking tool but also because privacy is at the heart of the very medium that the activism is trying to influence. With other issues, cyber-activism is just an instrument to advance a cause. In the advancement of privacy rights, cyber-activism is largely about the Internet. Cyber-activism is deeply affected if individuals cannot have assurances that their private communications are protected. The medium and the message are inextricably and mutually linked and implicated.

However, despite the success in embracing online tools of communication and networking, personal relationships have still endured and remained very important. Some of the respondents interviewed for this study have remained committed to the cause since the 1970s. A further enduring aspect of network building is the importance of the "traveling evangelists," the individuals who carry information across the network. They "zealously spread the ideology of any movement, promoting its ideas, reinforcing the beliefs of participants, exhorting them to action and helping them recruit newcomers and form groups, raise funds and mobilize against opponents" (Gerlach 2001, 296–297). Many of these evangelists do direct individual segments of the network, and are generally recognized by the media as leaders of the movement. However, they also spread the word—giving speeches to governmental, corporate, and civil society audiences and appearing in the traditional media. The personnel have changed over the years, but it is also instructive that some individuals that came to this issue in the 1970s have not wanted to move onto other pursuits.

At the same time and because this issue is endlessly fascinating, it is continually refreshed by the intellectual challenges posed by new technologies, and by the entrance of new actors into the network—new advocate/activists, advocate/consultants, advocate/academics, advocate/journalists, advocate/technologists, and advocate/artists. Hosein likes it that way: "You want a dynamic environment. You don't want a very well established environment with key players and so on and so forth. I like that there are people whom I have never heard of speaking on privacy issues. Some of them talk rubbish, and some of them are incredible. It is so dynamic."[34]

Privacy is also an issue that continues to attract younger people. There is evidence that a newer generation of privacy advocates has built some strong bonds of trust and affiliation as a result of similar educational experiences, especially within some of the major law schools. In the United States, the Boalt Law School, University of California, Berkeley, the Berkman Institute for the Internet and Society at Harvard, the Stanford Center for the Internet and Society, for example, have been important training grounds for students with broad interests in law and information technology. In Canada, the same can be said of the Canadian Internet Policy and Public Interest Clinic (CIPPIC) at the University of Ottawa. These kinds of programs were generally not available to earlier generations of privacy advocates. As a result of these experiences, as well as opportunities for internships with groups such as EPIC, ties have been forged among the more junior staff members within the privacy advocacy network.

The question in conclusion is whether this network constitutes a "social movement?" Is this segmentary and polycentric network something that will endure because of the nature of the issue? Or will it cohere, coalesce, develop, and mature in other ways? What can the scholarly literature tell us about the possible futures for the privacy advocacy network, and thus for the issue itself?

7 Movements and Futures

It is poor civic hygiene to install technologies that could someday facilitate a police state.
—Bruce Schneier

Privacy will be to the information economy of the next century what consumer protection and environmental concerns have been to the industrial society of the 20th century.
—Marc Rotenberg

Get a couple beers in them and [privacy advocates] will fantasize about what they call the "Privacy Chernobyl"—the one privacy outrage that will finally catalyze an effective social movement around the issue.
—Philip Agre

The analysis presented so far would lead to the following conclusions about privacy advocacy. The activities of civil society actors have tended to be marginalized in literature and by other actors in the policy community. Yet their activities are more important than people realize—the cases addressed in chapter 5 substantiate that point. Further, they are becoming more visible and more important, partly because of online activism, but also in some respects because of the need to pull together in response to the increasing surveillance post-9/11.

However, there is no concerted worldwide privacy movement that has anything like the scale, resources, or public recognition of organizations in the environmental, feminist, consumer protection, and human rights fields. In the privacy protection sector, there is a diverse, open-ended, and fluid range of groups and individuals, stretching from traditional civil liberties organizations, consumer associations, and groups established to promote freedom in cyberspace to more specialized groups involved with singles issues. When privacy conflicts arise, they tend to be waged by loose coalitions that come together for specific causes and then disband.

So far, the analysis has tended to support David Lyon's observation that "it is unlikely that in the case of resistance to surveillance items like data protection and privacy would ever become political 'hot button' issues. . . . It sounds as if the politics of surveillance is wishful thinking" (2001, 135).

But is this the way it has to be? Rotenberg's comparison with the environmental movement is premised on an assumption that today's privacy advocacy network will be transformed into a more coherent and recognizable social movement with similar visibility to that of environmentalism. An antisurveillance politics will continue to grow and challenge the bureaucratic and corporate tendencies to amass and process vast quantities of ever more refined personal information. In some interpretations, this will be catalyzed by a major scandal—the "Privacy Chernobyl." But will it, and if so when? It should always be remembered that there was a lag time of more than a century between the industrial revolution and the advent of an environmental politics.

The ultimate goal is to understand the conditions under which a more coherent international and mass-based social movement for privacy (against surveillance) might develop. Is the absence of such a movement inevitable and explicable because of the inherent properties of this issue, or is it something that might very well arise given the correct agents and strategic choices? The overwhelming question is whether the patterns exhibited within the histories of these and other social movements also are reflected in privacy protection. Or are there some inherent differences? Are there certain properties to privacy protection that inevitably will mean that advocacy through this loose and polycentric network is indeed the "way it has to be"? What insights about the future might we derive from the literature about social movements and collective action? And, perhaps more important, how do the advocates themselves view the issue, the network, and the future?

Could the Privacy Advocacy Network Become a Social Movement?

The privacy advocacy network has never been regarded as a "social movement" either by those within it, or by those observing from the outside. Indeed neither has any group activity associated with the communications and information revolution, whether it be broadcasting, telecommunications regulation, freedom of information, or intellectual property (Mueller, Page, and Kuerbis 2004). These issues tend to be seen as within the more specialized and technocratic realms of politics and policymaking. They are not likely to excite passions and adherence.

But what is meant by a social movement? Scholars have tended to expand the definition of a social movement in response to the kind of activism and protest they have seen around them. Clearly, the more inclusive the definition, the more scope there is to embrace privacy advocacy within its purview. The dominant school of sociological thought on social movements in the mid-twentieth century tended to focus on collective behavior, associating movements with phenomena such as riots, crowds, and mass hysteria. Shaped in part by the recent memory of the fascist movements in Germany, Italy, and Japan, the dominant effort was to explain the irrational dimensions of movements, seeing them as potentially dangerous and disruptive of stable social systems. They had their inception in conditions of dissatisfaction and unrest (Blumer 1939, 199) or relative deprivation (Gurr 1970). They were indistinguishable from "mass movements" that "mobilize people who are alienated from the going system, who do not believe in the legitimacy of the established order, and who therefore are ready to engage in efforts to destroy it" (Kornhauser 1959, 212).

More complex and varied concepts and approaches were, however, necessary as a result of the "new social movements" that emerged in the 1960s and 1970s. These movements were considered "new" because of a greater emphasis on nonmaterialistic values and lifestyles, and a tendency to emerge more from middle- than working-class constituencies (Inglehart 1977). This "silent revolution" was presumed to motivate those who, according to the Maslovian hierarchy of needs, have already attended to the material necessities of clothing, food, and shelter. Many new social movement theorists also emphasized a change from the industrial, heavy manufacturing based "Fordist" economy to a "post-industrial," "postmodern," or "post-Fordist" economy centered more on the service sector. For Touraine, for example, the passage to a post-industrial society, the conflicts and cleavages have been defined less by struggles between labor and capital, and more in terms of "ways of life" (Touraine 1988). Social movement development is therefore dependent upon the inherent and historical properties of the politics surrounding challenges to entrenched power (Touraine 1981; Tarrow 1998; Tilly 1984; Snow and Benford 1988).

Today's conception of a social movement is therefore very inclusive. It embraces those based on ascriptive identities—the women's movement, the civil rights movement, the gay and lesbian movement, as well as those surrounding particular issues—the environmental movement and the labor movement. Over time, others have been added, such as the antiglobalization movement. Other scholars have stressed the more ritualistic and symbolic dimensions of new social movements. Movements develop special patterns of expression and connection that distinguish them from the wider culture. The uniqueness of a social movement's culture is therefore determined by the shared values, styles, behaviors, languages, traditions, symbols, and/or other forms of group definition. But much of a movement's culture may be unspoken, invisible, such as a sense of connection based on shared past experiences (Lofland 1995).

For other analysts, the organizations and the structure of the conflict are secondary, as are any successes or failures in achieving policy goals. For some social movements, the essential role is an enabling one for the participants who seek to understand themselves and their relations with others. Social movements should permit self-actualization, an understanding of what it means to be a black in the United States, a woman, a gay man, a lesbian, or an aboriginal person. Thus, they not only seek to change laws and policies and focus on articulating and aggregating demands from the state, or replacing political elites, but also attempt to change social conditions and attitudes. They try to establish new meanings about the nature of the political and challenge entrenched power interests based on these new meanings. Contentious politics and the definition of an "us and a them" may be a contingency, but it is not central to the search for a new "political space" (Magnusson 1996).

Most of the social movement literature tends to be directed toward understanding and prescribing strategies of resistance for more "progressive" causes. Social movements are vehicles for "change," normally meaning change against the prevailing capitalist order. The literature is then directed toward trying to understand the conditions under which new social movements can find that new political space and change the terms of the discourse. However, the analysis should not be implicated by the normative preferences of the researcher. Social movements should not be confined to those associated with "progressive" causes, but defined in more objective terms. Tarrow, for instance, would prefer not to see social movements as expressions of extremism, violence, and deprivation but as "collective challenges, based on common purposes and social solidarities, in sustained interaction with elites, opponents and authorities" (1998, 4). This framework provides a useful analytical tool to assess the social movement properties of the privacy advocacy network.

Tarrow insists first that there should be a collective challenge—most often marked by "interrupting, obstructing or rendering uncertain the activities of others" (Tarrow 1998, 5). These challenges are "contentious" because movement leaders typically lack the stable resources that powerful interest groups can muster. They therefore seek to expand the scope of conflict, to become a focal point for supporters, and to create larger constituencies. There are many examples throughout this volume of instances of contentious politics representing collective challenges to state and corporate power. The key is not violence, but the disruption of ways of thinking and behaving, be it the performances of the New York Surveillance Camera Players, the campaign to flood the U.S. Department of Homeland Security with comments on Real ID, the peaceful protests against identification card systems in the streets of London and Tokyo, or the marches against data retention in Berlin and Frankfurt. There is plenty of collective challenge, plenty of attempted disruption, and an increasing amount of contention.

Second, Tarrow insists that social movements should have a "common purpose"; people join movements to mount "common claims against opponents, authorities or elites" (1998, 6). This attribute distinguishes the movement from the mob, the riot, or the crowd. Movements possess common and overlapping values or interests to animate their actions. "Privacy" indeed means a lot of things to a lot of people. Some advocates prefer to resist surveillance in collective terms, rather than promote privacy in individual terms. The common purpose is indeed flexible and vague, but any more so than environmentalism, feminism, or civil rights? Common to all privacy advocates is a fundamental belief that this is one of the defining issues of the modern era, and that there is a real need to place legal and technological controls on the abilities of organizations to capture, process, and disseminate personal information. There is a common, if broad, purpose.

Third, social movements should exhibit "solidarity and collective identity," again not in a temporary or ephemeral manner but in a sustained way over time. Collective identity is the name given to the tendency of many social movements to form a group self-image shaped by, but in turn shaping the consciousness of, individual participants. Leaders can only fashion a social movement when they "tap more deep-rooted feelings of solidarity or identity. This is almost certainly why nationalism and ethnicity or religion have been more reliable bases of movement organization than the categorical imperative of social class" (Tarrow 1998, 6). Thus, the common purpose does not necessarily lead to a common identity or sense of solidarity. It does not necessarily define who the "us" are in relation to the "them." And collective identities are not fixed, but are in constant construction and negotiation through repeated interactions among movement participants.

Collective identity is clearly a more difficult criterion to observe with respect to privacy advocacy. The glue that holds the network together is clearly not provided by any sense of ascriptive or affiliative identities (Gutman 2003). Ascriptive identity groups organize around characteristics that are largely beyond people's ability to choose: race, gender, class, physical handicap, ethnicity, sexual orientation, and age. Affiliative identities result from choices, such as academic discipline, schools, and employing institutions. Affiliative choices are of course limited by ascriptive identities, but none of these categories helps us understand what holds the privacy advocacy network together. Privacy advocates come from all ascriptive backgrounds and all walks of life.

Some movements are also held together by ideology, or a common framework of understanding about the respective roles of state, civil society, and market, and the relations among them. But privacy goes to the heart of those very questions, and the network has embraced groups and individuals with fundamentally different ideological understandings. It embraces those with a deep suspicion of the role of the state, as well as those who would insist that law and regulation are a prerequisite for sustained privacy protection. It embraces those who believe in, perhaps revere, the free market, to those who accept the freedom of the market but insist on its regulation, to those who would embrace an anticapitalist and antiglobalization agenda. The ideological underpinnings of the network are as diffuse as politics itself.

Neither can one identify the glue as a sense of shared grievance. Newly articulated grievances are generally the focal points around which movements are organized, and new grievances often emerge as movements evolve. Grievances stem from a shared perception that a group of individuals is being denied rights, opportunities, proper respect, safety, or some other form of social good simply because of who they are. It is generally true that those people whose privacy is more endangered are those from more marginalized communities. They tend to receive higher levels of surveillance, particularly from the state. After 9/11, for instance, there has been increasing levels of grievance among Arab Americans, and an increasing level of concern about discriminatory surveillance practices.[1]

However, the relationship between measures of social stratification and levels of surveillance is full of contradictions. Some surveillance practices, forms of direct marketing for instance, are explicitly targeted at those with higher levels of income. Identity theft will tend to hurt those with the most to lose. There are a range of tricky theoretical and empirical questions about the distribution of privacy protection within any society

(Bennett and Raab 2006, chap. 3). The extent to which shared grievances will translate into collective action will then depend on context and the specific perceptions of harm within specific contexts.

With respect to privacy, therefore, we return to the issue itself. Any sense of solidarity must be found not within the people themselves but within the politics. I have noted on many occasions the sense of belonging that is fostered by a common belief in a mission to shape the nature of new communications media. To be sure, this zeal is observed more in relation to Internet-related privacy issues, but it does produce some sense of solidarity, through a belief that privacy advocates are on the "electronic frontier" fighting back intrusive governments and corporations and shaping the future in profound and enduring ways. Therefore, young people became involved not only on the merits of the issue but out of a belief that this was a new and exciting issue upon which they could have an impact. It is "cool" to be involved in antisurveillance politics.[2] The solidarity is, to be sure, fragile. But it is present, and it has been sustained.

This brings us to Tarrow's fourth and final condition, the need to "sustain contentious politics" for it is only by "sustaining collective action against antagonists that a contentious episode becomes a social movement" (1998, 6). Tarrow does not specify a period in which movements must maintain their challenge, or else evaporate, rescind, or retreat into isolation and resentment. However, the sustenance of collective action marks the social movement from isolated acts of resistance. Identifiable groups that have framed their contention in terms of privacy can be dated back at least as far as the early 1970s. They accompanied, though followed, the emergence of the issue onto the agendas of advanced industrial states. The issue and the politics arose through two conditions of post-industrial society—information technology and complex organizations. It emerged at exactly the same time as other "post-materialistic" questions: environmentalism, feminism, gay and lesbian rights, civil rights, and so on. The issue has been sustained, and it has grown—even though it has not mobilized visible groups with broad mass memberships.

Some observers have theorized a natural life cycle to social movement politics, or an organizational ecology that contends that groups do rise and fall according to predictable patterns (Mueller, Page, and Kuerbis 2004). Growth takes place in the early stages as the organizational form is legitimated. It then declines as the competition for resources intensifies. The early stages of informality and loose relationships give way over time to higher levels of institutionalization. In some interpretations, this process might lead to a level of bureaucratic organization that loses contact with constituent groups and sight of the true and original purpose (Alberoni 1984).

However, it is very much an open question in an era of social networking and Internet activism whether or not patterns of movement institutionalization, observed in earlier eras, hold true. A more recent study of the organizational ecology of groups within the area of communications and information (including privacy groups), asks the explicit question whether a broad conception of communications and information policy can provide the basis for sustained social movement activism. Quantitative data indicate that the "answer is almost certainly 'no' if one looks backward, but very possibly 'yes' if one looks forward and extrapolates current trends" (Mueller, Page, and Kuerbis 2004, 182). These authors also see that the rise of Internet activism has been overcoming prior problems of movement segmentation.

Andrew Clement and Christie Hurrell have also contended from their studies of groups advocating community networking, free/open source software, and information privacy that there is potential for a broader "information/communications rights movement." There is, they argue, a conceptual and discursive equivalence between the environmental commons and the information commons, between the ecosphere and the "infosphere" (Clement and Hurrell 2005). In a further paper, Clement contends that the different strands of this movement are indeed becoming more gradually interwoven into this "infosphere": "by framing the infosphere as an embodied ecological environment, information rights movements can more easily articulate a set of rights and responsibilities for the citizens who operate within it, and can work together to develop and protect an information environment that is widely accessible and responsive to the needs and aspirations of computer users" (2006, 47).

Furthermore, the arguments of some social movement theorists would seem to predict the development of movements exactly like this. Surveillance is a central condition of postindustrial or postmodern society. It is manifested in a range of new technological practices. It attacks deep conceptions of individual, and indeed collective, identity. Challenges to surveillance are deeply rooted in wider challenges to state power (Fuentes and Frank 1989). There are multiple points of antagonism around the collection, use, and disclosure of one of the "currencies" of the post-industrial society—personal information. There appear to be many similarities between the properties of this issue and those of other "post-materialistic" questions that have produced more coherent, visible, and international new social movements from highly heterogeneous constituencies.

Perhaps, then, this can be a social movement. If we can talk in terms of a movement surrounding such vague concepts as "antiglobalization," then surely an "antisurveillance" politics can be embraced by the term. Furthermore, social movement theorists have always stressed the open, overlapping, and dynamic nature of social movement structures. They are "moving targets" (van de Donk et al. 2004, 3). Definitions stretch depending on the evidence observed. Nevertheless there is still a puzzle. There has been an enormous amount of policy activity: law, codes of practice, international agreements, privacy-enhancing technologies, and so on. There has been an international "trading-up" of international regulation (Bennett and Raab 2006). But little of this has occurred as a result of concerted grassroots pressure. To date, notwithstanding recent successful campaigns against specific practices, nobody would contend that the greater salience of the issue is attributable to the rise of a broader "pro-privacy" or "antisurveillance" politics. It is still generally an elitist issue within government, business, and civil society. Why this has been the case, is perhaps the more relevant question than whether this privacy advocacy network fits some amorphous definition of what a social movement is, or should be.

There are two explanations. First, the issue is conducive to a broader political development, but the participants themselves have not mobilized their resources in a sufficiently skilful manner. Or, there is something inherent in the issue, the properties of which can never elevate privacy and/or surveillance to a higher level of mass consciousness and political mobilization. Does the explanation lie in agency or in structure—or both?

Resource Mobilization

Much social movement literature tends to emerge from a European tradition, which is interested in locating the structural conditions for conflict, grievance, and contention. A different emphasis, of course, comes from that literature that would claim that the mere existence or framing of grievance or discontent, does not explain why particular movements arise in particular times and places. More a "strategy-oriented" paradigm, this literature focuses more on "resource mobilization" by entrepreneurial agents. Whether a movement develops or does not, succeeds or fails, is then more dependent on whether or not the group has its "act together." More precisely, success is contingent on how tangible and intangible resources might be marshaled in such a way as to resolve the familiar free rider dilemma within collective action theory; how to mobilize support when it makes little sense for any one individual to incur the costs of participation when he or she will receive the benefits of success from others (Olsen 1971).

Thus social movements do not just spread as a result of contagion. They are not a result of class conflict, or of relative deprivation. There is nothing inherent in the structural strains and cleavages of particular societies that will produce social movement politics. They arise because of rational and instrumental action on the part of social movement "entrepreneurs" who fashion social movement organizations (SMOs) and mobilize resources to the cause. The resource mobilization approach takes more seriously the strategies, tactics, and dilemmas that face the activists themselves. It claims to add a more realistic dimension to the macrosociological literature and, without prescribing recipes or handbooks for social change, allows those activists to see their tactical and instrumental choices in larger terms (Zald and McCarthy 1979, 1). This school is also interested in the direct and measurable impacts of movements on political issues, and less concerned with their more expressive identity-shaping and consciousness-raising dimensions, seeking to understand how the availability of resources and opportunities dovetails with the use of those symbolic meanings and with the creation of new social identities. The resource mobilization approach coexists with analyses of the political conditions under which movements arise, but focuses more on the opportunity structures. Collective action is therefore not seen as a symptom of abnormal and irrational politics, but as the response of actors taking advantage of new institutional and social conditions to push an agenda from the outside at the right time.

The term "resource" is conceived broadly. It embraces tangible resources such as finance, staff resources, and membership. It is presumed that there is a kind of competitive marketplace for these resources in any one country—and especially for money when conflicts of interest preclude financing from government or corporations. But groups also compete for committed and knowledgeable staff and often have trouble maintaining their allegiance against more attractive and lucrative career options in other sectors. Resource mobilization also refers, however, to more intangible factors such as knowledge, expertise, and communications skills. These factors in turn determine how social movements interact with external reference groups—their allies and opponents, state authorities, and the mass media. The political opportunity structures are not, then, stable arenas, like a kind of fixed playing-field upon which groups battle for influence. These structures can also be shaped by a skilful and resourceful group. The conflict is not only over the outcomes but also over the size and nature of the playing field itself.

What resources are possessed by the privacy advocacy network? Have they used them to their best advantage? In terms of financial support, the network has to make do with a pittance. There are, indeed, very few organizations within the entire network of privacy-centric or privacy-explicit groups that have enough resources to afford a permanent staff, and these are almost entirely United States–based. Further, and with the exception of the ACLU, the funding is always fragile and contingent on constant effort. In direct consequence, few organizations bother with a membership because they cannot afford the time and staff to solicit contributions, maintain a membership list, and remind people of renewals and so on. Some organizations would not want such a structure, even if they could, because constant referral to a membership inhibits their activist style. Conversely, the absence of a membership opens up the organization to the question of who exactly is being represented. There is indeed a further dilemma, of particular relevance to the privacy advocates. As Beth Givens reminds us: "It's very difficult to call yourself a privacy organization and solicit memberships because you have to go out and buy mailing lists. There's kind of an irony there. And that's one of the reasons I think there isn't really a large constituency around privacy advocacy. It's a real problem."[3]

So the resources of the privacy advocacy network are almost entirely intangible and chiefly related to expert knowledge—technical, legal, policy, and organizational. This expertise is marshaled in a variety of ways. It supports campaigns. It provides the raw material for research both within and outside the organization. It attracts the media. And it can be traded for access to relevant policymaking arenas, such as legislative hearings, governmental advisory committees, corporate advisory boards, and so on. The strategic and tactical dilemmas therefore rest on how to strike at the most opportune time, and in the most effective way.

No doubt individual tactical decisions can be critiqued. No doubt opportunities have been lost. But it would be extremely unfair to place the blame on organizational and strategic failures for the fact that the privacy advocacy network has not become more politically visible. Arguments do get advanced, suggesting that opportunities have been lost, and major scandals could, and should, have been constructed as the long-awaited "Privacy Chernobyl," that one enormous privacy disaster that raises the issue to a new level of mass consciousness and political mobilization. In reality, and in comparison with its resources, the privacy advocacy network has used its opportunities and has achieved successes. If a Privacy Chernobyl has been missed by poor judgments on the part of the network, it is difficult to determine what that crisis was, when it occurred, and what could have been done. The argument that the absence of a broad-based social movement is attributable to strategic error on the part of overworked and underfinanced privacy advocates simply cannot be sustained.

The Properties of Privacy

There is a strong current of opinion in the privacy advocacy network that this issue is "different." However framed, it entails some peculiar properties that are never going to promote a broader political activism. This issue *is* different, but different from what, and should the differences make a difference? A number of arguments have circulated around the network. It is now worth subjecting them to a more rigorous analysis.

The first objection is that privacy always has to be 'balanced' against a countervailing public interest that is typically more powerful. With few exceptions, there is always a justification for the capture and processing of personal information. National security arguments are invoked to justify the interception of communications. Safety is invoked to justify video surveillance. Equity is invoked to justify the collection of personal information for government services. The efficient conduct of marketing— "making sure the right people get targeted with the right ads"—is invoked to justify the collection and profiling of consumer data. The speedy and efficient access to Web sites is invoked to justify the logging of cookie technology on personal hard drives. The protection from fraud is invoked to justify the entire consumer credit industry. A desire for a productive and safe workplace is invoked to justify schemes for workplace monitoring. And even environmentalism can be invoked on occasion, for example, for the remote monitoring of home energy consumption or for the surveillance of vehicles as part of congestion charging schemes.

Privacy advocates have certainly had to struggle with a discourse that is often framed in terms of false dichotomies. They have also had to resist the very metaphor about "balancing" insisting that privacy protection is not incompatible with collective interests like security, efficiency, consumer satisfaction, and so on. Nevertheless, there is nothing inherent in this problem that is not also manifested within other areas. Environmentalism, for example, faces arguments about the need to reconcile conservation against powerful arguments concerning the protection of productive capacity in economic sectors, be it logging, fishing, automobile manufacture, or the use of open space for governmental projects. Just because there is a battle over language and interest between advocates and powerful interests should not mean that a broader political activism is not possible.

A further argument, which also tends to be advanced in comparison with environmentalism, concerns the visibility of harm. Whereas it is possible to observe and measure the direct results of much environmental pollution, arguments against excessive levels of surveillance often have to be pitched in terms of abstract rights and fears of hypothetical consequences. To be sure, many horror stories about the inappropriate collection and use of personal information can be marshaled to the cause (Smith 1993). However, as Philip Agre puts it: "With environmental pollution you can at least see the smoke and oily seabirds, but with invasions of privacy the information flows silently, out of sight, and then you can't figure out how they got your name, much less which opportunities never knocked because of the bad information in your file."[4] It is true that much of the harm from privacy invasions is latent. Most individuals will therefore see the intrusive direct-marketing call, the denial of a loan, the refusal of insurance, the subjection to extra security screening at the airport, or the inaccurate tax return, and will not view these problems as privacy problems. Yet each could have been directly, or indirectly, caused by the collection and processing of inaccurate, obsolete, or incomplete personal data. The cause and effect are often hidden and circuitous.

That is not to say, however, that other social movements do not have to grapple with similar dilemmas. The contemporary argument about global warming is exactly about making a link in the public mind between the burning of fossil fuels and the melting of the polar ice caps, and about interpreting complex science in ways that can change attitudes and behavior. Further, there are increasingly direct and visible manifestations of surveillance technology—video surveillance, identity cards, biometric scanning—which provide a direct moment of personal information capture. The increasingly frequent instances of data breaches can also be regarded as the privacy equivalent of the dumping of toxic waste. Indeed, the use of the term "data spills" deliberately invites this comparison.

A third argument concerns the highly subjective nature of privacy. The appropriate level of privacy protection is only something that can be decided at an individual level, and according to the highly variable instincts about what is, and is not, intrusive or sensitive. As was argued in chapter 1, the appropriate level of privacy that a society might legislate can never be based on an a priori determination of what is, and is not, sensitive. Context determines the level of risk. Public policy, in terms of laws and codes, is thus generally framed in procedural terms permitting individuals to exercise their privacy rights if they so wish, and against the practices they, as individuals, find most intrusive. The highly contextual and subjective nature of the issue makes it hard to measure levels of risk and difficult to produce collective action. As Caspar Bowden puts it: "If you want to say 'Hey chaps, let's go and storm the barricades for privacy so we can all be private together'—that doesn't make sense as a political proposition."[5]

It is difficult to deny that there are constraints imposed by the variable, subjective and contextual nature of the issue. On the other hand, there has been a historic convergence around the information privacy principles, and advocates can and do make judgments about privacy invasiveness using these yardsticks. Thus, Privacy International published in June 2007 an assessment of the privacy practices of the major Internet companies, ranking them according to ten variables of privacy friendliness and providing a color-coded score on a scale from "privacy-friendly and privacy-enhancing" to "comprehensive surveillance and entrenched hostility to privacy." The results achieved some media attention and stiff responses from Google, the only company given the lowest, and blackest, mark.[6] Over time, advocates have been able to frame the issue in more collective, and therefore measurable, terms.

A fourth argument relates to the kind of people who get interested in privacy. Bowden offers the following hypothesis: "It's because the people who value privacy by nature are perhaps more reticent than the average person, but also they are less 'groupie.' So to make privacy resonate as a political issue has so far been pretty insoluble. It may be that the character of society and surveillance has to become so oppressive and repugnant to a mass sensibility for spontaneous resistance to arise on a large scale."[7] Expressed in terms of privacy protection, the issue is likely to attract those people who are by nature less social, more individualistic, and less likely to wish to engage in collective action. Smith agrees: "I think perhaps the people who are attracted to this issue are not joiners."[8]

The argument is difficult to evaluate, one way or the other. Certainly the issue has attracted a high number of individual characters who may not be sympathetic to the demands and strictures of social movement organizations. Furthermore, many have not had experience of social organizing. Bowden again: "And so whereas in other social movements I think you have traditions flowing that provide models of social organization; so one thinks of the overlap of green politics and left politics for example. You don't have that in privacy because essentially people can approach the privacy issue from any point of the Left-Right political axis, and still be concerned with it. But there isn't anything like a ready model to sort of fit into."

A fifth argument concerns the diffuseness and multidimensionality of the issue. Valerie Steeves puts the problem like this:

I guess privacy is on the ascendancy but one of the problems with it from an organizational point view is that it pops up in so many different contexts.... So a part of the problem is that it is simply so decentralized and pervasive. Environmental issues tend to bundle around strip mining and air pollution; they bundle better but I think that reflects the fact that privacy is this social and democratic value. The environment is where we all live, whereas privacy is embedded in our social relations, it's embedded with how we interact with our kids, it's embedded in our workplace, it's embedded in our relationships with the government. Because of that I think our reaction to privacy invasions will be episodic by nature.[9]

Privacy is perhaps one of those issues that *is* a mile wide and an inch thick. In its diffuseness, it cannot attract deep and abiding commitments. It is always an issue, but never the top issue. It is at the heart of civil rights, civil liberties, health care policy, law enforcement, national security, employment law, and so on. But it is never sufficiently prominent to garner in-depth interest commitment. Smith has observed that privacy is always in "the top ten of American issues, but never in the top three. There are other priorities that they have. Everybody tells me how concerned they are about the issue, but will they put up $50 to join an organization ... I wonder?"[10]

This argument suggests nothing more than that privacy is another diffuse public interest issue that has the potential to attract a limitless number of supporters, were it not for the free-rider dilemma. In situations where the benefits of collective action accrue to members of the association, and only to those members, the material incentives for belonging are far stronger. Like other public interest groups, within the environmental, consumer, civil liberties, or human rights arenas, privacy advocacy groups need other nonmaterial incentives to get individuals to donate time and resources. This is a problem, but it is not one that is unfamiliar to other public interest organizations who advocate for issues of similar diffuseness and multidimensionality. Further, it can also be contended that this weakness is its strength. Privacy may be hidden in all political issues, and rarely asserted as a separate policy problem in its own right, but this suggests that the potential for coalition building is enormous.

Finally, there is the strong possibility that "political space" for privacy advocacy has been crowded out by the official (government-sponsored) agencies—the privacy and data protection commissioners performing their various investigative, auditing, complaints resolution, analytical, and enforcement responsibilities in various countries. These agencies, and the statutes that empower them, for the most part predated the emergence of privacy advocacy organizations. Thus, in countries like Canada, the network of federal and provincial privacy commissioners is seen by the media and the general public as the obvious spokespeople for the privacy issue. Steeves sees this very relationship from a Canadian perspective: "So as privacy has become more institutionalized as an issue, I think that in many ways it's made it more difficult to organize a civil society movement around privacy."[11] The same is the case in many European countries. In the United States, on the other hand, the absence of a federal privacy agency allows a multiplicity of groups to flourish.

The "crowding-out" hypothesis is again difficult to evaluate. The test would occur if privacy advocacy groups atrophied in the United States if ever Congress enacted legislation establishing such an agency, a step it has occasionally contemplated. On the other hand, the multiplicity of privacy advocacy groups in the United States is just as easily explained by the pluralistic political culture and constitutional environment that encourages freedom of association. It is doubtful that these advocacy groups would die if a governmental privacy protection agency were created. The existence of an Environmental Protection Agency or a Federal Trade Commission has not rendered environmental or consumer groups redundant. It is just as likely that privacy advocacy groups will continue and will develop the same kind of tense relationship that we see in Europe between the advocacy network and the official "data protectors." In some countries, that tension can be used to positive advantage by a strategic commissioner; it allows them to point to the extreme positions articulated by the outsiders and to accentuate the "reasonableness" of their recommendations and positions. Not all data protection authorities see the relationship in those terms, however.

Each of these arguments has some merit, but none is peculiar to the privacy question. There is a tendency within the network to argue that privacy is "different." This analysis suggests, however, that any differences should not necessarily make a "difference." Everything in this account suggests that this issue is on an upward trajectory in advanced industrial states. It might not reach the same importance as environmental or consumer protection, as Rotenberg suggests at the outset of this chapter. And it should be remembered that it took more than a century after the advent of industrialism, for an environmental politics to emerge. Nor may we see the great "privacy Chernobyl" that will produce a broader, and mass-based, social movement. But the issue is here to stay, and it will probably enjoy a growth in public and political consciousness and interest.

What this study has described and evaluated is not a social movement, but a transnational advocacy network, which has striking parallels in other sectors (Keck and Sikkink 1998). The network might become more cohesive and institutionalized over time, with less pragmatic and ad hoc methods for setting priorities and engaging in campaigns. It will undoubtedly grow through more horizontal connections. But it might never become a social movement—not because of anything inherent in privacy protection, but because the advocacy network is becoming the dominant mode of organization in international relations. Perhaps a mass-based social movement will not develop, precisely because there is a transnational advocacy network (Keck and Sikkink 1998, 204). Hence the standard for comparison has changed, and the comparisons to 1960s social movements are perhaps misplaced. How can we become like "environmentalism" or "civil rights" or "feminism" are not the questions to ask. If the privacy advocacy network does not transform into a social movement, with significant mass mobilization, then perhaps it does not matter. The network society has changed the meaning of what a social movement is and has affected the standards of evaluation.

These descriptions of the privacy advocacy network, whilst admittedly an incomplete snapshot, are strikingly consistent with conclusions about transnational advocacy from other studies of other international political issues. Keck and Sikkink's case studies, for example, reveal that "networks are difficult to organize transnationally, and have emerged around a particular set of issues with high value content and transcultural resonance. But the agility and fluidity of networked forms of organization make them particularly appropriate to historical periods characterized by rapid shifts in problem definition" (Keck and Sikkink 1998, 200).

They note how activists may "shop around the entire global scene for the best venues to present their issues, and seek points of leverage at which to apply pressure" (Ibid.). The successful activists, as we have noted, apply the correct blend of information, symbolic, leverage, and accountability politics. They predict that the role of networks in international politics will grow, posing some severe conceptual and theoretical questions for those who still conceive of the global order and international system as one characterized by sovereign states.

Keck and Sikkink's observations about network structure also resonate with the findings here. They note how the notion of the network as a structure infuses much of what individual actors do and say: "However much an individual or representative of a particular organization may speak and act in the name of a network without necessarily consulting its other members regularly, the synergy of networking nonetheless transforms the timbre of his or her voice. The "voice" of the network is not the sum of the network component voices, but the product of an interaction of voices" (Keck and Sikkink 1998, 207). Thus, the agents are consulted not as individuals, but as "privacy advocates." Whether or not these actors have formerly consulted the network matters little. The existence of the network, and the relations among the network participants, gives the agents a voice and often allows them to "punch beyond their weight."

Further, power and resource imbalances matter less within network structures. This is not to say that stronger and more powerful groups do not have a greater voice. But the more powerful actors are often transformed by their participation in the network. The increasingly close relationship between the ACLU and Privacy International, two groups that superficially have little in common from a structural point of view, is support for this proposition. On privacy and surveillance issues, the ACLU is a network member. It brings resources, membership, and organization to the network. It is in turn transformed by its relations with smaller groups. The relations are often lopsided and asymmetrical, but they are not hierarchical.

Consequently, and here there are lessons for privacy advocates, Keck and Sikkink conclude that "networks are more effective when they are strong and dense. Network strength and density involves the total number and size of organizations in the network, and the regularity of their exchanges" (1998, 206). The question of the development of a larger and integrative SMO, with a mass membership and so on, is less important than whether the existing network can continue to collaborate, share its resources, and extend and solidify its contacts and exchanges, in a complementary, reciprocal, and "networked" fashion. Those linkages must also obviously be global. The continued growth of the privacy advocacy network is also deeply contingent on involving more actors from different countries within the network, and broadening the hitherto European/North American emphasis and flavor of its work.

Conclusions from Privacy Advocates

Academic research and social activism are not separate and discrete activities. The business of trying to change the way the world is run, is inherently "theoretical." Even though activists insist on their practical and down to earth approaches, they are always theorizing because they are always thinking about the underlying causes behind visible problems. They develop models of how the world works in order to change it. And they reflect deeply and consistently on how to build the kinds of organization that can make that change possible. By the same token, much of what academia treats as theoretical has been put on the agenda by social movements. There is a critical and a reflexive relationship between scholarship about and the actions of social movements. Privacy is no different, and the advocates interviewed for this project are testament to the fact that practice and scholarship are, and should be, inseparably intertwined.

At the same time, there is also an improvisational quality to contemporary activism. This book has also been testament to the unavoidable tendency among privacy advocates to "make things up as they go along." Some of the more traditional groups surely have more established modus operandi that produce some decision rules for campaigning. Most do not. The improvisational quality of contemporary privacy advocacy therefore means unpredictability, both for supporters and opponents. These observations echo other generalizations about social movement politics: "Since social movements, like street theater, write their own scripts, if any, as they go along, any prescription of agendas or strategies, let alone tactics, by outsiders—not to mention intellectuals—is likely to be irrelevant at best and counterproductive at worst (Fuentes and Frank 1989, 179).

Hence, the critical concluding question is not what scholarly literature from other domains might say about the future of this network and this issue. The crucial issue is how those within the movement view the future, and what interpretations they offer about the larger questions raised in this chapter. These advocates are not just "subjects" whose views are waiting to be unearthed and presented for academic consumption. They also read the same literature and reflect on its meaning. They develop assumptions and understandings about the causes and consequences of surveillance, about the meanings of privacy and about the most effective ways to effect change. So what lessons do we learn from the advocates themselves? There is a great deal of deep and considered reflection, but there is little consensus.

There is one body of opinion that tends to hold that the status quo is as good as it has ever been. The privacy advocacy network is broader and more effective than at any time since the issue arose to the agenda. Simon Davies of PI holds such a view:

We have a vibrant, active, diverse field at the moment that is guerilla-like. It's responsive, it's efficient. . . . I'm talking about the whole universe of privacy activists and advocates. Remember that the difference between now and twenty years ago is that then, privacy advocates were privacy advocates. Now there's a bit of a privacy advocate in an awful lot of people for different circumstances and under different conditions. And what is wonderful about the vibrant nature of modern activism is that you don't know where it's going to spring from. It can happen spontaneously. The links can just spark and in that way, it's remarkably efficient because it's honed by everybody. We have a vibrant, active, diverse field at the moment that is guerilla-like. It's responsive, it's efficient.[12]

Davies has observed this movement for over twenty years. He does not want these individual groups to coalesce and institutionalize. They would become turgid and unresponsive.

Others are skeptical that such a cohesive group would do any good in the absence of a reframing of the issue. Deidre Mulligan of the UC Berkeley School of Law contends: "I think that Pris Regan's book *Legislating Privacy* is very helpful in understanding that privacy viewed as an individual right in and of itself, rather than something that we have a collective interest in or as something that is an enabler of other things that we care about in society, tends to not have a lot of traction . . . At the legislative level it's still unclear whether or not, even if you had a more cohesive group, whether or not single issue advocacy around privacy is going to be the way to best utilize that organized group. Privacy may still be in service of other issues, and in combination with people who are working on other issues."[13]

Others believe that a greater level of coordination is absolutely necessary. Beth Givens of Privacy Rights Clearinghouse would like to see "an ACLU of informational privacy—a large membership group that has hundreds of thousands, if not millions of members who pay dues and get newsletters and alerts."[14] Others see it as inevitable given their observations of the dynamics of other social movements. Ari Schwartz of CDT, for instance: "I see the potential for a larger movement... because I think it is similar to how the environmental movement grew up, in which there were some medium sized organizations, and it was not until the 60s and 70s until those organizations became much bigger... With privacy you can look back and say that we are at the point where the environmental movement was in the 1960s, and expand from there."[15]

Yet others, such as Roger Clarke of APF, think it will, and should, happen but not for a long time: "Now a formal peak body of public interest organizations that could be decades away. I might be a dead man before that ever arises. But we have much better communications across the twenty or so major players, and we have much better coordination across them. But it's emergent and we've been working on it for sometime.... Yes, I think it will emerge.[16] Others think it should happen, but probably won't. Here's Barry Steinhardt of the ACLU: "The question is what is preventing the creation of a privacy equivalent to Amnesty International, for example. Is that going to happen eventually? Maybe. Or are we going to slip quietly into the surveillance society without a large-scale revolt? I don't know the answer to that question and I fear that we will go quietly into that dark night. We'll just keep slipping further and further into the surveillance society and then we'll just wake up in the middle of it." Whereas some scoff at Scott McNeally's famous remark that "you have zero privacy anyway, get over it," Steinhardt takes it very seriously. The ACLU Web site now displays a ticking clock with predictions left about the short amount of time before the United States slips into a state of total surveillance.[17]

Others do see the answer, not in a formal peak association, but in a continual broadening of the coalition. Lillie Coney of EPIC, a quite recent addition to the privacy community and the main organizer of the Privacy Coalition, draws parallels with the civil rights movement and sees a pressing need to draw lessons from that experience and to draw upon its resources and expertise.[18] There are, however, costs, as Jim Dempsey explains: "From my perspective, the privacy community and the civil rights or antidiscrimination community have not worked together not for a lack of mutual respect, but just we're busy and they're busy. To get them involved in our work would mean that they would have to drop something they're doing, and for us to get involved in their work means we would have to drop something that we are doing."[19]

Many countries, of course, do not have a civil rights tradition. That is why, according to Pam Dixon of World Privacy Forum:

It's crucial that we frame our ideas of privacy in a global manner. When you talk to people from other countries, particularly developing countries and particularly countries that don't have the same culture that you happen to have grown up in, they may have different cultural norms of what privacy is. India is an excellent example. Russia is an extraordinary example.... In Russia, privacy is not getting a knock on your door in the dead of night. How can we develop an idea of privacy that encompasses all these viewpoints, which are very deeply embedded within each culture... Where are the commonalities?

Then there is the local perspective, offered by Rich Neumeister from Minnesota: "before we start thinking internationally, we've got to get our shit together nationally."[20]

There is a widespread recognition that the privacy advocates will not be successful unless privacy resonates more effectively with the mass public. Opinion polls indicating high levels of concern in the abstract are not sufficient. Shifts in attitudes must affect behavior to the extent that the refusal to provide personal information on demand is not regarded as odd or suspicious, but a quite commonplace and understandable response to a reasonable request. Just as employees in restaurants have developed sensibilities to the needs of certain people to refuse certain foods, because of religious affiliation or because of allergic reactions, so a shift in consciousness is needed such that other employees "get it" when someone refuses to provide an address, a social security number, or some other identifier.[21]

If education is the sine qua non of progress, then perhaps the answer lies in sensitizing young people to the privacy issue from the earliest ages. Here is Mulligan:

We took a long time to get to the point where environmental considerations were something that was on the mind of every kindergartener.... If you look at the experience of students growing up today with MySpace and Gmail, and cell phones, and FLICKR, they're experiencing the ways in which technology can track them, monitor them and expose them, but also the power that it allows them to project images of themselves and to build communities. So they are experiencing the intense power in both positive and negative ways. So I think they are going to have a better understanding of the relationship between technological design and privacy.[22]

Perhaps this is true. By the same token, there are just as many people who despair at the cavalier way that young people display personal information about themselves on social-networking Web sites.

It is unsurprising that hardworking advocates have not developed a consensus on these intractable questions. There is no agreement on whether a more cohesive movement is desirable, no agreement on what it should look like, no agreement on whether it is going to happen, no agreement on what it would do, and no agreement on the appropriate frame. No advocate has a comprehensive picture either of the issue or of the actors and groups involved. That is the nature of an open and horizontal network. No one participant has the overview. Thus, the reflections, while deep, considered, and grounded in "theory," are always shaped by personal lessons and perspectives. It is indeed striking how many advocates respond to larger questions about the network, the issue, and the movement in terms of the behaviors and characters of specific personalities.

There is also a tendency for advocates to define their positions in terms of optimism or pessimism about "the future." There are some who believe that the privacy argument will win out over those organizations who believe that they should be allowed to do whatever they wish with peoples' personal information. Chris Hoofnagle is optimistic, because of this: "I think one luxury for privacy advocates is that if you look at the issues, if you look at the facts, the privacy advocates have compelling arguments. I don't think advocates need to spin the situation. Ultimately, the privacy side is going to be more convincing."[23] The optimists point to the greater number of privacy protection laws, the expanding policy community, the increasing fear of negative publicity that can arise from being labeled hostile to the issue, and the visible successes such as those documented in chapter 5. The "pessimists" point to the relentless set of forces, bureaucratic, corporate, political, and technological, which are increasingly aligned to produce more creative, extensive, and intrusive methods of surveillance. They despair at the cavalier way in which individuals, and especially young people, surrender their personal data without a second's thought.

I contend, however, the question of who is an optimist and who a pessimist is largely irrelevant, because there is no one trajectory by which we can measure the progress or regress of privacy protection at any one time. The variety of issues, the multiple ways in which the problem is framed, and the bewildering variety of organizational and national contexts in which it arises mean that it is misleading to derive simplified conclusions about the state of the issue. As we have concluded elsewhere, "the governance of privacy in the global economy through such multiple modes of regulation and coordination means that it is thoroughly misleading to try to observe a balance between privacy and surveillance on a global scale" (Bennett and Raab 2006, 295). It is this pluralism of issues, institutions, contexts, and actors that explain why different advocates can observe progress and regress at the same time. They can disagree not only on the question of whether the ACLU's "Surveillance Clock" is telling the correct time but also on the question of what exactly is supposed to happen at midnight.

The Future of Privacy Advocacy

The network of civil society actors described here is, of course, part of a larger policy community engaged with the development and implementation of policy on privacy and data protection. There is a complex and dynamic regime of participants that include regulatory bodies, data controllers, data subjects, technology developers and providers, government policymakers, the media, and, of course, privacy advocacy groups (Bennett and Raab 2006, 220). There are a lot of people with a stake in the issue. The effectiveness of the system of privacy protection, both nationally and internationally, will depend on the attitudes and behavior of all of these participants, all engaged in what we have called the "governance of privacy." The advancement of this value requires a strong, comprehensive, and unambiguous law; an active and assertive regulatory authority; a strong commitment to privacy by data controllers; a set of market incentives that drive companies to be pro-privacy and to adopt strong self-regulatory mechanisms; a vigilant, concerned, and activist citizenry; and the understanding and application, at the outset of system development, of privacy-enhancing technologies.

What is also clear is that a strong and vibrant privacy advocacy network rooted in civil society is indispensable. An alert and informed network must coexist with the official data protection agencies and the institutionalized chief privacy officers within corporations. It is not simply that the civil society advocates have more freedom to express the more fundamental privacy argument, unencumbered by the pragmatic needs to reconcile that position with social, political, and corporate interests. It is not only that the articulation of a more radical position from the outside permits the institutionalized privacy advocates within government and business to advance the cause, even if in a more compromising way. It is also the case, supported by the preceding analysis, that the nongovernmental and noncorporate actors can also push the limits of the discourse and bring new issues to the domestic and international agendas. They also, of course, contribute to shifts in policy and in changes in the behavior of target actors. More crucially, they exist on the cutting edge, seeing the trends, warning of the dangers, pushing and cajoling in public arenas and private negotiation. However, the ability of the privacy advocacy network to grow is contingent on a number of conditions. This analysis suggests six, which should be read not as prescriptions but as observations of promising trends.

First, there must always be in any network and any campaign an appropriate blend of information, symbolic, leverage, and accountability politics. The stories described in chapter 5 did not result in successes solely, or even primarily, because of the work of privacy advocates. In each, there was a coincidence of political and economic factors that permitted the privacy advocates' efforts to make a difference. In each as well, privacy advocates marshaled information to the debates, linked the issues to symbolic events that resonated within the political culture, applied leverage where possible, and in particular forced organizations to live up to their own rules and those of the jurisdictions in which they were operating. There are many legal and nonlegal rules about privacy protection. Some are strong, and others are weak. Any public statement or commitment to privacy protection, however weak and qualified, provides an opportunity to test whether words are supported by actions and practices. No doubt privacy advocates could do more to use the rights and obligations stated in privacy policies to force higher levels of compliance.[24]

A second lesson relates to the operation of the network itself. Keck and Sikkink (1998) contend that networks are more successful when they exhibit strength and density. By this, they point to the regularity and frequency of interactions within the network. There have been serious efforts in recent years to bring some of the privacy-centric and privacy-explicit groups together to discuss strategy and priorities. The advent of a newer generation of privacy advocates has facilitated these interactions. Nevertheless, there is still a culture of improvisation. The priorities are never established in any coherent way. They emerge because one or two actors decide to do something and ask around for support.

A third lesson relates to the value of broadening the coalition. The efforts to expand the network to privacy-marginal and privacy-potential groups have accelerated in recent years. There is now a broader recognition that an awful lot of interests can be attracted to particular causes, and thus make the network appear far wider and politically significant than in the past. The extension of the network is often temporary, however. New groups may stay for one campaign, and leave for the next. If these groups embrace a privacy protection campaign one month, they often have to drop something else. Broad campaigns, such as that against data retention, take enormous time and effort. They cannot be regular occurrences. Nevertheless, slow adjustment to the realities of the issue, and the potential of the Internet, has produced a broad realization that such broad-based campaigns are beneficial for the network and the issue. Common cause should continue to be made with privacy marginal and privacy potential groups—those actors for whom the issue is rarely, if ever, prominent.

Fourth, many social movements suffer from what is often called "Founders' Syndrome," the inability of the group to project an image and mission beyond that of the personality who created it. Sometimes this syndrome is manifested in conflict between founders and newcomers. Sometimes it causes groups to atrophy after their original creators have moved from the scene. Many groups within the privacy advocacy network are closely associated with the image of their creators. Many are only one person shops. To survive, however, organizations (and especially nonprofits) continue to evolve through their life-cycle change. They must often experience a shift from the improvisational and entrepreneurial to more planned and managed development. There is evidence that some of the groups established in the early 1990s have survived initial conflicts and disruptions in personnel. Many have successfully brought a younger generation of advocates into the community. The strength of the network stems, as noted in the last chapter, from the horizontal and "thin ties." There is also an encouraging pattern of bringing younger people into these groups to enliven and refresh the debate and the mission.

Fifth, there is evidence that the network is beginning to reach out to countries beyond the advanced industrial world. Surveillance is not a national phenomenon; and neither is privacy protection. While the emphasis of this study has been located within the industrialized states of North America, Western Europe, and Australia, privacy advocacy does exist elsewhere, as chapter 2 demonstrated. These advocates are often embedded within larger human rights organizations and frequently have far more immediate priorities. Many of them are unknown to the more established actors in the advanced industrialized world. The globalization of the network has not occurred to the extent that privacy advocates had originally hoped. Experience from other issues, however, suggests that the broader the network, the easier it is to "shop around" for opportunities to challenge surveillance practices. For example, if a law in one country does not offer an opportunity to challenge the practices of a multinational company, then the network might use actors located in another. The globalization of network activity not only permits mutual understanding and lesson drawing but also broadens the opportunities for accountability and leverage politics.

Finally, the question of how the issue should be "framed" will never be resolved, nor should it. Certainly no scholarly analysis, however persuasive, can settle ultimately the meaning of privacy and provide, once and for all, the precise conceptual formula for political and legal success. It is probable, however, that the ability of advocates to advance the cause will depend on being able to frame the question more in collective than in individual terms, and to encourage wider debate, nationally and internationally, about the kind of society in which we want to live. Advocacy tends to be more persuasive when individual cases are projected to societal trends and common experience.

This study has held a mirror up to the individuals and groups, who in the face of enormous social and technological pressures, have tried to advance a complex argument about the erosion of a fundamental human right. Given their lack of resources, the fact that any successes have been achieved is indeed remarkable. This study does not support the proposition that "you have zero privacy anyway; get over it." It does not support the contention that there is an irreversible slide into the "surveillance society." Even though privacy advocates may feel that they are engaging in a continual game of "whack a mole," hitting down one challenge only to find others immediately cropping up,[25] there is much to be celebrated from this history. But the future of this network lies not in emulating other social movements, nor in waiting for the great privacy Armageddon. It lies in the persistent, relentless, and informed articulation of the very simple proposition that individuals have a right to control the information that relates to them. Few would deny this right. Everybody wants it for themselves. The cause is a just one. The issue is not going to disappear, and neither will the men and women who advocate it.

Appendix 1: List of Interviewees

Name	Organization	Date	Place of interview
Albrecht, Katherine	Consumers Against Supermarket Privacy Invasion and Numbering (CASPIAN)	May 4, 2006 June 28, 2007	Washington, D.C., USA, and telephone
Bittmer, Peter	Forum Informatikerinnen für Frieden and gesellshaftliche Verandtwortung (FIFF)	June 24, 2006	Berlin, Germany
Bowden, Caspar	Former director of Foundation for Information Policy Research (FIPR)	May 18, 2007	telephone
Bruch, Christoph Kant, Martina	Die Humanistische Union (HU)	June 22, 2006	Berlin, Germany
Clarke, Roger	Australian Privacy Foundation (APF)	March 28, 2007	telephone
Coney, Lillie	Electronic Privacy Information Center (EPIC) and Privacy Coalition	June 12, 2007	telephone
Davies, Simon	Privacy International (PI)	May 3, 2007	Montreal, Q.C., Canada
Dempsey, Jim	Center for Democracy and Technology (CDT)	February 15, 2007	Berkeley, Calif., USA
Dixon, Pam	World Privacy Forum (WPF)	March 7, 2007	Carlsbad, Calif., USA
Gellman, Bob	Independent consultant	June 20, 2007	telephone
Givens, Beth	Privacy Rights Clearinghouse (PRC)	March 8, 2007	San Diego, Calif., USA
Greenleaf, Graham	Australian Privacy Foundation (APF)	August 16, 2007	Victoria, B.C., Canada
Guerra, Robert	Privaterra	March 27, 2006	Toronto, ON, Canada
Hoofnagle, Chris	Samuelson Law, Technology & Public Policy Clinic, U. of California, Berkeley	February 5, 2007	Berkeley, Calif., USA

Name	Organization	Date	Place of interview
Holvast, Jan	Holvast and Associates	June 29, 2006	Amsterdam, Netherlands
Hosein, Gus	Privacy International (PI)	June 17, 2006	Toronto, ON, Canada
Lawford, John	Public Interest Advocacy Centre (PIAC)	March 31, 2006	Ottawa, ON, Canada
Lawson, Philippa	Canadian Internet Policy and Public Interest Clinic (CIPPIC)	September 27, 2006	Ottawa, ON, Canada
Mulligan, Deidre	Samuelson Law, Technology & Public Policy Clinic, Berkeley Center for Law and Technology at the University of California, Berkeley	April 17, 2007	Berkeley, Calif., USA
Neumeister, Rich	Private Citizen, Inc.	May 25, 2006	St. Paul, Minn., USA
New York Surveillance Camera Players		August 27, 2006	New York, N.Y., USA
Pierce, Deborah	Privacy Activism	May 17, 2007	San Francisco, Calif., USA
Rotenberg, Marc	Electronic Privacy Information Center (EPIC)	May 3, 2006	Washington, D.C., USA
Smith, Robert Ellis	*Privacy Journal*	August 29, 2006	Providence, R.I., USA
Steeves, Val	University of Ottawa	September 28, 2006	Ottawa, ON, Canada
Steinhardt, Barry	American Civil Liberties Union (ACLU)	June 1, 2007	telephone
Schwartz, Ari	Center for Democracy and Technology (CDT)	May 5, 2006	Washington, D.C., USA
Tangens, Rena	FoeBuD	June 27 2006	Bielefeld, Germany
Tien, Lee	Electronic Frontier Foundation (EFF)	February 26, 2007	Berkeley, Calif., USA
van Amersfoort, Rick	Buro Jansen and Janssen	June 28, 2006	Amsterdam, Netherlands
Wessling, Maurice van Hoboken, Joris	Bits of Freedom (BoF)	June 28, 2006	Amsterdam, Netherlands

Appendix 2: Standard Interview Questions

Background

What is your background and expertise?
Tell me how you first became involved with the privacy issue.

Privacy Advocacy

Do you regard yourself as a privacy advocate?
If so, what do you mean by that term?
How do you distinguish between your role in this community and that of others?
Privacy is a notoriously broad and vague concept; how do you define it?
How do you know a privacy breach when you encounter one?
What principle or principles guide your advocacy?

Organization

What is the stated mission of your organization?
How broad/large is it? In what countries do you operate?
Do you have a membership?
From where do you obtain resources?

Techniques and Tactics

First there are a set of activities related to official government bodies:

- Consultation and commentary on government proposals
- Lobbying
- FOI requests
- Expert witnesses
- Complaints to information and privacy commissioners
- Litigation

Second, media relations:

- Offline: op-eds, letters, books
- Online: weblogs, lists, electronic petitions, etc.

Third, advice and education:

- Advice on development of personal information systems
- Advice on internal policies/codes
- Training of employees
- Working on behalf of members of the public

Fourth, resistance strategies:

- Transparency
- Outing
- Boycotts
- Clogging the system activism (e.g., junk faxes)
- Art and symbols

Is there anything else?
What strategies are the most successful for you?

The Issue and the Network

What sorts of privacy issues do you become involved with?
What sorts of privacy issues do you avoid?
What are the boundaries of the privacy issue for you?
How does this issue conflict with access/freedom of speech issues?
How do you prioritize the issues that you take on?
How do you keep up with what is going on?
What are the major constraints in advocating this issue?
Do you join with other groups both within and outside the privacy movement to make common cause?
Do you think there is the potential for a broader international movement to support the privacy issue?

Notes

1 Framing the Problem

1. Articles 25 and 26 of the EU Data Protection Directive stipulate that personal data on Europeans should only flow outside the boundaries of the EU to countries that can guarantee an "adequate level of protection." (European Union 1995).

2. *The Concise Oxford Dictionary*, for example: "supervision, close observation, invigilation, esp. of suspected person."

3. See, for example, the work of Susan Sibley on the role of law and inspection of laboratories: "Governing Green Laboratories: Trust and Surveillance in the Cultures of Science," paper presented to the Center for the Study of Law and Society, University of California, Berkeley, January 16, 2007.

4. Steve Mann, "Sousveillance," 2002, http://wearcam.org/sousveillance.htm. See also the blog on sousveillance, "On the Identity Trail," May 8, 2007, http://idtrail.org/.

5. Rate my Professors, http://www.ratemyprofessor.com.

6. Steve Mann, "Sousveillance," 2002, http://wearcam.org/sousveillance.htm.

7. See the examples at "Sousveillance," Wikipedia, http://en.wikipedia.org/wiki/Sousveillance.

8. Not Bored!, http://www.notbored.org. The activities of the Surveillance Camera Players are discussed in chapter 3.

9. "Report TIPS Informants," Operation TIPS—Tips, http://www.all-the-other-names-were-taken.com/tipstips.html.

10. "Interim Report to Members 1990–1991," Privacy International, November 25, 1991, http://www.privacyinternational.org/article.shtml?cmd[347]=x-347-145834.

11. "Definitions," BC Freedom of Information and Privacy Association (FIPPA), http://fipa.bc.ca/rights/.

12. Center for Digital Democracy, http://www.democraticmedia.org.

13. Global Internet Liberty Campaign, http://www.gilc.org.

14. Electronic Privacy Information Center, http://www.epic.org.

15. The Privacy Coalition, http://www.privacycoalition.org.

16. Australian Privacy Foundation, http://www.privacy.org.au/About/Background.html.

17. Center for Democracy and Technology, http://www.cdt.org.

18. Electronic Frontier Foundation, http://www.eff.org.

19. Center for Digital Democracy, http://www.democraticmedia.org.

20. Health Privacy Project, http://www.healthprivacy.org.

21. "Privacy and Technology" Web page, American Civil Liberties Union, http://www .aclu.org/privacy/index.html.

22. Bits of Freedom, http://www.bof.nl/index_uk.html.

23. Not Bored!, http://www.notbored.org.

24. International Campaign Against Mass Surveillance (ICAMS), http://www.i-cams.org.

2 The Groups

1. The London School of Economics and Political Science, "What Is Civil Society?," http:// www.lse.ac.uk/collections/CCS/what_is_civil_society.htm.

2. In the United States, for instance, many groups are classified as nonprofit, tax-exempt educational foundations under Section 501(c) 3 of the Internal Revenue Code.

3. Personal interview, Graham Greenleaf, Victoria, B.C., August 16, 2007. Greenleaf had to arrange a small conference associated with the 1992 International Privacy Commissioners conference in Sydney to help pay off these expenses.

4. Privacy International, "Interim Report to Members," November 25, 1991, http://www .privacyinternational.org/article.shtml?cmd[347]=x-347-145834.

5. Ibid.

6. Personal interview, Gus Hosein, June 16, 2006.

7. Personal interview, Simon Davies, May 7, 2007.

8. Personal interview, Gus Hosein, June 16, 2006.

9. "Background," Australian Privacy Foundation, http://www.privacy.org.au/About/ Background.html.

10. CPSR was established in June 1982, and up until the mid-1980s, it focused on the dangers posed by the massive increase in the use of computing technology in military applications. Since then, however, CPSR's program has broadened considerably. In 1986, the Privacy and Civil Liberties Project began really in response to requests for research support from Washington-based organizations that lacked CPSR's computing expertise. This work then made it possible for CPSR to open a Washington-based privacy office in 1988. Marc Rotenberg was named the director of that office, which grew rapidly and in June 1994 spun off into EPIC.

11. Personal interview, Marc Rotenberg, May 3, 2006.

12. *Cy pres* is derived from the French "Cy près comme possible," meaning "as near as possible." These monies result from successful class action lawsuits where it is impossible to distribute all the funds directly to the injured parties. The court may then order that the funds be used for grants to benefit the class members indirectly or "as nearly as possible" in order to compensate for the harm to the class members indirectly. The settlement or judgment will often specify the "next best use" that the funds should be used for. See http://www .cypresfunds.net.

13. "Privacy," Electronic Privacy Information Center, http://www.epic.org/privacy/. See "Privacy by Topic: The A to Z's of Privacy."

14. Privacy Rights Clearinghouse, http://www.privacyrights.org.

15. Personal interview, Beth Givens, March 8, 2007.

16. Ibid.

17. Personal interview, Deborah Pierce, May 17, 2007.

18. Privacy Activism, http://www.privacyactivism.org.

19. World Privacy Forum, http://www.worldprivacyforum.org.

20. Personal interview, Pam Dixon, March 7, 2007.

21. Arge Daten Privacy Service, http://www.argedaten.at.

22. Personal interview, Barry Steinhardt, June 1, 2007.

23. Note, for example, the controversy that erupted in the 1988 presidential election campaign when then Vice-President Bush "outed" Governor Michael Dukakis as a "card-carrying member of the ACLU," implying a softness on crime and a lack of patriotism.

24. "Privacy and Technology," American Civil Liberties Union, http://www.aclu.org/privacy/index.html.

25. In 2004, for instance, the ACLU launched a "no spy pledge campaign" that urged consumers to write to stores, airlines, banks, and car rental companies and request that they not hand over their personal data to the government unless required by law. See "No Spy Pledge" Campaign, American Civil Liberties Union, http://www.aclu.org/privatize/companylist.html.

26. "Is the U.S. Turning into a Surveillance Society?," American Civil Liberties Union, http://www.aclu.org/privacy/gen/index.html.

27. "About Us," CATO Institute, http://www.cato.org/about/about.html.

28. Jim Harper, "Understanding Privacy—and the Real Threats to It," *Policy Analysis*, no. 520, August 2004, http://www.cato.org/pubs/pas/pa520.pdf.

29. Solveig Singleton, "Privacy and Human Rights: Comparing the United States to Europe," Cato Institute, December 1, 1999, http://www.cato.org/pubs/wtpapers/991201paper.html.

30. http://libertycoalition.net.

31. "Privacy Project Home," Canadian Civil Liberties Association, http://www.ccla.org/privacy/index.html.

32. "Civil Liberties Advocates and the Origins of the BCCLA," B.C. Civil Liberties Association, http://www.bccla.org/originsofbccla.htm.

33. Interview, Christoph Bruch and Martina Kant, Die Humanistische Union, June 22, 2006.

34. "About," Liberty and the Civil Liberties Trust, http://www.liberty-human-rights.org.uk/about/index.shtml.

35. Statewatch, http://www.statewatch.org.

36. European Civil Liberties Network, http://www.ecln.org/about3.html.

37. European Civil Liberties Network, http://www.ecln.org/.

38. Buro Jansen and Janssen, http://www.burojansen.nl/.

39. "Act Now," Amnesty International, http://web.amnesty.org/pages/internet-index-eng.

40. Rights and Democracy, http://www.ichrdd.ca.

41. The name was chosen because of its common impact in English, French, Spanish, Italian, and so on. Similar services are provided by the CryptoRights Foundation, http://www.cryptorights.org/operations/.

42. Personal interview, Robert Guerra, March 26, 2006.

43. See Pablo Palazzi's blog, "Habeas Data," http://dataprotection.blogspot.com/, as well as Data Protection Laws, http://www.dataprotectionlaws.com.ar/.

44. In Peru, an organization called Alfa-Redi, http://www.alfa-redi.org, as well as a chapter of CPSR. In Chile, Digital Rights (Derechos Digitales), http://www.derechosdigitales.org. In Argentina, the Open Source Foundation (Fundacion via Libre) has begun to campaign against data retention, http://www.vialibre.org.ar/. In Guatemala, there is a human rights organization called Seguridad en Democracia (SEDEM). There is also an Ibero-American Data Protection network coordinated by the Spanish data protection authority, http://www.agpd.es. I am grateful to Katitza Rodriguez of CPSR Peru for explaining the Latin American landscape to me.

45. "Human Rights and the Internet," NGO Privacy Ukraine, http://www.internetrights.org.ua/index.php?page=about&lang=en.

46. Big Brother Awards International, http://www.bigbrotherawards.org. Key organizations in Eastern Europe are Iuridicum Remedium (Czech Republic), http://www.iure.org, and Internet Society Bulgaria, http://www.isoc.bg/index_en.html.

47. Privacy Mongolia, http://www.privacymongolia.org. A representative showed up at the 2007 Annual Meeting of the International Conference of Data Protection and Privacy Commissioners in Montreal.

48. Personal interview, Valerie Steeves, September 26, 2006.

49. "Which?" http://www.which.co.uk/reports_and_campaigns/consumer_rights/index.jsp.

50. Verbraucherzentrale Bundesverband 2004.

51. "About Us," Consumer's Association of Canada, http://www.consumer.ca/index.php4?id=1480.

52. For example, L'Organisation Générale des Consommateurs in France, http://www.orgeco.net/; the Consumentenbond in the Netherlands, http://www.consumentenbond.nl; the Movimento Comsumatori in Italy, http://www.movimentoconsumatori.it; and the Consumer Federation of America, http://www.consumerfed.org.

53. See Ed Mierzwinski's blog, "U.S. PIRG Consumer Blog," Federation of State PIRGs, http://www.uspirg.org/html/consumer/archives/protecting_privacy/index.html.

54. Consumers Against Supermarket Privacy Invasion and Numbering (CASPIAN), http://www.nocards.org, and Spychips, CASPIAN, http://www.spychips.org.

55. Personal interview, Katherine Albrecht, May 3, 2006.

56. Ibid.

57. Ibid.

58. Trans Atlantic Consumer Dialogue, http://www.tacd.org.

59. "About EFF," Electronic Frontier Foundation, http://www.eff.org/about/.

60. John Perry Barlow, "A Declaration of the Independence of Cyberspace," Electronic Frontier Foundation, http://homes.eff.org/~barlow/Declaration-Final.html.

61. One of the first EFF T-shirts contained a simple rendering of the First Amendment.

62. Electronic Frontier Canada, http://www.efc.ca, and Electronic Frontiers Australia, http://www.efa.org.au.

63. Personal interview, Lee Tien, February 26, 2007.

64. Center for Democracy and Technology, http://www.cdt.org/about/.

65. Jerry Berman, "Letter from the President," in "Accomplishments and Objectives 2004–06," Center for Democracy and Technology, January 2006, http://www.cdt.org/mission/2006annualreport.pdf.

66. Personal interview, Ari Schwartz, May 4, 2006.

67. "CDT Mission and Principles," Center for Democracy and Technology, http://www.cdt.org/mission/.

68. "About," Center for Democracy and Technology, http://www.cdt.org/about/.

69. Robert Gellman, "New Report on RFID and Privacy," *Direct Marketing News*, August 9, 2006, http://www.dmnews.com/cms/dm-news/legal-privacy/37789.html.

70. Center for Digital Democracy, http://www.democraticmedia.org.

71. Netjus, http://www.netjus.com; IRIS (Imaginons en Réseau Internet Solidaire), http://www.iris.sgdg.org/; Digital Rights Denmark, http://www.digitalrights.dk; Digital Rights Ireland, http://www.digitalrights.ie.

72. BoF was initially funded through the sale of an Internet Service Provider developed for the hacker community (XS4ALL).

73. Telephone interview, Caspar Bowden, May 18, 2007.

74. In 2002, Bowden left FIPR to head the privacy work for Microsoft's Trusting Computing Initiative across Europe, the Middle East, and Africa.

75. Cyber-Rights and Cyber-Liberties, http://www.cyber-rights.org.

76. The CCC hacked the German Bildschirmtext computer network and succeeded in transferring DM 134,000 from a Hamburg bank to the account of the CCC; the money was returned the next day at a press conference. In 1996, CCC members successfully hacked Microsoft's ActiveX technology. And most famously in 2001, the CCC celebrated its twentieth birthday with an interactive light installation (Project Blinkenlights), which turned the Haus des Lehrers building in Berlin into one huge computer screen.

77. See "How to Fake Fingerprints?" Chaos Computer Club e.V., October 26, 2004, http://www.ccc.de/biometrie/fingerabdruck_kopieren.xml?language=en.

78. Interview with Peter Bittner, FIFF, June 24, 2006. See Forum InformatikerInnen für Frieden und gesellschaftliche Verantwortung e.V. (Forum for Computer Professionals for Peace and Social Responsibility), http://fiff.hbxt.de.

79. "EDRI Members," European Digital Rights, http://www.edri.org/about/members.

80. "About European Digital Rights," European Digital Rights, http://www.edri.org/about.

81. Early examples would be Jason Catlett of Junkbusters, David Chaum of Digicash, Phil Zimmerman, the inventor of the Pretty Good Privacy (PGP), and Austin Hill, the founder of Zeroknowledge.

82. Simon Davies, "On Campaigns of Opposition to ID Card Schemes," Privacy International, January 1, 1996, http://www.privacyinternational.org/issues/idcard.

83. NO2ID, http://www.no2id.net/.

84. Amador Books Albuquerque, http://www.amadorbooks.com/nocards.htm.

85. Californians against Telephone Solicitation (CATS), http://www.stopjunkcalls.com.

86. Coalition Against Unsolicited Commercial Email (CAUCE), http://www.cauce.net.

87. Private Citizen, Inc., http://privatecitizen.com.

88. Speed Cameras Dot Org, http://www.speedcameras.org/.

89. http://www.speedcam.co.uk/index2.htm.

90. Patient Privacy Rights Foundation, http://www.patientprivacyrights.org.

91. Health Privacy Project, http://www.healthprivacy.org/.

92. Medical Privacy Coalition, http://www.medicalprivacycoalition.org.

93. TheBigOptOut, http://www.thebigoptout.org.

94. The Identity Project, http://www.papersplease.org.

95. "Travel Advice from Edward Hasbrouck, The Practical Nomad," The Practical Nomad, http://hasbrouck.org/.

96. LeaveThemKidsAlone, http://www.leavethemkidsalone.com.

97. Brittan Elementary School in Northern California won a Big Brother Award for this practice in 2005. See "Children and RFIP Systems," Electronic Privacy Information Center, http://www.epic.org/privacy/rfid/children.html.

98. Take, for instance, the Global Internet Liberty Campaign, http://www.gilc.org.

99. For the British group Genewatch, privacy was a very marginal concern until the government established the Police National DNA Database in 2004 (www.genewatch.org).

3   The Actors

Epigraphs: Rotenberg's statement was made at the First Conference on Computers, Freedom and Privacy (CFP), San Francisco, March 26–28, 1991. Flaherty's statement appeared in countless speeches while he was information and privacy commissioner of British Columbia. Quoted in the *Wall Street Journal*, April 12, 2001, on the occasion of Bush directing the Department of Health and Human Services to implement new medical privacy regulations in the United States.

1. Personal interview, Valerie Steeves, September 26, 2006.

2. Personal interview, Philippa Lawson, September 27, 2006.

3. Personal interview, Graham Greenleaf, August 21, 2007.

4. Personal interview, Ari Schwartz, May 5, 2006.

5. Personal interview, Simon Davies, May 7, 2007.

6. Personal interview, Lee Tien, February 26, 2007.

7. "Part 11. Communications and Liaison, Chapter 2, Privacy Advocate," Internal Revenue Service, United States Department of the Treasury, http://www.irs.gov/irm/part11/ch02s01.html.

8. "Privacy Statement," Network Technologies Inc., http://www.networktechinc.com/privacy-statement.html.

9. Personal interview, Rich Neumeister, May 24, 2006.

10. Personal interview, Gus Hosein, June 16, 2006.

11. The University of Georgia.

12. Personal interview, Chris Hoofnagle, February 5, 2007.

13. Personal interview, Jim Dempsey, February 15, 2007.

14. Personal interview, Robert Ellis Smith, August 27, 2006.

15. Sarah D. Scalet, "Privacy Q&A: Alan Westin on Protecting Corporate Data," *CIO*, June 15, 2003, 3–4, http://www.cio.com/archive/061503/balancing.html.

16. Personal interview, Robert Ellis Smith, August 27, 2006.

17. Telephone interview, Katherine Albrecht, June 28, 2007.

18. Metromail, the dominant mail-list company at the time, hired prisoners in Texas to process consumer-survey data. One of the prisoners phoned one of the survey respondents, Beverley Dennis, and harassed her using the knowledge he had gained from the survey. Dennis won a multimillion-dollar settlement in her lawsuit and decided to devote $1 million to grassroots privacy advocacy.

19. A term coined by Davies at the First Conference on Computers, Freedom and Privacy (CFP), San Francisco, March 26–28, 1991. Rebecca Mercuri, "Computers, Freedom, Privacy Trip Report," *The Risks Digest* 11, no. 39, April 4, 1999, http://catless.ncl.ac.uk/Risks/11.39.html.

20. For an analysis of the various meanings of the word "balance," see Raab 1999.

21. Personal interview, Simon Davies, May 7, 2007.

22. Personal interview, Rich Neumeister, May 24, 2006.

23. "The Twin Cities' Privacy Crusader," *Business Week Online*, February 6, 2003, http://www.businessweek.com/bwdaily/dnflash/feb2003/nf2003026_9425_db025.htm.

24. As quoted by State Senator Steve Kelley (Ibid).

25. "The Devil and Ms. Jansen and Other Tales from Our Least Likely Lobbyists," *Minneapolis/St. Paul City Pages*, January 30, 2002, http://citypages.com/databank/23/1104/article10105.asp.

26. Rachel E. Stassen-Berger, "Public Life, Private Man: Man Shows You Don't Have to Run for Public Office to Represent Public Interests," *St. Paul Pioneer Press*, March 17, 2002.

27. "And he causeth all, both small and great, rich and poor, free and bond, to receive a mark in their right hand, or in their foreheads. And that no man might buy or sell, save he

that had the mark, or the name of the beast, or the number of the beast." *Revelation* 13:16–18. "And there fell a noisome and grievous sore upon the men which had the mark of the beast, and upon them which worshipped his image." *Revelation* 16:1–2. "If any man worship the beast and his image, and receive his mark, or in his forehead, or in his hand, the same shall drink of the wine of the wrath of God, which is poured out without mixture into the cup of his indignation; and he shall be tormented with fire and brimstone in the presence of the holy angels, and in the presence of the Lamb and the smoke of their torment ascendeth up for ever and ever and they have no rest day nor night, who worship the beast and his image, and whosoever receiveth the mark of his name." *Revelation* 14:9–11. See further references at AntiChips, http://www.antichips.org/what-is-verichip.htm.

28. Katherine Albrecht, Caspian Newsletter, May 4, 2007, http://www.newsletterarchive.org/2007/05/04/151159-%5BCaspian-newsletter-l%5D+Your+help+is+needed+to+stop+human+microchipping.

29. AntiChips, http://www.antichips.org.

30. "Drivers License Photo Challenged on Religious Grounds," *CBC News* October 22, 2004, http://www.cbc.ca/canada/story/2004/10/21/bothwell041021.html.

31. Personal interview, Deborah Pierce, May 17, 2007.

32. Arik Hesseldahl, "Privacy Nuts, Chill Out," *Forbes*, April 22, 2005, http://www.forbes.com/personaltech/2005/04/22/cx_ah_0422tentech.html; David Coursey, "How a Broadband Provider Got Slimed by Privacy Nuts," *ZDNet*, February 15, 2002, http://review.zdnet.com/4520-6033_16-4206955.html.

33. David Braun, "FBI Calls Privacy Extremists Elitist," TechWire, September 25, 1997, http://www.jya.com/fbi-elite.htm.

34. Lyle Hawkins, "Opposition to National ID: Giving Comfort to Terrorists," *Edmonton Journal*, November 8, 2001.

35. Heather McDonald, "The Privacy Jihad," *Wall Street Journal*, April 1, 2004 (emphasis in original). The date might have suggested that this article should not be taken too seriously. But in a later piece she attacked the "privacy extremists" and "privacy charlatanism." Heather MacDonald, "Perils of Privacy," *The New York Post*, April 26, 2004.

36. Heather MacDonald, "The Escalating Triumph of Privacy Advocacy over Common Sense," *Washington Post*, May 31, 2004.

37. Personal interview, Simon Davies, May 7, 2007.

38. Recent examples include Schwartz and Reidenberg 1996; Swire and Litan 1998; Bygrave 2002; Solove 2004.

39. See, for instance, Gandy 1993; Lyon 2001, 2003a,b; Marx 1988; Rule 2007.

40. See, for example, Bennett 1992; Bennett and Grant 1999; Bennett and Raab 2006; Regan 1995; Gilliom 2001; Whitaker 1999.

41. Examples include Schoeman 1992; Hansson and Palm 2005; Boling 1996; Nissenbaum 2004; van den Hoven and Weckert 2005.

42. See examples of the work of the Data Privacy Lab, http://privacy.cs.cmu.edu/index.html.

43. The influence of these individuals and others is traced in Bennett 1992.

44. Examples include the Privacy Foundation at the University of Denver's College of Law; the Centre de Recherche Informatique et Droits at Namur University, Belgium; the Harvard Information Infrastructure Project; the Berkeley Center for Law and Technology; the Oxford Institute for the Internet and Society; and many others.

45. Examples include the Canadian Internet Policy and Public Interest Clinic at the University of Ottawa and the Samuelson Law, Technology and Public Policy Clinic at the University of California, Berkeley.

46. Personal interview, Deidre Mulligan, April 17, 2007.

47. Stanley Fish, "Why We Built the Ivory Tower," *New York Times*, May 21, 2004.

48. The surveys conducted under the stewardship of Alan Westin, and funded through Equifax, have been particularly controversial. See, for instance, Oscar Gandy's critique of Westin's surveys (Gandy 2003).

49. A topical example is the battle in the United Kingdom over the British ID card scheme and the attempt by the government to discredit a report written under the auspices of the London School of Economics and Political Science, *The Identity Project: An Assessment of the UK Identity Cards Bill and Its Implications*, June 27, 2005, http://is2.lse.ac.uk/idcard/identityreport.pdf.

50. "The mission of the IAPP is to define, promote, and improve the privacy profession globally. The International Association of Privacy Professionals (IAPP) is the world's largest association of privacy professionals. Based in York, Maine, the organization represents over 4,000 members from businesses, governments and academia across 32 countries. Founded in 2001, the IAPP was established to define, promote and improve the privacy profession globally. The IAPP is committed to providing a forum for privacy professionals to share best practices, track trends, advance privacy management issues, standardize the designations for privacy professionals, and provide education and guidance on opportunities in the field of privacy." It therefore attracts many professionals in addition to consultants. International Association of Privacy Professionals, http://www.privacyassociation.org.

51. "Supporting EPIC," Electronic Privacy Information Center, http://epic.org/epic/support.html.

52. The Ponemon Institute, LCC, would be an example. See http://www.ponemon.org/.

53. A point often made by Alan Westin, the founder of Privacy and American Business in 1993, for instance during his keynote address to the Visions of Privacy conference, Victoria, B.C., May 1996.

54. In the interests of full disclosure, I have performed this role on a number of occasions, having written reports for the Canadian Standards Association, the Standards Council of Canada, the European Union, and various agencies of the Government of Canada.

55. Telephone interview, Roger Clarke, March 28, 2007.

56. A position associated with the theories of Langdon Winner (1986). It is also inherent in Lawrence Lessig's (1999) basic argument that computer code has legal and regulatory properties.

57. Eric Hughes, "A Cypherpunk's Manifesto," Activism.net, March 9, 1993, http://www.activism.net/cypherpunk/manifesto.html.

58. Gilmore actually lost his suit in federal court, and the Supreme Court refused to hear his appeal on the question of whether the TSA could enforce these rules through a secret law. See "Want to Fly? Papers, Please," PapersPlease.org, http://papersplease.org/gilmore/facts.html.

59. PGP Corporation, http://www.pgp.com.

60. The Zfone Project, http://zfoneproject.com/.

61. See Bruce Schneier's blog, http://www.schneier.com/blog/archives/2005/09/secure_flight_n_1.html.

62. Privacy Journal, http://www.privacyjournal.net/.

63. Personal interview, Robert Ellis Smith, August 29, 2006.

64. Privacy Times, http://www.privacytimes.com.

65. Access Reports, edited by Harry Hammitt, is an example; see http://www.accessreports.com/about.html.

66. TRAC Immigration, http://trac.syr.edu/immigration/index.html.

67. The metaphor preferred in Solove 2004.

68. Other illustrations include *The Matrix*, a 1999 film in which a simulated reality is created by sentient machines in order to subdue then human population with cybernetic

implants; *Equilibrium*, a 2002 film wherein a dystopic future society surviving the third world war takes an emotion-suppressing drug named "prozium" and where the general public is constantly watched by the Grammaton Clerics to make sure that no one—breaks the equilibrium; *V for Vendetta*, a 2005 film about a future-day England that has been transformed into a *1984*-style dystopia; and *Gattaca*, a 1997 film about an aerospace firm in the future that analyzes DNA and determines where people belong in life.

69. See further listings at "Resource Base," Surveillance & Society, http://www.surveillance-and-society.org/pages/resources/a.htm.

70. "Rhetorics of Surveillance: From Bentham to Big Brother," CTRL [SPACE], http://hosting.zkm.de/ctrlspace/e/intro.

71. Bit product database, http://bureauit.org/bitindex.html.

72. Cheryl Sourkes, *Public Camera*, exhibit at the National Gallery of Canada, April–October, 2007, http://www.gallery.ca/english/default_4239.htm. See also Sourkes 2007.

73. Jill Magid, http://jillmagid.net/index.php.

74. http://elahi.rutgers.edu.

75. FoeBuD e.V., http://www.foebud.org.

76. Personal interview, Rena Tangens, June 27, 2006.

77. See Surveillance Camera Players 2006, 35. This book provides a complete record of their performances, their campaigns and the reaction of law enforcement authorities.

78. The author took such a tour of New York City Hall on a rainy Sunday afternoon on August 27, 2006.

4 The Strategies

Epigraphs: On the history of the CCLA, see http://www.ccla.org/his/. Lawson's statement made at the Conference on Private Sector Privacy in a Changing World, Vancouver, September 20–21, 2007.

1. Statement of Barry Steinhardt, Director of Technology and Liberty Program, American Civil Liberties Union, on government data mining before the Technology, Information Policy, Intergovernmental Relations and the Census subcommittee of the House Committee on Government reform, May 20, 2003, http://www.aclu.org/safefree/general/17262leg20030520.html.

2. Personal interview, Chris Hoofnagle, February 5, 2007.

3. Ibid.

4. Personal interview, Caspar Bowden, May 18, 2007.

5. Personal interviews, Christoph Bruch and Martina Kant, Die Humanistische Union, Berlin, June 22, 2006.

6. See the Policy Laundering Project, http://www.policylaundering.org.

7. See Alan Davidson, John Morris, and Robert Courtney, "Strangers in a Strange Land: Public Internet Advocacy and Internet Standards," 2002, http://www.cdt.org/publications/piais.pdf.

8. Colin J. Bennett and Robin Bayley, "Saying What You Do and Doing What You Say: Arguments and Prospects for an International Privacy Standard," paper prepared for the Annual Meeting of the International Privacy and Data Protection Commissioners, Montreal, Quebec, September 27, 2007.

9. See *EPIC Alert*, 14.04, February 27, 2007. As EPIC reported: "There are any number of scenarios under which it would make sense for the vendors, with TSA's support, to record the images, including the desire to build a database of images of suspected weapons so that image processing techniques could be developed to improve the screening process."

10. The story is told by Shirley Lynn Scott, as "The Video Tape," in Crime Library, http://www.crimelibrary.com/classics3/bulger/.

11. "RFID: Tracking Everything, Everywhere," Katherine Albrecht, Spychips, http://www.spychips.com/rfid_overview.html.

12. Spychips, http://www.spychips.com/index.html.

13. Chris Jay Hoofnagle, "Big Brother's Little Helpers: How ChoicePoint and Other Commercial Data Brokers Collect, Package and Process Your Data for Law Enforcement," http://www.epic.org/privacy/choicepoint/cp_article.pdf.

14. http://www.bigbrotherinside.org.

15. Davies recalls that the idea stemmed from an argument in a bar with a company representative and his final parting shot—"there ought to be an award for people like you." Personal interview, Simon Davies, May 3, 2007.

16. Big Brother Awards, http://www.bigbrotherawards.org.

17. "Big Brother Awards, Germany," Digital Civil Rights in Europe, October 25, 2006, http://www.edri.org/edrigram/number4.20/bba-germany.

18. "Hungarian Big Brother Award for Data Protection Commissioner," December 2, 2004, http://www.edri.org/edrigram/number2.23/BBA.

19. "Happy Birthday George Orwell!," EPIC Alert, Electronic Privacy Information Center, volume 10.13 (June 25, 2003), http://www.epic.org/alert/EPIC_Alert_10.13.html.

20. "Surveillance Campaign," American Civil Liberties Union, http://www.aclu.org/pizza/.

21. Observing Surveillance, http://www.observingsurveillance.org.

22. NO2ID, http://www.no2id.net.

23. Privacy International, http://www.privacyinternational.org.

24. "The Center for Democracy & Privacy Quiz: Privacy on Trial," Center for Democracy & Privacy, http://www.cdt.org/privacy/quiz/.

25. At Abika (www.abika.com), one can purchase background checks, and personality profiles; search criminal, tax records, and vehicle license records; and obtain DNA profiles and many others.

26. "PIPEDA Complaints," Canadian Internet Policy and Public Interest Clinic, http://www.cippic.ca/en/projects-cases/privacy/pipeda-complaints/.

27. Personal interview, Pippa Lawson, September 27, 2006.

28. "PI Launches Campaign to Suspend Unlawful Activities of Finance Giant," Privacy International, June 28, 2006, http://www.privacyinternational.org/article.shtml?cmd[347]=x-347-538985.

29. See these and other cases described as "EFF's Legal Victories," Electronic Frontier Foundation, http://www.eff.org/legal/victories/more.php.

30. The lengthy and complex history of cases is described as "EFF's Class-Action Lawsuit against AT&T for Collaboration with Illegal Domestic Spying Program," Electronic Frontier Foundation, http://www.eff.org/legal/cases/att/.

31. Privacy & Technology, American Civil Liberties Union, http://www.aclu.org/privacy/index.html.

32. The Gramm-Leach-Bliley law covering financial institutions, the Telephone Consumer Protection Act, the Video Rentals legislation, the Fair Credit Reporting Act, and so on.

33. Quoted in Privacy Journal 33, no. 6, April 2007.

34. Anti-Spyware Coalition, http://www.antispywarecoalition.org.

35. Personal interview, Jim Dempsey, February 15, 2007.

36. Joris Evers, "Advertisers May Face Public Humiliation over Adware," ZDNET, February 10, 2006, http://news.zdnet.com/2100-1009_22-6037662.html?tag=zdfd.newsfeed.

37. This correspondence can be found at "DoubleClick, Abacus, Direct and Privacy," http://www.junkbusters.com/DoubleClick.html.

38. "About Us," Sypchips, http://www.spychips.com/about_us.html.

39. Telephone interview, Katherine Albrecht, June 28, 2007.

40. Boycott Benetton, http://www.boycottbenetton.com.

41. Boycott Gillette, http://www.boycottgillette.com/.

42. Kim Zetter, "Yo, Mr. CEO, Get Our Point Now?" *Wired*, October 24, 2003, http://www.wired.com/news/business/0,1367,60964,00.html.

43. Jaikumar Vijayan, "Privacy Advocate Targets Mass. Secretary of State's Website," *Computerworld*, April 6, 2007. See also The Virginia Watchdog, http://www.thevirginiawatchdog.com.

44. Margaret Johnston, "Take Net Privacy into Your Own Hands," CNN, April 19, 1999, http://www.cnn.com/TECH/computing/9904/09/netprivacy.idg/.

45. "Japan Launches ID Scheme," BBC News World Edition, August 5, 2002, http://news.bbc.co.uk/2/hi/asia-pacific/2173003.stm.

46. Sinclair Stewart, "Privacy Protestor Pays Visa Bill with Pennies," *Globe and Mail*, November 23, 2005.

47. Jason Catlett, "Open Letter (9/13) to P3P Developers," JunkBusters, Technical Standards and Privacy, September 13, 1999, http://www.junkbusters.com/standards.html.

48. "Pretty Poor Privacy: and Assessment of P3P and Internet Privacy," Electronic Privacy Information Center, June 2002, http://www.epic.org/reports/prettypoorprivacy.html.

49. Drew Clark, "A Public Feud by Privacy Advocates," *National Journal*, September 1, 2001.

5 Cases and Conflicts

Epigraphs: Bruce Sterling on the fight over the Clipper Chip at CFP '94. "So, people, we have a fight on our hands," *Wired*, Issue 2.07 (July 1994), http://www.wired.com/wired/archive/2.07/sterling.cfp.html. "Largest Anti-Surveillance Street Protest in Germany in Over Twenty Years," http://www.edri.org/edrigram/number5.18/liberty-instead-of-fear.

1. Personal interview, Graham Greenleaf, August 16, 2007.

2. The full story is told in "The Federal Government Calls It a 'Human Services Access Card': We Call It What It Is: A National ID Card System," The Australia Privacy Foundation, http://www.privacy.org.au/Campaigns/ID_cards/HSAC.html#APFPolicy.

3. Telephone interview, Roger Clarke, March 28, 2007.

4. NO2ID, http://www.no2id.net.

5. "La pétition pour le retrait de la carte d'identité biométrique," INES, http://www.ines.sgdg.org.

6. Pièces et Main d'Ouevre, http://pmo.erreur404.org/spip.php?page=plan.

7. "Trouble over Privacy in Japan," *The Economist*, August 8, 2002.

8. Simon Davies, "The Loose Cannon: An Overview of Campaigns of Opposition to National Identity Card Proposals," Australian Privacy Foundation, February 2004, http://www.privacy.org.au/About/Davies0402.html.

9. Graham Greenleaf has argued that this is really the "Australia Card" in disguise. "If it quacks like a duck" has proved a useful piece of rhetoric in the contemporary debate (Greenleaf 2007).

10. American Civil Liberties Union, http://www.realnightmare.org/.

11. Congressional testimony of Whitfield Diffie of Sun Microsystems, "The Impact of a Secret Cryptographic Standard on Encryption, Privacy, Law Enforcement and Technology," May 11, 1993, http://www.epic.org/crypto/clipper/diffie_testimony.html.

12. Other arguments can be found in "The Clipper Chip," Electronic Privacy Center, http://www.epic.org/crypto/clipper/.

13. "Information Policy Fact Sheet: *Encryption and the Clipper Chip*," Computer Professionals for Social Responsibility, http://trout.cpsr.org/publications/factsheet/clipper.htm.

14. "Communications Privacy in the Digital Age," Center for Democracy and Technology, June 1997, http://www.cdt.org/digi_tele/9706rpt.html#intro.

15. John Markoff, "Flaw Discovered in Federal Plan for Wiretapping," *New York Times*, June 2, 1994, http://query.nytimes.com/gst/fullpage.html?res=9502E4D6103BF931A35755 C0A962958260.

16. BIOS is the acronym for the basic input/output system, the built-in software that determines the basic functions of the computer. The BIOS contain all the code required to control the keyboard, screen, disk drives, and serial communications.

17. Cyber-Rights and Cyber-Liberties, "Report on the Intel Pentium III Processor Serial Number Feature," by Dr. Brian Gladman, Technology Policy Advisor, February 1999, http://www.cyber-rights.org/reports/intel-rep.htm."

18. See http://www.bigbrotherinside.org.

19. This letter amounted to a questionnaire, the responses to which they intended to publish. Were these companies: refusing to ship Pentium III systems until Intel disabled the PSN in the Pentium III hardware; not currently planning to ship Pentium III systems for other reasons; planning to ship Pentium III systems with the PSN disabled (turned off) in the BIOS; planning to ship Pentium III systems with the PSN enabled in the BIOS (turned on), but disabled (turned off) by default in the Operating System Control Utility provided by Intel or another software mechanism; planning to ship Pentium III systems with the PSN enabled by default after startup, but with an Operating System Control Utility provided by Intel or another software mechanism through which the user can disable (turn off) the PSN; planning to ship Pentium III systems with the PSN enabled (turned on) by default, but with the ability for the user to disable (turn off) the PSN in the BIOS; or planning to ship Pentium III systems with the PSN enabled (turned on) by default, with no built-in mechanism to disable (turn off) the PSN? See "CDT Asks Computer Manufacturers How They Plan to Implement the ID Feature," Center for Democracy & Technology, February 6, 1999, http://www.cdt.org/privacy/issues/pentium3/990216oem.letter.shtml.

20. All correspondence is available in "The Intel Processor Serial Number Letters," Junkbusters, http://www.junkbusters.com/ht/en/intel.html#halt.

21. Declan McCullagh, "Intel Nixes Chip-Tracking ID," *Wired*, April 27, 2000, http://www.wired.com/politics/law/news/2000/04/35950.

22. DoubleClick Inc. and Abacus Direct Corporation joint press release. "DoubleClick Inc and Abacus Direct Corporation to Merge in a $1 Billion Stock Transaction," June 14, 1999, reprinted by SEC Info, http://www.secinfo.com/duwTa.62Pu.b.htm#1stPage. For a discussion of the DoubleClick controversy, see David J. Todd, *Politicizing Privacy: Focussing Events and the Dynamics of Conflict*. University of Victoria, M.A. thesis, 2001.

23. The campaign seems to have been led by Jason Catlett of Junkbusters. These letters can be found at "DoubleClick, Abacus Direct and Privacy," Junkbusters, http://www.junkbusters.com/doubleclick.html.

24. "DoubleClick Puts Off Its Plans for Wider Use of Personal Data," *New York Times*, March 3, 2000.

25. "Safe Harbor List," Department of Commerce, United States of America, http://web.ita.doc.gov/safeharbor/shlist.nsf/webPages/safe+harbor+list.

26. Details of the advocacy campaign can be found at http://www.epic.org/privacy/consumer/microsoft/passport.html.

27. "Microsoft Passport Investigation Docket," Electronic Privacy Information Center, http://www.epic.org/privacy/consumer/microsoft/ftcletter10.23.01.html.

28. Letter from Marc Rotenberg, Jason Catlett, and Chris Hoofnagle, Electronic Privacy Information Center, November 5, 2001, http://www.epic.org/privacy/consumer/microsoft/subcomltr11.5.01.html.

29. Letter from Marc Rotenberg, Chris Hoofnagle, and Nathan Mitchler, Electronic Privacy Information Center, January 29, 2002, http://www.epic.org/privacy/consumer/microsoft/stateagletter.html.

30. "Microsoft Settles FTC Charges Alleging False Security and Privacy Promises," media release, Federal Trade Commission, August 8, 2002, http://www.ftc.gov/opa/2002/08/microsoft.htm.

31. "Comments of the Electronic Privacy Information Center (EPIC); U.S. Public Interest Research Group; Remar Sutton, President; The Consumer Task Force for Automotive Issues, JunkbustersCorp.; Computer Professionals for Social Responsibility; Privacy International, Consumers Union; Center for Digital Democracy; and The Media Access Project, September 9, 2002 (Submission to the Federal Trade Commission), Electronic Privacy Information Center, http://www.epic.org/privacy/consumer/microsoft/ordercomments.html.

32. http://www.wrf.com/publication_newsletters.cfm?sp=newsletter&year=2003&ID=10&publication_id=9764&keyword=.

33. See the Laws of Identity at Kim Cameron's blog, http://www.identityblog.com.

34. "Microsoft Advocates Comprehensive Privacy Legislation," http://www.microsoft.com/presspass/press/2005/nov05/11-03DataPrivacyPR.mspx.

35. Brian Kreps, "Microsoft Calls for National Privacy Law," http://blog.washingtonpost.com/securityfix/2005/11/microsoft_calls_for_national_p_1.html.

36. See http://www.privacyrights.org/ar/ChronDataBreaches.htm.

37. See the ChoicePoint page at http://www.epic.org/privacy/choicepoint/.

38. http://www.ftc.gov/opa/2002/01/elililly.htm.

39. Office of the Privacy Commissioner of Canada, "CIBC's Privacy Practices Failed in Case of Misdirected Faxes," http://www.privcom.gc.ca/incidents/2005/050418_01_e.asp.

40. Clarke has insisted that "identity theft is the acquisition and use of sufficient evidence of identity relating to a particular person that the thief can operate as though they were that person. This can be as simple as stealing a wallet or purse, with or without passing the contents via an intermediary or 'fence'. Alternatively, it can be achieved by mail theft, the 'fishing' of credit card slips and loan or credit applications from rubbish-bins, or through an 'inside job', e.g., at a financial institution." Many data breaches might result in fraudulent activity without the assumption of another person's identity. Roger Clarke, "Information Privacy On the Internet: Cyberspace Invades Personal Space," http://www.anu.edu.au/people/Roger.Clarke/DV/IPrivacy.html.

41. See the Identity Theft Resource Center, http://www.idtheftcenter.org/index.shtml.

42. Personal interview, Roger Clarke, March 28, 2007.

43. Personal interview, Chris Hoofnagle, February 5, 2007.

44. Personal interview, Simon Davies, May 7, 2007.

45. Simon Davies, "The Loose Cannon: An Overview of Campaigns of Opposition to National Identity Card Proposals," February 2004, http://www.privacy.org.au/About/Davies0402.html.

46. Telephone interview, Roger Clarke, March 28, 2007.

6 The Networks

Epigraphs: As recalled by Roger Clarke, "Just Another Piece of Plastic for Your Wallet: The 'Australia Card' Scheme," 1987, http://www.anu.edu.au/people/Roger.Clarke/DV/OzCard.html. Graham Greenleaf recalls "strange bedfellows," personal interview, August 16, 2007.

Perhaps Hawke said both. The key point is that he tried to disparage the coalition thus allowing them to respond by saying "yes, this may be an odd coalition of interests but that is the nature of Australia ... mate!"

1. Personal interview, Gus Hosein, June 17, 2006.

2. Personal interview, Robert Ellis Smith, August 29, 2006.

3. Wendy Grossman, "Computers, Freedom and Privacy, Mk XII," *The Inquirer*, April 26, 2002, http://www.theinquirer.net/default.aspx?article=3379.

4. Roger Clarke, "Personal Notes on Computers, Freedom & Privacy 2002," http://www .anu.edu.au/people/Roger.Clarke/DV/NotesCFP02.html.

5. Lorrie Faith Cranor, "Ten Years of Computers, Freedom and Privacy: A Personal Retrospective," AT&T Labs Research, http://www.cfp2000.org/papers/2cranor.pdf.

6. For instance, in London in 2006, the commissioners issued a declaration on the importance of adequate data protection in the context of law enforcement cooperation. In Montreux in 2005, they passed a resolution calling for a universal convention for the protection of individuals with regard to the processing of personal data. In Wroclaw in 2004, they passed a resolution on the importance of privacy standardization.

7. World Summit on the Information Society, "Declaration of Principles: Building the Information Society, a Global Challenge in the New Millenium" (Document WSIS-03/ GENEVA/DOC/4-E, para. 35), December 12, 2003, http://www.itu.int/wsis/docs/geneva/ official/dop.html.

8. World Summit on the Information Society, Tunis Agenda for the Information Society (Document: WSIS-05/TUNIS/DOC/6(Rev. 1)-E, para. 46), November 18, 2005, http:// www.itu.int/wsis/docs2/tunis/off/6rev1.html.

9. Ralph Bendrath and Rikke Frank Jørgensen, "The World Summit on the Information Society: Privacy Not Found?" *Script-ed*, AHRC Research Centre for Studies in Intellectual Property and Technology Law, http://www.law.ed.ac.uk/ahrc/script-ed/vol3-4/rikke.asp.

10. Global Internet Liberty Campaign, http://www.gilc.org.

11. Marc Rotenberg, "EPIC Testimony on Crypto Legislation" (to the Senate Committee on Commerce, Science & Transportation, subcommittee on Science, Space & Technology, on the Promotion of Commerce On-line in the Digital Era Act of 1996, s. 1726), Electronic Privacy Information Center, June 26, 1996, http://www.epic.org/crypto/export_controls/epic _testimony_696.html.

12. Personal interview, Lee Tien, February 26, 2007.

13. In Defense of Freedom, http://www.indefenseoffreedom.org/.

1. On September 11, 2001 thousands of people lost their lives in a brutal assault on the American people and the American form of government. We mourn the loss of these innocent lives and insist that those who perpetrated these acts be held accountable.

2. This tragedy requires all Americans to examine carefully the steps our country may now take to reduce the risk of future terrorist attacks.

3. We need to consider proposals calmly and deliberately with a determination not to erode the liberties and freedoms that are at the core of the American way of life.

4. We need to ensure that actions by our government uphold the principles of a democratic society, accountable government and international law, and that all decisions are taken in a manner consistent with the Constitution.

5. We can, as we have in the past, in times of war and of peace, reconcile the requirements of security with the demands of liberty.

6. We should resist the temptation to enact proposals in the mistaken belief that anything that may be called antiterrorist will necessarily provide greater security.

7. We should resist efforts to target people because of their race, religion, ethnic background, or appearance, including immigrants in general, Arab Americans, and Muslims.

8. We affirm the right of peaceful dissent, protected by the First Amendment, now, when it is most at risk.

9. We should applaud our political leaders in the days ahead who have the courage to say that our freedoms should not be limited.

10. We must have faith in our democratic system and our Constitution, and in our ability to protect at the same time both the freedom and the security of all Americans.

14. The relevant documentation for the campaign can be found at "Gmail Privacy Page," Electronic Privacy Information Center, http://www.epic.org/privacy/gmail/faq.html.

15. Joint letter to Attorney General Lockyer, Chris Jay Hoofnagle, Beth Givens, and Pam Dixon, Electronic Privacy Information Center, May 3, 2004, http://www.epic.org/privacy/gmail/agltr5.3.04.html.

16. "More on Gmail and Privacy," Google, http://mail.google.com/mail/help/about_privacy.html.

17. Summaries of the First Conference on Computers, Freedom and Privacy, March 26–28, 1991, Steve Cisler and Rebecca Mercuri, Electronic Frontier Foundation, http://www.eff.org/Privacy/?f=cfp1_convention.summaries.

18. The Privacy Coalition, http://www.privacycoalition.org.

19. "Notice of Proposed Rulemaking: Privacy Act of 1974: Implementation of Exemptions: The Homeland Security Operations Center Database," Department of Homeland Security Privacy Office, http://www.epic.org/privacy/homeland/dhs_hsocd_final.pdf.

20. Regulations.gov, http://www.regulations.gov/fdmspublic/component/main.

21. "Who We Are," Patientprivacyrights, http://www.patientprivacyrights.org/site/PageServer?pagename=Who_We_Are.

22. "Civil Liberties: Development of a Concern," Canadian Friends Service Committee, http://cfsc.quaker.ca/pages/documents/CivilLibertiesPolicy.pdf.

23. "The Emergence of a Global Infrastructure for Mass Registration and Surveillance: 10 Signposts," International Campaign against Mass Surveillance, http://www.i-cams.org/Surveillance_intro.html. See also Webb 2007.

24. Stoppt die Vorratsdatenspeicherung!, http://www.vorratsdatenspeicherung.de/.

25. Personal interview, Deborah Pierce, May 17, 2007.

26. Personal interview, Robert Ellis Smith, August 2, 2006.

27. Personal interview, Deidre Mulligan, April 17, 2007.

28. The Intel Pentium III Processor Serial Number, http://www.cdt.org/privacy/issues/pentium3/.

29. "Demonstration in Berlin am 22. September 2007," AK VORRAT, http://wiki.vorratsdatenspeicherung.de/Demonstration_in_Berlin_am_22._September_2007.

30. Personal interview, Deborah Pierce, May 17, 2007.

31. Simon Davies, "Don't Mourn; Organize," WIRED 4, no. 3, March 1996, 86.

32. The title also resonates with the very influential piece (Granovetter 1973).

33. Telephone interview, Roger Clarke, March 28, 2007.

34. Personal interview, Gus Hosein, June 17, 2006.

7 Movements and Futures

Epigraphs: Bruce Schneier, from his book *Secrets and Lies*. Rotenberg quoted in *New York Times*, September 29, 1996. See Philip E. Agre, Department of Information Studies, University of California, Los Angeles, December 26, 1999, http://polaris.gseis.ucla.edu/pagre/notes/99-12-26.html.

1. In August 2004, for instance, the Arab American Institute coordinated a campaign against the provision of tabulations on the Arab American population, prepared by the Census Bureau to the Department of Homeland Security and to the Bureau of Customs and Border Protection. See statements, correspondence, and media coverage at http://www.aaiusa.org/issues/civil-liberties/dhs.

2. An observation about the motivations of the participants in the September 22, 2007, protests in Berlin, made at the Civil Society Workshop, Montreal, September 25, 2007.

3. Personal interview, Beth Givens, March 8, 2007.

4. Phil Agre, Department of Information Studies, University of California, Los Angeles, http://polaris.gseis.ucla.edu/pagre/notes/99-12-26.html.

5. Telephone interview, Caspar Bowden, May 19, 2007.

6. See Privacy International, "A Race to the Bottom: Privacy Ranking of Internet Service Companies, A Consultation Report," June 9, 2007, http://www.privacyinternational.org/article.shtml?cmd[347]=x-347-553961.

7. Telephone interview, Caspar Bowden, May 19, 2007.

8. Personal interview, Robert Ellis Smith, August 29, 2006.

9. Personal interview, Valerie Steeves, September 28, 2006.

10. Personal interview, Robert Ellis Smith, August 29, 2006.

11. Personal interview, Valerie Steeves, September 28, 2006.

12. Personal interview, Simon Davies, May 3, 2007.

13. Personal interview, Deidre Mulligan, April 17, 2007.

14. Personal interview, Beth Givens, March 8, 2007.

15. Personal interview, Ari Schwartz, May 5, 2006.

16. Personal interview, Roger Clarke, March 28, 2007.

17. "Surveillance Society Clock," American Civil Liberties Union, http://www.aclu.org/privacy/spying/surveillancesocietyclock.html.

18. Telephone interview, Lillie Coney, June 12, 2007.

19. Personal interview, Jim Dempsey, February 15, 2007.

20. Personal interview, Rich Neumeister, May 25, 2006.

21. An analogy suggested by Katherine Albrecht. Telephone interview, June 28, 2007.

22. Personal interview, Deidre Mulligan, April 17, 2007.

23. Personal interview, Chris Hoofnagle, February 5, 2007.

24. For example, not enough attention is paid to the exercise of access rights. Most privacy policies assert that individuals have a right to access their own personal information, and to correct or amend it if necessary. Most organizations state this commitment because they know that it will rarely, if ever, be tested.

25. This analogy has been used by Bruce Schneier, among others: "Sometimes being a privacy advocate is like playing whack-a-mole, you knock one down and four more pop up." Dylan Tweney, "Words of Wisdom from the Electronic Frontier Foundation Pioneer Awards," *Wired Magazine*, March 27, 2007, http://blog.wired.com/business/2007/03/words_of_wisdom.html.

Bibliography

Agre, Philip E. "Surveillance and Capture: Two Models of Privacy." *Information Society* 10 (1994): 101–127.

Agre, Philip E., and Marc Rotenberg. *Technology and Privacy: The New Landscape.* Cambridge, Mass.: MIT Press, 1997.

Alberoni, Francesco. *Movement and Institution.* New York: Columbia University Press, 1984.

Albrecht, Katherine, and Liz McIntyre. *Spychips: How Major Corporations and Government Plan to Track Your Every Move with RFID.* Nashville: Nelson Current, 2005.

Albrecht, Katherine, and Liz McIntyre. *The Spychips Threat: Why Christians Should Resist RFID and Electronic Surveillance.* Nashville: Nelson Current, 2006.

Allen, Anita L. *Uneasy Access: Privacy for Women in a Free Society.* Totowa, N.J.: Rowman and Littlefield, 1988.

Appel, Roland, and Dieter Hummel. *Vorsicht Volkszählung!* Cologne: Kolner Volksblatt, 1987.

Ash, T. Garton. *The File: A Personal History.* New York: Vintage Books, 1997.

Ayres, J. "From the Streets to the Internet: The Cyber-diffusion of Contention." *Annals of the American Academy of Political and Social Sciences* 566, no. 1 (1999): 132–143.

Barney, Darin. *The Network Society.* Cambridge: Polity Press, 2004.

Bennett, Colin J. *Regulating Privacy: Data Protection in the United States and Europe.* Ithaca: Cornell University Press, 1992.

Bennett, Colin J. "The Public Surveillance of Personal Data: A Cross-National Analysis." In *Computers, Surveillance and Privacy*, edited by David Lyon and Elia Zureik, 237–259. Minneapolis: University of Minnesota Press, 1996.

Bennett, Colin J. "Convergence Revisited: Toward a Global Policy for the Protection of Personal Data?" In *Technology and Privacy: The New Landscape*, edited by Philip E. Agre and Marc Rotenberg, 99–123. Cambridge, Mass.: MIT Press, 1997.

Bennett, Colin J. "What Happens When You Book an Airline Ticket? The Collection and Processing of Passenger Data Post 9/11." In *Global Surveillance and Policing: Borders, Security, Identity*, edited by Elia Zureik and Mark B. Salter, 113–138. Portland, Ore.: Willan Publishing, 2005.

Bennett, Colin J., and Rebecca Grant, eds. *Visions of Privacy: Policy Choices for the Digital Age.* Toronto: University of Toronto Press, 1999.

Bennett, Colin J., and David Lyon. *Playing the Identity Card: Security, Surveillance and Identification in Global Perspective.* London: Routledge, 2008.

Bennett, Colin J., and Charles D. Raab. *The Governance of Privacy: Policy Instruments in Global Perspective.* Cambridge, Mass.: MIT Press, 2006.

Bennett, Colin J., and Priscilla M. Regan. "Surveillance and Mobilities." *Surveillance and Society* 1, no. 4 (2004): 449–455.

Bennett, Lance. "Communicating Global Activism: Strengths and Vulnerabilities of Networked Politics." In *Cyberprotest: New Media, Citizens and Social Movements*, edited by Brian D. Loader, Wim van de Donk, Paul G. Nixon, and Dieter Rucht, 123–146. London: Routledge, 2004.

Blumer, Herbert. "Collective Behavior." In *An Outline of the Principles of Sociology*, edited by Robert E. Park, 219–280. New York: Barnes and Noble, 1939.

Boling, Patricia. *Privacy and the Politics of Intimate Life*. Ithaca: Cornell University Press, 1996.

Brunsting, Suzanne, and Tom Postmes. "Social Movement Participation in the Digital Age: Predicting Offline and Online Collective Action," *Small Group Research* 33, no. 5 (2002): 525–554.

Burnham, David. *The Rise of the Computer State*. New York: Random House, 1983.

Butz, William P. "Data Confidentiality and Public Perceptions: The Case of the European Censuses." Paper presented to the American Statistical Association, 1985. http://www .amstat.org/sections/SRMS/proceedings/papers/1985_016.pdf.

Bygrave, Lee. *Data Protection Law: Approaching its Rationale, Logic and Limits*. New York: Kluwer Law International, 2002.

Canadian Standards Association (CSA). *Model Code for the Protection of Personal Information*, CAN/CSA-Q0830–96, Rexdale: CSA, 1996.

Castells, Manuel. *The Rise of the Network Society*. Oxford: Blackwell, 1996.

Center for Democracy and Technology (CDT). "Communications Privacy in the Digital Age." 1997. http://www.cdt.org/digi_tele/9706rpt.html#intro.

Center for Democracy and Technology (CDT), and Ontario, Office of the Information and Privacy Commissioner (Ontario IPC). 2000. "P3P and Privacy:An Update for the Privacy Community," http://www.cdt.org/privacy/pet/p3pprivacy.shtml.

Chaum, David. "Achieving Electronic Privacy." *Scientific American* 267, no. 2 (1992): 96–101.

Chester, Jeff. *Digital Democracy: New Media and the Future of Democracy*. New York: New Press, 2007.

Chick, Cindy L. "Lexis/Nexis Held Hostage by the Internet: The P-Trak Debacle." LLRX, November 18, 1996. http://www.llrx.com/features/ptrak.htm.

Clarke, Roger. "Another Piece of Plastic for Your Wallet: The Australia Card Scheme." 1987. http://www.anu.edu.au/people/Roger.Clarke/DV/OzCard.html.

Clarke, Roger. "Information Technology and Dataveillance." *Communications of the ACM* 31, no. 5 (1988): 498–512.

Clarke, Roger. "Introduction to Dataveillance and Information Privacy, and Definitions of Terms." 1997 (revised 2006). http://www.anu.edu.au/people/Roger.Clarke/DV/Intro.html.

Clement, Andrew. "Toward an Integrated Information Rights Movement: Conceptual Foundations from Environmentalism." Paper presented to the Information Rights and Organizational Accountabilities Workshop, Faculty of Information Studies, University of Toronto, June 16–17, 2006.

Clement, Andrew, and Christie Hurrell. *Information/Communications Rights as a new Environmentalism?* Working paper, Canadian Research Alliance for Community Innovation and Networking, Toronto, 2005.

Cohen, Stanley. *Folk Devils and Moral Panics*. New York: Routledge, 1972.

Council of Europe (CoE). *Convention for the Protection of Individuals with Regard to Automatic Processing of Personal Data*. Strasbourg: Council of Europe, 1981.

Culnan, Mary J. "The Lessons of the Lotus Marketplace: Implications for Consumer Privacy in the 1990's." 1991. www.cpsr.org/prevsite/conferences/cfp91/culnan.html.

Davies, Simon. *Big Brother: Australia's Growing Web of Surveillance.* Sydney: Simon and Schuster, 1992.

Davies, Simon. "Re-engineering the Right to Privacy: How Privacy Has Been Transformed from a Right to a Commodity." In *Technology and Privacy: The New Landscape,* edited by Philip E. Agre and Marc Rotenberg, 161–162. Cambridge, Mass.: MIT Press, 1997.

Davies, Simon. "CCTV: A New Battleground for Privacy." In *Surveillance, Closed Circuit Television and Social Control,* edited by Clive Norris, Jade Moran, and Gary Armstrong, 243–254. Aldershot: Ashgate Publishing, 1998.

Davies, Simon. "Spanners in the Works: How the Privacy Movement is Adapting to the Challenge of Big Brother." In *Visions of Privacy: Policy Choices for the Digital Age,* edited by Colin J. Bennett and Rebecca Grant, 244–261. Toronto: University of Toronto Press, 1999.

Deleuze, Giles. "Postscript on the Societies of Control." *October 59* (Winter 1992): 3–7.

Diebert, Ron. "International Plug n' Play? Citizen Activism, the Internet, and Global Public Policy." *International Studies Perspective* 1, no. 3 (2000): 255–272.

Diffie, Whitfield, and Susan Landau. *Privacy on the Line: The Politics of Wiretapping and Encryption.* Cambridge, Mass.: MIT Press, 1998.

Dixon, Pam. *Be Your Own Headhunter Online: Get the Job You Want by Using the Information Superhighway.* New York: Random House/Times Books, 1995.

Donahue, William. *The Politics of the Civil Liberties Union.* New Brunswick, N.J.: Transaction Books, 1985.

Drinan, Robert. *The Mobilization of Shame: A World View of Human Rights.* New Haven: Yale University Press, 2001.

Edelman, Murray. *The Symbolic Uses of Politics.* Urbana: University of Illinois Press, 1964.

Electronic Privacy Information Centre (EPIC). *Privacy and Human Rights.* Washington, D.C.: EPIC and Privacy International, 2007.

Electronic Privacy Information Centre (EPIC). *Ensuring Accuracy and Privacy: EPIC 2005–2006 Annual Report.* Washington, D.C.: EPIC, 2006.

European Union. *Directive 95/46/EC of the European Parliament and of the Council on the Protection of Individuals with Regard to the Processing of Personal Data and on the Free Movement of Such Data.* Brussels: European Commission, OJ No. L281.24, October 1995.

Flaherty, David. *Protecting Privacy in Surveillance Societies.* Chapel Hill: The University of North Carolina Press, 1989.

Foucault, M. "Governmentality." Trans. Rosi Braidotti and revised by Colin Gordon. In *The Foucault Effect: Studies in Governmentality,* edited by Graham Burchell, Colin Gordon, and Peter Miller, 87–104. Chicago: University of Chicago Press, 1991.

Franklin, Ursula M. *The Real World of Technology.* Toronto: Anansi, 1999.

Fried, Charles. *An Anatomy of Values: Problems of Personal and Social Change.* Cambridge, Mass.: Harvard University Press, 1970.

Fried, Charles. "Privacy." *Yale Law Journal* 77, no. 3 (1968): 475–493.

Froomkin, Michael. "The Metaphor is the Key: Cryptography, the Clipper Chip and the Constitution." *University of Pennsylvania Law Review* 143 (1995): 709–712. www.law.miami.edu/~froomkin/articles/clipper.htm.

Fuentes, Marta and Andre Gunder Frank. "Ten Theses on Social Movements." *World Development* 17, no. 2 (1989): 179–189.

Funder, Anna. *Stasiland: Stories from Behind the Berlin Wall.* London: Granta, 2003.

Gandy, Oscar H., Jr. *The Panoptic Sort: A Political Economy of Personal Information.* San Francisco: Westview Press, 1993.

Gandy, Oscar H., Jr. "Public Opinion Surveys and the Formation of Privacy Policy." *Journal of Social Issues* 59, no. 2 (2003): 283–299.

Garey, Diane. *Defending Everybody: A History of the American Civil Liberties Union.* New York: Harper Collins, 1998.

Garfinkel, Simson. *Database Nation: The Death of Privacy in the 21st Century.* Sebastopol, Calif.: O'Reilly & Associates, 2000.

Gerlach, Luther P. "The Structure of Social Movements: Environmental Activism and its Opponents." In *Networks and Netwars: The Future of Terror, Crime and Militancy*, edited by John Arquilla and David Ronfeldt, 289–310. Santa Monica: Rand, 2001.

Gilliom, John. *Overseers of the Poor: Surveillance, Resistance and the Limits of Privacy.* Chicago: University of Chicago Press, 2001.

Gilliom, John. "Struggling with Surveillance: Resistance, Consciousness, and Identity." In *The New Politics of Surveillance and Visibility*, edited by Kevin D. Haggerty and Richard V. Ericson, 111–129. Toronto: University of Toronto Press, 2006.

Goffman, Erving. *Frame Analysis: An Essay on the Organization of Experience.* Cambridge, Mass.: Harvard University Press, 1974.

Graber, Doris A. *Verbal Behavior and Politics.* Urbana: University of Illinois Press, 1976.

Granovetter, Mark. "The Strength of Weak Ties." *American Journal of Sociology* 78, no. 6 (1973): 1360–1380.

Greenleaf, Graham. "The Australia Card: Towards a National Surveillance System." 1987. http://austlii.edu.au/itlaw/articles/GGozcard.html.

Greenleaf, Graham. "Stopping Surveillance: Beyond Efficiency and the OECD." *Privacy Law and Policy Reporter* 3, no. 8 (1996): 148–152.

Greenleaf, Graham. "APEC's Privacy framework: A New Low Standard." *Privacy Law & Policy Reporter* 11, no. 5 (2005): 121–124.

Greenleaf, Graham. "Quacking Like a Duck: The National ID Card Proposal (2006) Compared with the Australia Card (1986–87)." 2007. http://austlii.edu.au/~graham/.

Grossman, Wendy M. *Net.Wars.* New York: New York University Press, 1997.

Gurak, Laura. *Persuasion and Privacy in Cyberspace: The Online Protests over Lotus Marketplace and the Clipper Chip.* New Haven: Yale University Press, 1997.

Gurr, Ted R. *Why Men Rebel.* Princeton, N.J.: Princeton University Press, 1970.

Gutman, Amy. *Identity in Democracy.* Princeton: Princeton University Press, 2003.

Haggerty, Kevin D., and Richard V. Ericson. "The Surveillant Assemblage." *British Journal of Sociology* 51, no. 4 (2000): 605–622.

Haggerty, Kevin D., and Richard V. Ericson, eds. *The New Politics of Surveillance and Visibility.* Toronto: University of Toronto Press, 2006.

Hannan, Michael T. and John H. Freeman. *Organizational Ecology.* Cambridge, Mass.: Harvard University Press, 1989.

Hansson, Sven Ole, and Elin Palm, eds. *The Ethics of Workplace Privacy.* Brussels: Peter Lang, 2005.

Hopgood, Stephen. *Keepers of the Flame: Understanding Amnesty International.* Ithaca: Cornell University Press, 2006.

Hosein, Gus. "The Sources of Laws: Policy Dynamics in a Digital and Terrorized World." *Information Society* 20, no. 3 (2004): 187–199.

Howlett, Michael, and M. Ramesh. *Studying Public Policy: Policy Cycles and Policy Subsystems.* Oxford: Oxford University Press, 2003.

Inglehart, Ronald. *The Silent Revolution: Changing Values and Political Styles Among Western Publics.* Princeton: Princeton University Press, 1977.

Keane, John. *Global Civil Society?* Cambridge, U.K.: Cambridge University Press, 2003.

Keck, Margaret, E., and Kathryn Sikkink. *Activists Beyond Borders: Advocacy Networks in International Politics.* Ithaca: Cornell University Press, 1998.

Kennedy Cuomo, Kerry. *Speak Truth to Power: Human Rights Defenders Who Are Changing Our World.* New York: Umbrage Editions, 2005.

Kornhauser, William. *The Politics of Mass Society.* Glencoe: Free Press, 1959.

Kuerbis, Brandon. *Case Study: The Electronic Privacy Information Center.* 2005. www .thepublicvoice.org/events/EPIC_Case_Study2.pdf.

Laniel, Laurel, and Pierre Piazza. "The Ines Biometric Card and the Politics of National Identity Assignment in France." In *Playing the Identity Card: Security, Surveillance and Identification in Global Perspective*, edited by Colin J. Bennett and David Lyon. London: Routledge, 2008.

Leizerov, Sagi. "Privacy Advocacy Groups' versus Intel: A Case Study of How Social Movements are Tactically Using the Internet to Fight Corporations," *Social Science Computer Review* 18, no. 7 (2000): 461–483.

Lessig, Lawrence. *Code and Other Laws of Cyberspace.* New York: Basic Books, 1999.

Levy, Steven. *How the Code Rebels Beat the Government—Saving Privacy in the Digital Age.* New York: Viking Adult, 2001.

Li, Joyce H.-S. *The Center for Democracy and Technology and Internet Privacy in the U.S.: Lessons of the First Five Years.* Lanham, Md.: Scarecrow Press, 2003.

Lofland, John. "Charting Degrees of Movement Culture: Tasks of the Cultural Cartographer." In *Social Movements and Culture*, edited by H. Johnston and B. Klandermans, 188–216. Minneapolis: University of Minnesota Press, 1995.

London School of Economics (LSE). *The Identity Project: An Assessment of the UK Identity Cards Bill and Its Implications.* June 27, 2005. http://is2.lse.ac.uk/idcard/identityreport.pdf.

Luker, Kristin. *Abortion and the Politics of Motherhood.* Berkeley: University of California Press, 1984.

Lyon, David. *The Electronic Eye: The Rise of Surveillance Society.* Minneapolis: University of Minnesota Press, 1994.

Lyon, David. *Surveillance Society: Monitoring Everyday Life.* Buckingham: Open University Press, 2001.

Lyon, David, ed. *Surveillance as Social Sorting: Privacy, Risk and Digital Discrimination.* New York: Routledge, 2003a.

Lyon, David. *Surveillance after September 11th.* Cambridge: Polity Press, 2003b.

Lyon, David. *Surveillance Studies: An Overview.* Cambridge: Polity Press, 2007.

Magnusson, Warren. *The Search for Political Space.* Toronto: University of Toronto Press, 1996.

Marx, Gary. *Undercover: Police Surveillance in America.* Berkeley: University of California Press, 1988.

Marx, Gary. "A Tack in the Shoe: Resisting and Neutralizing the New Surveillance." *Journal of Social Issues* 59, no. 2 (2003): 369–390.

Marx, Gary. "Technology and Gender: Thomas I. Voire and the Case of the Peeping Tom." In *Sociology Quarterly* 43, no. 3 (2003): 407–433.

Miller, Arthur. *The Assault on Privacy: Computers, Data Banks and Dossiers.* Ann Arbor: University of Michigan Press, 1971.

Moore, Barrington. Privacy: Studies in Social and Cultural History. Armonk NY: M. E. Sharpe, 1984.

Mueller, Milton, Christiane Page, and Brandon Kuerbis. "Civil Society and the Shaping of Communication-Information Policy: Four Decades of Advocacy." *Information Society* 20, no. 3 (2004): 169–185.

Neier, Aryeh. *Dossier: The Secret Files They Keep on You.* New York: Rowman and Lillienfeld, 1974.

New York Surveillance Camera Players. *We Know You Are Watching.* New York: Factory School, 2006.

Nissenbaum, Helen. "Privacy as Contextual Integrity." *Washington Law Review* 79, no. 1 (2004): 119–158.

Ogasawara, Midori. "Dataveillance Defines Who Is a Desirable Citizen: National Identification (Card) Systems in Japan." In *Playing the Identity Card: Security, Surveillance and Identification in Global Perspective*, edited by Colin J. Bennett and David Lyon. London: Routledge, 2008.

O'Harrow, Robert. *No Place to Hide: Behind the Scenes of Our Emerging Surveillance Society.* New York: Free Press, 2005.

Olsen, Mancur. *The Logic of Collective Action: Public Goods and the Theory of Groups.* Cambridge, Mass.: Harvard University Press, 1971.

Organization for Economic Cooperation and Development (OECD). *Guidelines on the Protection of Privacy and Transborder Flows of Personal Data.* 1981. http://www.oecd.org/document/18/0,2340,en_2649_34255_1815186_1_1_1,00.html.

Organization for Economic Cooperation and Development (OECD). *Cryptography Policy: The Guidelines and the Issues.* 1997. http://www.oecd.org/document/11/0,2340,en_2649 _34255_1814721_1_1_1_1,00.html.

Piazza, Pierre. *Histoire de la Carte Nationale d'Identité.* Paris: Odile Jacob, 2004.

Raab, Charles. "From Balancing to Steering: New Directions for Data Protection." In *Visions of Privacy: Policy Choices for the Digital Age*, edited by Colin J. Bennett and Rebecca Grant, 68–93. Toronto: University of Toronto Press, 1999.

Regan, Priscilla. *Legislating Privacy: Technology, Social Values and Public Policy.* Chapel Hill: University of North Carolina Press, 1995.

Ribeiro, G. J. "Cybercultural Politics: Political Activism at a Distance in a Transnational World." In *Cultures of Politics, Politics of Cultures: Re-Visioning Latin American Social Movements*, edited by S. E. Alvarez and A. Escobar, 325–352. Boulder, Colo.: Westview Press, 1998.

Rosen, Jeffrey. *The Unwanted Gaze: The Destruction of Privacy in America.* New York: Vintage Books, 2000.

Rosen, Jeffrey. *The Naked Crowd: Reclaiming Security and Freedom in an Anxious World.* New York: Random House, 2004.

Rule, James. *Privacy in Peril: How We Are Sacrificing a Fundamental Right in Exchange for Security and Convenience.* New York: Oxford University Press, 2007.

Rule, James, Douglas McAdam, Linda Stearns, and David Uglow. *The Politics of Privacy: Planning for Personal Data Systems as Powerful Technologies.* New York: Elsevier, 1980.

Rule, James, Douglas McAdam, Linda Stearns, and David Uglow. "Documentary Identification and Mass Surveillance in the United States." *Social Problems* 31, no. 2 (1983): 222–234.

Sabatier, Paul, and Hank Jenkins-Smith. "An Advocacy Coalition Framework of Policy Change and the Role of Policy-Oriented Learning Therein." *Policy Sciences* 21 (1988): 129–168.

Samarajiva, Rohan. "Surveillance by Design: Public Networks and the Control of Consumption." In *Communication by Design: The Politics of Information and Communication Technologies*, edited by R. Mansell and R. Silverstone, 129–156. Oxford: Oxford University Press, 1996.

Schneier, Bruce. *Beyond Fear: Thinking Sensibly about Security in an Uncertain World.* New York: Copernicus Books, 2003.

Schneier, Bruce. *Secrets and Lies: Digital Security in a Networked World.* Indianapolis: Wiley, 2004.

Schattschneider, Elmer. *The Semi-Sovereign People: A Realist's View of Democracy in America.* New York: Holt, Rinehart and Winston, 1960.

Schoeman, Ferdinand. *Privacy and Social Freedom.* Cambridge, U.K.: Cambridge University Press, 1992.

Schwartz, Paul. "The Computer in German and American Constitutional Law: Towards an American Right of Informational Self-Determination." *American Journal of Comparative Law* 37, no. 4 (1989): 687–689.

Schwartz, Paul. "Privacy and Democracy in Cyberspace." *Vanderbilt Law Review* 52, no. 6 (1999): 1610–1702.

Schwartz, Paul, and Edward Janger. "Notification of Data Security Breaches." *Michigan Law Review* 105, no. 5 (2007): 913–984.

Schwartz, Paul, and Joel Reidenberg. *Data Privacy Law: A Study of United States Data Protection.* Charlottesville: Michie, 1996.

Sieghart, Paul. *Privacy and Computers.* London: Latimer, 1976.

Smith, Robert E. *War Stories: Anecdotes of Persons Victimized by Invasions of Privacy.* Providence, R.I.: Privacy Journal, 1993.

Snow, David. "Frame Alignment Processes: Micromobilization and Movement Participation." *American Sociological Review* 51, no. 4 (1986): 464–481.

Snow, David, and Robert D. Benford. "Ideology, Frame Resonance and Participant Mobilization." In *International Social Movement Research: From Structure to Action*, edited by Bert Klandermans, Hanspeter Kriesi, and Sidney Tarrow, 197–218. Greenwich, Conn.: JAI Press, 1988.

Solove, Daniel. *The Digital Person: Technology and Privacy in the Information Age.* New York: New York University Press, 2004.

Solove, Daniel. "A Taxonomy of Privacy." *University of Pennsylvania Law Review* 154, no. 3. (2006): 477–560.

Spar, Deborah. "The Spotlight and the Bottom Line: How Multinationals Export Human Rights." *Foreign Affairs* 77, no. 2 (1998): 7–12.

Stalder, Felix. "Privacy Is Not the Antidote to Surveillance" *Surveillance and Society* 1, no. 1 (2002): 120–124.

Surveillance Studies Network. *A Report on the Surveillance Society.* 2006. http://www .ico.gov.uk/upload/documents/library/data_protection/practical_application/surveillance _society_full_report_2006.pdf.

Swire, Peter, and Robert Litan. *None of Your Business: World Data Flows, Electronic Commerce and the European Privacy Directive.* Washington, D.C.: Brookings Institution Press, 1998.

Sykes, Charles. *The End of Privacy.* New York: St. Martin's Press, 1999.

Tarrow, Sidney. *Power in Movement: Social Movements and Contentious Politics.* Cambridge, U.K.: Cambridge University Press, 1998.

Tilly, Charles. "Social Movements and National Politics." In *Statemaking and Social Movements: Essays in History and Theory*, edited by Charles Bright and Susan Harding. 297–317. Ann Arbor: University of Michigan Press, 1984.

Touraine, Alain. *The Voice and the Eye: An Analysis of Social Movements.* Trans. by Alan Duff. Cambridge, U.K.: Cambridge University Press, 1981.

Truman, David. *The Governmental Process: Political Interests and Public Opinion.* New York: Alfred A. Knopf, 1951.

U.K. National Consumer Council (NCC). *The Glass Consumer: Life in a Surveillance Society.* London: NCC, 2005.

van de Donk, Wim, Brian D. Loader, Paul G. Nixon, and Dieter Rucht. *Cyberprotest: New Media, Citizens and Social Movements.* New York: Routledge, 2004.

van den Hoven, Jeroen, and Joh Weckert. *Information Technology and Moral Philosophy.* Cambridge, U.K.: Cambridge University Press, 2005.

Verbraucherzentrale Bundesverband. *Glaserne Verbraucher: Hysterie oder schon bald Alltag.* Berlin: VZBV, 2004.

Vitaliev, Dmitri. *Digital Security and Privacy for Human Rights Defenders.* Dublin: Frontline: International Foundation for the Protection of Human Rights Defenders, 2007.

Walker, Samuel. *In Defense of American Liberties: A History of the American Civil Liberties Union.* Carbondale: Southern Illinois University Press, 1999.

Warren, Samuel, and Louis Brandeis. "The Right to Privacy." *Harvard Law Review* 4 (1890): 193–220.

Webb, Maureen. *Illusions of Security: Global Surveillance and Democracy in the Post-9/11 World.* San Francisco: City Light Books, 2007.

Westin, Alan. *Privacy and Freedom.* New York: Atheneum, 1967.

Westwood, John. "Life in the Privacy Trenches: Experiences of the British Columbia Civil Liberties Association." In *Visions of Privacy: Policy Choices for the Digital Age*, edited by C. J. Bennett and R. Grant, 231–243. Toronto: University of Toronto Press, 1999.

Whitaker, Reg. *The End of Privacy: How Total Surveillance Is Becoming a Reality.* New York: New Press, 1999.

Winner, Langdon. *The Whale and the Reactor: A Search for Limits in an Age of High Technology.* Chicago: University of Chicago Press, 1986.

Wood, David. "People Watching People." *Surveillance and Society* 2, no. 4 (2004): 474–478.

Zald, Mayer, and John McCarthy. *The Dynamics of Social Movements: Resource Mobilization, Social Control and Tactics.* Cambridge, Mass.: Winthrop Publishers, 1979.

Index